MAHAN ABEDIN

CN01508516

Iran Resurgent

The Rise and Rise of the Shia State

HURST & COMPANY, LONDON

First published in the United Kingdom in 2019 by
C. Hurst & Co. (Publishers) Ltd.,
41 Great Russell Street, London, WC1B 3PL

Printed in India

Distributed in the United States, Canada and Latin America by Oxford University Press, 198 Madison Avenue, New York, NY 10016, United States America.

A Cataloguing-in-Publication data record for this book is available from the British Library.

ISBN: 9781849049559

www.hurstpublishers.com

CONTENTS

INTRODUCTION

In the past two decades the Islamic Republic of Iran has emerged as the preeminent indigenous power in the Middle East. This is despite decades of revolutionary turmoil and isolation on the international stage. How can this success be explained? Moreover, is this success sustainable? These are the key questions studied in depth in this book.

Iran's diplomatic and strategic success is all the more remarkable given that it has unfolded against the backdrop not only of fierce US opposition but of equally considerable regional pushback. Both Saudi Arabia and Israel view Iran as an enemy and have pulled no punches in their attempts to arrest Iranian strategic momentum.

Whilst ideology is often characterised as an impediment to Iran's internal political development, in terms of foreign policy it has been a key instrument of Iranian power projection. In strategic terms, Iran's idiosyncratic version of political Islam—born out of the 1979 revolution—is a key energiser and force multiplier.

In the last decade, this revolutionary ideology has taken distinctly sectarian tones by its strident adoption of Shia ideology and imagery. This has bolstered Iranian nationalism, since Shia Islam is a central pillar of Iranian national identity. Moreover, the enthusiastic embrace of the Shia cause has increased Iran's appeal to the wider region's disenfranchised Shia community.

It is by appealing to this community and by intervening in their conflicts with local regimes and other powers that Iran has been able to embed itself in all of the region's tension points, ranging from the Gaza Strip, Yemen and Bahrain to Syria and Lebanon. Intervening in conflicts—and thus becoming indispensable to conflict resolution— has been a key Iranian regional policy.

Ideology is also important in that it is a constant factor in Iranian strategic affairs, playing a consistent role through political vicissitudes and shifts in the balance of power within the Iranian establishment. Indeed, the nation's revolutionary ideology has not only survived unscathed but it has in fact strengthened against the backdrop of considerable political instability in Tehran. From May 1997 power in Iran has repeatedly switched hands, moving from conservatives to reformists to populists and subsequently to the ruling centrists led by President Hassan Rouhani.

All these political currents—and their underlying philosophies— have widely divergent views and approaches to politics and the economy. They have all tried to reshape the country in accordance with their beliefs and interests, some with greater success than the others. However, none of these currents have so much as attempted to fundamentally reshape the Islamic Republic's foreign policy. This speaks to the strength and resilience of the state ideology and of the institutions that propagate its doctrine. Institution-building has been one of the key features of post-revolutionary Iran, and has led to the formation of a dense institutional environment in the Islamic Republic that guarantees complex policy development and implementation. Institutional density also produces a consensual approach toward policymaking, which in turn facilitates accountability, if not transparency. In stark contrast, policymaking in pre-revolutionary Iran was relatively straightforward, and was often developed by the Shah and his closest advisors.

An important development in the past two decades has been the entrenchment of hard power institutions and the tentative emergence of an Iranian 'deep state'. This has been a largely indigenous process, in part reflecting the state's institutional density. It is also a reaction by ideological forces in the Islamic Republic to the chaos and factionalism often associated with contemporary Iranian political society. The rationale is simple: a cohesive national security community is an indispensable counterbalance to a fragmented political society.

Composed essentially of the Islamic Revolutionary Guard Corps (IRGC), the Ministry of Intelligence and Security (MOIS), and working in tandem with sympathetic elements in the foreign ministry and allied think-tanks, this deep power nexus operates at both formal and informal levels. At the formal—and hence relatively transparent – level this nexus has set about formulating and implementing realisable foreign policy objectives. By assigning an ideological tenor to these objectives they have made the job easier, not only for illuminating the national interest but also for finding local partners across the region to do Iran's bidding. In essence, the Iranian deep state is a coalition of ideological compatriots, spread across sensitive institutions and whose overriding achievement has been the establishment of hegemonic influence over national security discourse.

Iran as a revolutionary and ideological state has considerable and surprisingly enduring strategic momentum—one that the United States and its key regional allies Saudi Arabia and Israel have failed to stop. It remains to be seen at what point—and under what conditions— this momentum will finally stall. But the contention here is that post-revolutionary Iran has developed a sufficiently mature policymaking environment for it to maintain an advantage over regional rivals and foes that would survive even without this ideology-driven momentum.

Clearly ideology alone does not explain Iran's success. In fact, it is impossible even to begin to understand Iran's regional role and its global ambition without developing a deep understanding of the essential features of the country. This is the starting point of this book, namely a close look at the country's strategic profile, its location, human and natural resources, and its history.

Central to this analysis is the Islamic Revolution of 1979 which toppled the Shah and ushered in the dawn of the Islamic Republic. Often described by political scientists as the last real revolution of the modern era, the Iranian revolution fundamentally changed every aspect of the country. The biggest change, of course, was at the political level where the profile of the state changed from a nominally constitutional monarchy to an Islamic Republic. This change is crucial to understanding the role of ideology in reshaping Iranian ambitions, in that the Shah's regime was ideologically neutral (at least in foreign policy terms) whereas the Islamic Republic is profoundly ideological.

Arguably the greatest long-term impact of the revolution has been the development of a relatively sophisticated political society. The second chapter comprises the study of this political society and its relationship to the country's foreign policy. Criticisms of post-revolutionary Iranian democracy often focus on the perceived flaws of the system from a Western perspective. These critics are missing the forest for the trees, for Iran does not set out to emulate the West. In fact, much of Iranian politics is in opposition to Western political discourse, not simply for the sake of it, but because an independent path to political development and international standing is central to the goals of the Iranian revolution.

How is political society connected to foreign policy? In practically every major country, domestic politics ultimately impacts foreign policy, if not at a foundational ideological level, then at least in more practical ways in terms of rotation of power and elites, new national priorities, and so forth. In Iran's case the connection between domestic and foreign policy is greater than in most states, primarily because of the nation's revolutionary heritage and the establishment's perennial need to flaunt the country's advances with a view to validating the revolution.

In more immediate terms, the relative vibrancy of Iranian political society gives weight to the country's international ambitions insofar as Iran's democracy (flawed as it may be) stands in stark contrast to political atrophy and atavism across the region, particularly in Saudi Arabia, Iran's chief Arab adversary. Iran's political stability has come at a high cost – notably the suppression of a broad range of political forces and interest groups that have over the course of the past thirty-five years fallen foul of the establishment. But the Islamic Republic has set down firm roots, to the extent that political change in Iran is unfolding gradually and against the backdrop of a resilient state and society.

Looking ahead, the political instability that began with the ascent of the reformists twenty years ago may finally be coming to an end. The reformists have softened their position and formed a coalition with technocrats and centrists led by President Rouhani. This coalition has hitherto proved remarkably successful in the face of stiff conservative and principlist opposition, first in the Majlis (parliamentary) elections of March 2016 and then more convincingly in the May 2017 presidential elections.

Rouhani is the clearest expression of the bond between domestic and foreign policies in the Islamic Republic. He has spent decades at the heart of the Iranian national security establishment and in 2003 was the head of Iran's nuclear negotiating team. Rouhani's centrist approach veers away from the rhetoric of the revolution and instead aims at stabilising foreign policy gains and the pursuit of realisable goals in the context of the international order.

Iran's practical, as opposed to formal, acceptance of the prevailing international order is important in that it indicates a decisive move away from revolutionary dogma and ideals. But it does not necessarily signify the abandonment of ideology, not least because ideology has been key to Iran's regional success. More broadly, taking into account Iran's ambition to establish a global standing, a more proactive and accepting approach toward key international institutions and a willingness to work with key Western powers such as the US and the UK are crucial to Iran's success. In terms of advancing its global ambitions, the Islamic Republic may prove to be an arch-realist.

Iran employs a dual role of spoiler and troubleshooter to maintain and expand its regional influence. It is a spoiler in the sense that it has the resources, skills and local connectivity to frustrate US and Western goals in the region. Conversely, Iran can mobilise its considerable diplomatic and intelligence resources to solve regional problems. Western governments hope for a resolution of this dual position by offering cautious support to the centrists and technocrats allied to Rouhani. This double role as both good cop and bad cop is less a reflection of the actual nature of the Islamic Republic than a response to—and indeed a manipulation of – the West's decades-long inability to fully understand the Iranian system, evidenced by the persistent, reductive division of Iranian leaders and elites into 'moderates' and 'hardliners'.

But Western aspirations of finding a reliable focal point in the Iranian system are a forlorn hope, at least for the foreseeable future. The bifurcation of the Iranian system into 'moderates' and 'hardliners' is more wishful thinking than a reflection of reality. The West's continual misdiagnosis of the Iranian system stems, at least in part, from a desire to co-opt the Islamic Republic into the Western camp, in other words to restore the status quo ante. In this respect, Iranian leaders are correct to point out that the United States has never come to terms with the Iranian revolution.

The centrists so favoured by the West are not a minority voice within Iran's defence and foreign policy institutions. For example, the MOIS is currently in the grip of Rouhani proteges. More broadly, the bulk of the national security infrastructure is aligned to the Rouhani administration.

To be sure, the IRGC is a highly autonomous entity with a propensity to formulate and implement niche regional policies independently of the country's formal policymaking institutions. This is an important feature of Iranian modus operandi and the subject of study in the third chapter. In pushing an energetic regional policy, the IRGC essentially relies on a range of asymmetric capabilities. Through its expeditionary Qods Force, the IRGC organises, trains, arms and directs a multitude of non-state actors throughout the region. Most of these are concentrated in Iraq and the Levant region.

In Iraq, an array of Shia-dominated militias have been organised under the Popular Mobilisation Units (PMU) umbrella, backed by the IRGC. The PMU has been the spearhead in the fight against the so-called Islamic State (IS) group and following Iranian strategy has transformed the massive security threats beginning in early 2014 into strategic opportunities. This line of thought is reflected in the PMU's deep push into Arab Sunni areas of Anbar and Nineveh provinces. Furthermore, many signs point to the PMU's emergence as a state within a state in Iraq. The most important in regional strategic terms is the PMU's dominant position at key points of the Iraq–Syria border.

The trajectory of the PMU is not dissimilar to that of Lebanese Hezbollah in the 1980s and early 1990s, when with massive Iranian help Lebanon's once beleaguered Shia community overcame historical obstacles to emerge as the dominant force in the country's politics. This model is also being pursued in Yemen, albeit with a much lighter footprint. The Ansarullah movement (or the 'Houthis') consciously models itself on Lebanon's Hezbollah and fully deploys the 'resistance' narrative developed jointly by Iran and Hezbollah.

The so-called 'axis of resistance' forms the conceptual and ideological basis of the IRGC's regional policy. By framing Iran's regional outlook in oppositional terms, vis-à-vis the United States and Israel, and by mobilising the region's besieged Shia minorities (and, in the case of Iraq and Bahrain, Shia majorities), the IRGC has set out the blueprint for a highly energised and multi-faceted strategy whose momentum has intensified in recent years.

The fourth and fifth chapters look at two key countries where the IRGC model of deploying asymmetric tactics within the broader context of the 'resistance' narrative has proved remarkably successful. In Iraq, following the Anglo-American invasion in March–April 2003, Iran moved quickly to alter the country's profile from proximate enemy to friend and even potential ally. This Iranian strategy intensified at the end of 2011 with the formal withdrawal of US forces from Iraq. It intensified further still in early 2014 with the sweeping advance of IS across north-western and western Iraq. Already in a commanding position with respect to the Iraqi government, and specifically to the dominant Shia parties comprising the fledgling post-war Iraqi establishment, Iran turned the IS blitzkrieg to its advantage by mobilising the multitude of Shia militias under its full or partial control into a cohesive force: the PMU.

The PMU's skilful exploitation of the security and military crisis in Iraq—exemplified above all by its innovative military tactics and penetration of the deepest pockets of Arab Sunni Iraq—has consolidated Iraq's status within Iran's strategic orbit. These developments have far-reaching repercussions, not least the near total collapse of Arab Sunni political leadership and by extension the unprecedented empowerment of Iraqi Shias. A key challenge for Iranian policy is to manage this transition in the context of communal fragmentation and potential state breakup.

In Syria, the situation is even more complex. Syria is Iran's only formal ally, reflecting a deep relationship stretching back to the early years of the Iran–Iraq War, when Syria dissented from the Arab fold by openly backing Iran. Maintaining this alliance has been a key preoccupation of Iranian policy for decades. Apart from a deep affinity for Syria's ruling regime rooted in the experience of the Iran–Iraq War, Iran is fully committed to Syria for a broad range of ideological and pragmatic reasons. Above all, Syria is crucial to the cohesion of the 'axis of resistance', specifically the continual empowerment of Lebanese Hezbollah.

It is in this context that the full spectrum of asymmetric assets has been mobilised in Syria, ranging from the deployment of experienced Qods Force personnel (ostensibly in an advisory role), to the mobilisation of Shia militias from across the region and beyond, as well as, crucially, the development of parallel defence and security structures in Syria in the form of the National Defence Forces.

In terms of the Syrian intervention, the key question for Iranian policy is whether the expected and potential dividends match or exceed the investment in blood and treasure. It is noteworthy that in the course of saving its key ally, the Islamic Republic has paid a considerable reputational price, effectively alienating itself in the eyes of the Sunni Arab public. Nevertheless, the existing gains are not insubstantial. For a start, Iran has been forced to diversify its diplomacy by engaging with a wide range of powers involved in the Syrian conflict, ranging from Russia and Turkey to the United States and Qatar. The intervention in Syria may come to be recognised as the moment when post-revolutionary Iran developed a truly global diplomacy.

Looking ahead, Iranian regional and global diplomacy has three country-specific challenges, and these are studied in depth in the final chapters. First, Saudi Arabia is Iran's key regional rival, seeking to challenge the Islamic Republic on multiple fronts, ranging from proxy warfare to engaging at the sectarian level with a view to pushing back against the Shia-grounded 'resistance' narrative. Whilst a 'hot' war is not imminent, in the short term at least this confrontation is set to escalate, potentially to the point of limited military clashes. The outcome of this confrontation—however incomplete or partial—will have huge repercussions for the region. At the centre of it all is the tug of war in Bahrain, where an indigenous protest movement—and lately an emerging low-level insurgency—will inevitably present tough yet appealing choices to Iranian strategists and policymakers. There can be little doubt that Iran would consider a direct intervention in Bahrain if it felt strong enough, a prospect that carries global ramifications.

After Saudi Arabia, Israel is Iran's most determined foe. In contrast to its perspective on Saudi Arabia (which is mostly seen as a historical rival and not necessarily as a diehard enemy), the Islamic Republic considers Israel a great civilisational foe. For nearly four decades Iranian propaganda has called for the destruction—or, failing that, the abolition—of the Jewish state. Like Saudi Arabia, Israel competes with Iran for regional strategic space and influence. This competition is mostly focused on the Levant, and here Iran has the upper hand in the shape of Lebanese Hezbollah. By as good as placing itself on the Israel–Lebanon border, the Islamic Republic appears to directly threaten the Jewish state.

But are these two states natural enemies? A careful study of recent history as well as of the foundational dynamics shaping the regional landscape suggest otherwise. This begs the question as to the circumstances under which Iran and Israel could de-escalate their conflict. The answer lies in Iran's much more significant and far more fraught relationship with the United States. The final chapter looks at whether the Islamic Republic could ever come to terms with the 'Great Satan'. The developments of the past two decades, and especially since the Anglo-American invasion of Iraq in 2003, have shown that Iran can sustain strategic growth whilst at the same time managing multiple tension points with the US, both in the region and beyond.

The nuclear accord of July 2015 is important in that it marked the first time Iran and the US engaged in intense and consistent multilateral and bilateral diplomacy. Briefly there was great hope that the positive dynamics flowing from the nuclear accord could be expanded and replicated in other areas, potentially heralding a partial Iranian–American rapprochement. Not surprisingly these hopes were quickly dashed by the rise of Donald Trump and a renewal of tough US rhetoric.

I argue that despite these obstacles, in order to achieve a sustainable dominant position in the region, as well as wider international standing, Iran will need to secure relations with the US on a stable footing. On balance, nearly four decades of estrangement from the world's sole superpower have been to Iran's detriment. But how realistic is partial rapprochement in the context of the multiple and very serious disagreements between these two powers? This is arguably the greatest challenge for Iranian diplomacy in the years ahead, namely to identify and pursue realistic points of agreement and cooperation with the US.

Whilst Iran is committed to global multipolarity—and is thus naturally drawn to powers like China and Russia—it can nevertheless find the space to engage more with the US.

Provided Iranian strategists, policymakers and diplomats continue to make the correct decisions—and to fully exploit opportunities and threats as they arise –there is no reason to doubt that Iran could emerge as an important power in the twenty-first century, with the ability to contribute and shape events beyond the region. A key driver towards a bigger geopolitical profile will be Iran's demographic changes, namely the expected growth in population. Iran's population nearly doubled in the decade after the revolution, but after the end of the Iran–Iraq War the government stabilised the birth rate.

The political and cultural grounds on which the birth control programme of the early 1990s was anchored is under close scrutiny and is being slowly deconstructed. Indeed, the Iranian leader, Ayatollah Khamenei, has repeatedly called for a doubling of the population (which currently stands at around 80 million), arguing that the country has both the space and resources to accommodate many more people. Crucially, Khamenei links population growth to national prestige and power.

It remains to be seen whether Khamenei's aspiration will be translated into policy, but any significant increase in the population would clearly raise a broad range of resource-centred issues. Despite significant diversification in the past couple of decades, the Iranian economy continues to be dominated by oil, natural gas and their derivatives. A substantial and prolonged drop in the price of oil will have significant ramifications for the economy and, by extension, Iran's foreign policy.

Dwindling water sources is another resource-centred issue and one that is being slowly identified as a national security threat. The management of a potential water crisis, in addition to better management of the economy, possibly in the context of significant demographic changes, is of central importance to the Islamic Republic's regional ambitions and global standing.

The breakdown of the JCPOA and the re-imposition of sanctions by the Trump administration compound Iran's demographic, environmental and economic challenges. To sustain an expansive regional policy—and by extension to continually increase Iran's ecological footprint—requires consistent economic growth. Sustainable economic growth is in turn dependent on expert management and expansive engagement with the global economy.

Sanctions are clearly a major impediment to economic and financial engagement with the world. Even if the latest round of brutal US sanctions is eased at some point in the near future, Iran is still faced with the prospect of indefinite US economic and financial harassment. Indeed, absent a dramatic shift in Iranian strategic posture, the US is set to continually sanction the Islamic Republic in one form or another.

The mismanagement of the economy may not be directly attributable to sanctions but nevertheless it cannot be entirely divorced from it either. Iran's rentier economy and the corruption and lack of transparency associated with it are by-products of the country's embattled economic environment. The paucity of financial and commercial engagement with the outside world has enabled the emergence and consolidation of an unmeritocratic economic elite.

Hitherto Iran has managed to formulate and implement an ambitious foreign policy in the midst of continual economic crisis. It remains to be seen whether this model is sustainable, especially as the US doubles down on its plans to sabotage Iran's economy.

IRAN'S BACKGROUND

Iran, by virtue of its size and history, is a natural regional power. The country is unique in the Middle East in that it is an 'authentic' nation-state—its polity and national identity have evolved slowly over millennia. No other country in the region can claim such a long history. Israel professes ancient roots but the Jewish people were displaced from their original homeland for centuries before they resettled largely Arab Palestinian territories in the late nineteenth and early twentieth centuries.

Egypt can also be regarded as an ancient culture but not necessarily as an ancient nation-state. The ancient Egyptian polity was overthrown following the demise of the Pharaohs and the country did not truly develop a modern political consciousness until the nineteenth century. Moreover, it did not achieve modern independence until the 1940s.

By contrast, the Iranian state evolved continuously over two millennia and has had a distinct cultural and political identity since the advent of the Achaemenid (Hakhamaneshian) Empire in 550 BC. To be sure, Iran has been the subject of violent overthrow on many occasions, notably at the hands of Alexander the Great, the Muslim Arabs of the seventh century AD and the Mongols in the thirteenth century. But despite these catastrophic events, the Iranian state was revived in due course, owing not in small part to the country's resilient and rich culture.

The Muslim Arab invasion of the seventh century is arguably Iran's best example of a national catastrophe. It was followed by centuries of occupation, punctuated by a period of national revival that led to the reunification of Iran as an independent state by the Safavids. The Arab Muslim invasion is uniquely important insofar as it is the single invasion most remembered and lamented by modern Iranians. Whilst many observers detect a strong anti-Arab bias in Iranians' selective historical memory, it is the cultural aspects of this episode that resonate deeply with the Iranian people.

Whilst the ancient Iranians either enthusiastically embraced Islam or converted over a long period for socio-economic or political reasons, the country refused to relinquish its national identity, embodied most importantly by its national language Farsi, in the face of a sustained colonisation campaign by the Arab conquerors and rulers. This resistance constituted a radical departure from trajectories in other areas conquered by the early Muslims, notably the Levant and North Africa, where indigenous languages—and attendant identities—were swept away by the Arabic language and Arab culture. Even ancient Egypt could not resist and adopted Arabic, thereby relinquishing a substantive connection with its ancient history.

In Iran, this consciously maintained connection with the ancient past would also have been lost had it not been for the revival of the national language, a movement spearheaded by the tenth-century poet Ferdowsi, who produced the epic *Shahnameh* (Book of Kings). Although it was based largely on mythology, *Shahnameh* reproduced Iranian political consciousness within recognisable cultural terms and boundaries, as embodied by the division of 'Iran' and 'Turan' (the latter encompassing the lands beyond the Iranian frontier, roughly corresponding to Central Asia today). Moreover, Ferdowsi adapted the Persian language so that it absorbed new Arabic words and terms whilst retaining its linguistic core. This was a new Farsi that took into account the seismic events of the past 350 years, beginning with the collapse of the mighty Sassanid Empire, the sweeping away of the national religion, Zoroastrianism, and its replacement with Islam, the colonisation of the country by Arabs from the Arabian Peninsula and Mesopotamia and a 300-year-long occupation.

Iran's recovery from Arab Muslim occupation and the re-emergence of localised Iranian states from the tenth century onwards set the stage for an imperial revival 450 years later in the form of the Safavid Empire. What is crucial is that despite multiple occupations— and ensuing national, demographic and cultural devastation – the idea of Iran has endured. This idea in turn helps to build a powerful state underpinned by a uniquely rich culture and confident national identity.

This historical continuity is widely recognised by Iranian historians as well as by historians of Iran. This basic consensus notwithstanding, a debate continues to rage on whether Iran is a nation or an empire. Inevitably the debate has been highly politicised, with the country's adversaries trying to present Iran as an empire whilst most Iranians consider themselves to belong to a nation, finding Iran's imperial dimensions to figure only incidentally as part of their long and chequered history.

The accounts of Iran's critics aim to reduce contemporary Iran to a Persian linguistic and cultural core, with a view to energising separatist movements on the country's periphery. This tactic is founded on a deep appreciation of the country's centrifugal forces—its perennial centre–periphery tension. This friction is a key feature of the Iranian political landscape and recurs during periods of extreme political stress, most recently in the aftermath of the 1979 Islamic revolution.

These tensions aside, it is reductionist to frame Iran as an empire. This approach takes no account of the country's strong national identity and culture, in which a great majority of the country's population are deeply invested. Moreover, it displays a misunderstanding of ethnic identities in an Iranian context. For example, the Persian-speaking majority do not consider themselves an ethnic group. Moreover, the second-largest linguistic group, namely the Azeri Turks, are so deeply embedded into the fabric of national life as to be indistinguishable from Persian speakers in their interests, at least insofar as national affairs are concerned.

Whilst Iran is indeed composed of an ethnic mosaic, with some groups, particularly the Kurds and the Baloch, displaying strong ethnic identities, the country's national identity is overarching and supersedes parochial affiliations. In this respect, Iran is radically different from its Arab neighbours, as tribalism has largely disappeared from the Iranian national landscape. This was largely due to the aggressive nation-building project of Reza Shah in the 1920s and 1930s. While there are still residual and stubborn pockets of tribalism in the country—amongst some Arab communities in the western Khuzestan province and some Baluchis in the south-eastern Sistan va Baluchistan province—these are exceptions rather than the norm. By and large, tribalism does not influence modern Iranians' political behaviour or indeed any significant aspect of their lives.

The centre–periphery tension cannot be reduced to an inter-ethnic struggle between a Persian-speaking majority and marginalised ethnic groups fighting for their rights. It is, more accurately, a struggle for power, as marginalised groups—led by narrow and ambitious elites—fight for more resources, and potentially even for greater autonomy, possibly in a federal national structure. This will to power takes on ethnic and cultural forms as an identity marker and for motivational and mobilisational effect.

The best recent example was the large-scale fighting that erupted in Kurdish-majority regions following the revolutionary victory in February 1979. Spearheaded by the Kurdish Democratic Party of Iran (KDPI)—led at the time by the charismatic Abdul-Rahman Ghassemlou—the KDPI took over military bases and other state institutions with the stated intention of carving out autonomy, which many interpreted as a dash for independence.

The centre re-asserted itself quickly by taking back occupied areas, but a low-level insurgency by the KDPI and other narrow elitist groups purporting to champion Kurdish rights dragged on until the mid-1980s. In fact, these groups were never totally eradicated and a new generation of Kurdish separatists continues to wage intermittent and low-level violence against the Iranian state.

But the centre–periphery cleavage transcends ethnic-centred quests for empowerment and potential separation. It is also about culture and modes of living, which ultimately reflects the nature of modern state-building in Iran. The modern Iranian state can be traced to the emergence of the Pahlavi monarchy, founded by Reza Khan in the early 1920s. Once crowned Shah in 1924, Reza Khan set about implementing an ambitious modernisation programme which transformed Iranian national life. Indeed, much of the country's critical infrastructure, including roads and other transportation networks, was built during that period.

Like other grand modernisation programmes at the time, Reza Shah's project was underpinned by far-reaching cultural engineering which sought to overthrow many traditional modes of living. The Persian-speaking core of the country, in addition to the Azeri provinces and the Caspian region, generally responded well to this cultural engineering project. But the Kurdish-majority region, some Arab communities and the Baluchi element in the impoverished Sistan va Baluchistan province responded less well.

Notwithstanding Reza Shah's harshness, the modernisation campaign in Iran was less brutal than in other countries, notably neighbouring Turkey, which under Kemal Ataturk was experiencing a painful transition from a caliphate to a modern republic. This was accompanied by continual repression of minority identities, particularly of the Kurds. By contrast, in Iran the minorities were rarely (if ever) subjected to such harsh measures, which in Turkey's case went as far as denial of the existence of a national Kurdish identity and instead calling the Kurds 'mountain Turks'. In Iran, starting from Reza Shah's reign, the focus of the state was to supresses narrow elitist groups that purported to represent minority rights. By and large, minorities were left alone to practise their culture with minimal state interference in their way of life.

That is not to say that all aspects of minority culture were accepted at an official level or reflected in the practices of state institutions. Linguistic minorities have long complained of discrimination in the education sector, since other languages or dialects are not on a par with the official state language Farsi. These minority demands are being met, albeit intermittently and in ways that do not undermine national cohesion.

The differences in modern state-building between Turkey and Iran are worth considering further. In Turkey, the modern Kemalist state adopted a harsh and totalitarian approach toward minorities because it feared disintegration and national collapse. This spoke to a lack of national confidence, arguably a reflection of the less than formidable roots of the Turkish nation state. By contrast, modern state-builders in Iran were more confident of reconciling the past with the present with a view to developing modern statecraft.

Nevertheless, it can be argued that the Pahlavis went too far in their drive to 'revive' ancient Iranian culture and identity. The constant evocation of the glory of ancient Persian kings, and of pre-Islamic values and standards more broadly, inevitably created a clash between the two poles of Iranian identity, namely Iranian nationalism and Shia Islam. Eventually, this conflict would—in the late 1970s—contribute to the emergence of a national revolt against the Pahlavi system, culminating in the success of the Islamic revolution.

But despite all its faults—above all the failure to resolve centre–periphery tensions—modern state-building in Iran has been a largely successful enterprise. The country's modern institutions reflect both national identity and the shared heritage of Iran's rich history. This has contributed to the endurance of these institutions, notably the modern national army (founded in the 1920s), and the education and justice systems. The strength of these institutions in part explains Iran's relative stability. Moreover, it has enabled the country to formulate and implement ambitious foreign policies.

The Cohesive Effect of Shia Islam

No study of Iranian statecraft and foreign policy is complete without a detailed consideration of the role of Shia Islam in Iranian state formation and the resulting impact on Iranian national identity, attitudes and external policy drivers and choices. The drivers for Shia Islam's advent in Iran are open to dispute. Devout Iranian Shias point to Shiism's emphasis on justice and continual struggle against oppression as a central point of appeal. According to this view, Iranians invariably prioritise the quest for justice over the quest for liberty and other political objectives. Others argue that Iranians were drawn to Shiism from its earliest days not only on account of agreement with its tenets but also, perhaps more importantly, because of a desire to stand out from the crowd. From this point of view, Shiism was a tool with which Iranians could defend their national identity in the face of a concerted Arab colonisation project.

In terms of the faith itself, there have been many attempts to find similarities or at least draw parallels between Shia doctrine and ancient Iranian beliefs and values. Much of this effort has been undertaken by modern Iranian nationalists keen to fully reconcile what is essentially a foreign religion with the country's pre-Islamic heritage. This ambition is not as esoteric as it might be in other parts of the world, for, as discussed earlier, Iranians maintain a conscious link with their pre-Islamic past, as expressed through national celebrations such as the Nowruz new year festival.

The contention here is that Shiism is Iranians' most important identity-marker. This statement obviously needs qualification, not least because around 10 per cent of the Iranian population is non-Shia, being either Sunni Muslims or from non-Islamic religious minorities, notably Armenian Christians, Zoroastrians and Jews. Moreover, there are many elements that comprise Iranian identity, not least the country's pre-Islamic heritage and the rituals, festivals and complex set of myths and semi-myths embedded in that imagined history.

However, Shiism is central to Iranian identity insofar as the majority's core beliefs and values are rooted in the history, traditions and doctrines of that heterodox branch of Islam. Shiism essentially informs the Iranian worldview and Iranians' understanding of social and political justice. It defines Iranians' place in the world, both how they relate to each other and, more importantly, how they relate to the outside world. This foundational role is buttressed and formalised by the fact that Twelver Shiism is the country's official state religion.

What is striking is how a relatively recent development in the nation's long history has had such profound and transformational impact on Iranian identity, socio-political organisation and geopolitical profile. The advent of Twelver Shiism as Iran's official state religion took place just over 500 years ago, beginning with the rise to power of the Safavid dynasty in the early sixteenth century. Before this Shiism had existed in Iran—and in some cases formed the basis of local states, particularly in the Caspian region—but it was rarely a cohesive and unifying force. Moreover, Shiism in Iran came in many shapes and forms before the establishment of the Safavid dynasty, with Twelver Shias a distinct minority in the Iranian plateaux.

This historical reality undermines the arguments of the 'nativist' school, whose foundational belief revolves around the notion that Shiism, at least in some respects, forms a continuum with Zoroastrianism and other pre-Islamic Iranian belief systems such as Mithraism. It also disproves the arguments of many Arab nationalists, who hold that Shiism is essentially an Iranian creation, designed to meet Iran's cultural and political needs, especially in respect of the country's interaction with its Arab neighbours.

In fact, in purely historical and doctrinal terms, there is nothing intrinsically Iranian about Shiism, as the heterodox faith emerged and developed in a distinctly Arab milieu, particularly in southern and central regions of Mesopotamia, where the bulk of Shia history, mythology and accompanying shrines and holy sites are concentrated. Whilst a cogent argument can be made that foundational Iranian beliefs were more easily reconciled with Shia doctrines than with orthodox Sunni ones, the notion that there were deeper primordial connections between pre-Islamic Iran and Shiism is not based on fact.

The connection becomes even more complex when we consider that the Safavids were a Turkic dynasty of Turkmen Sufi descent. This further belies the myth of a 'Persian' conspiracy either to concoct or corrupt Shiism with a view to transforming it into a tool of cultural and political domination. Whilst the Safavids—like many Turkic tribes before and after them—adopted the Persian language, their original identity and culture were formed in the steppes of Central Asia, as opposed to the sophisticated towns and communities of the Persian-speaking heartlands of the Iranian plateaux.

The Safavids' adoption of Twelver Shiism was arguably motivated more by political considerations than by doctrinal and devotional passion. While by most accounts the Safavids were fanatical Shias, their decision to elevate the importance of the Shia religion and to frame modern Iranian identity around it was doubtless influenced in no small measure by their hostile external environment. The most proximate threat to Iran's new Turkic rulers was the mighty Ottoman Empire, which was also originally comprised of Turkic tribes from the Central Asian steppes.

The Ottoman Empire was the seat of the Islamic Caliphate and, by extension, the champion and arbiter of orthodox Sunni Islam. By adopting Twelver Shiism as the state religion, the Safavids above all made an astute geopolitical choice: a revived Iranian Empire could justify its existence—and set about expanding—by posing as an ideological and religious alternative to the Ottomans. This strategy was remarkably successful; not only did it prevent the absorption of the Iranian heartland into the Ottoman Empire, but equally importantly it created the setting for the flourishing and expansion of the modern Iranian state.

The Safavids were undoubtedly Iran's most important post-Islamic ruling dynasty. They created the first cohesive and expansive Iranian Empire since the pre-Islamic Sassanid dynasty, which was swept into oblivion by Arab Muslim armies in the seventh century. By reviving an ancient empire, the Safavids lent credence to Iran's enduring political integrity—which had survived nearly a millennium of occupation and fragmentation—and proved the country's perennial geopolitical potential. The characterisation of contemporary Iran as a 'Sassanid-Safavid entity' by modern Salafi-Jihadis like al-Qaeda and the Islamic State (IS) may be malicious, but it is not entirely off the mark.

Aside from reviving the idea of Iran as a powerful state, the Safavids created many of the foundational institutions that form the bedrock of Iranian state and society. Foremost amongst these were the Shia clerical institutions, with their hierarchical structures (at least in relation to their Sunni counterparts). These bodies went on to exert decisive influence at key moments in modern Iranian history, notably during the two Iranian revolutions of the twentieth century: the constitutional revolution of 1908–1909 and the Islamic revolution seventy years later.

Through its patronage of Twelver Shia clericalism—advanced in no small part by importing Shia clerics from southern Lebanon and Iraq—the Safavids not only played a central role in cementing Shiism in the deepest fabrics of Iranian society, but they also unwittingly introduced deep and centrifugal tensions into the heart of Iranian statecraft. The empowerment of Shia clergy came at a huge cost: this clerical class was politically astute, and in view of their proximity to the centres of power, leading clerics would inevitably develop political ambitions of their own.

The Shia clerical class played a central role in key national moments, including the tobacco concession protest of 1890–91, led by Grand Ayatollah Mirza Hassan Shirazi; the constitutional revolution of 1909; the oil nationalisation movement in the early 1950s; and, of course, the 1979 Islamic revolution. The Islamic revolution finally resolved the tensions between the clergy and the state by propelling the clerical class into the commanding heights of the Iranian government. By capturing the higher reaches of the state, so the argument goes, the clerics were able to remould state and society in their own image.

But the 'theocracy' argument—beloved by many Western reporters and analysts—fails to take sufficient stock of the reality of power structures in post-revolutionary Iran. For a start, only a minority of clerics are involved in politics and government. Whilst it is true that the Shia clerical class enjoys an elevated status—and associated benefits—because of the revolution, the fact remains that the vast majority of clerics are based at the seminaries where they are engaged in teaching and learning.

Moreover, a significant number of clerics—including leading Ayatollahs—have expressed opposition toward the ruling system and paid dearly for it. The most famous example is the late Ayatollah Hossein Ali Montazeri—once the late Ayatollah Khomeini's designated successor—who fell out of favour because of his critique of certain state policies, especially those concerning political prisoners. He was ostracised and confined to house arrest for prolonged periods.

Still, the strongest counter-argument to the 'theocracy' thesis—and the attendant discourse on the resolution of centuries-old tensions at the heart of Iranian statecraft—is provided by the presence of structural tensions within the ruling system, notably the cleavage between the Supreme Leader and the presidency. *Velayat-e Faqih* (Rule of the Jurisconsult), or the guardianship of the country by an Islamic jurist, is the cornerstone of Iran's idiosyncratic system of Islamic government. The Supreme Leader, or *Valiyeh Faqih* (ruling jurisconsult), enjoys sweeping powers, conferred on him by the constitution, including commanding the armed forces and appointing the heads of major state institutions (such as the state broadcaster), the head of the judiciary and Friday prayer leaders across the country.

By contrast to the *Valiyeh Faqih*, the head of the executive branch of government is directly elected through universal suffrage. As such, he has a mandate from the electorate to implement his proposed policies and to run the country. This mandate inevitably clashes with the higher powers of the *Valiyeh Faqih*, especially if the latter continuously interferes in the domestic and foreign policies. The history of the Islamic Republic—barring the first revolutionary decade—bears out this analysis.

The 1980s were an exception inasmuch as the towering charismatic figure of Ayatollah Ruhollah Khomeini concealed systemic tensions. Following Khomeini's death in June 1989 and the rise to power of his successor Ayatollah Seyed Ali Hosseini Khamenei, these tensions came to the fore, at first gradually and then, since 1997, in increasingly aggravated forms. Indeed, the current *Valiyeh Faqih* has had major issues with all elected heads of government since 1989, including Ali Akbar Hashemi Rafsanjani (1989–1997), Seyed Mohammad Khatami (1997–2005), Mahmoud Ahmadinejad (2005–2013) and Hassan Rouhani (2013–present).

In recent years, these tensions have reached a high point, especially following Rouhani's convincing victory in the May 2017 presidential elections, where he comfortably defeated the establishment favourite Seyed Ebrahim Raissi. The key question is whether this tension constitutes a centrifugal force in Iranian politics, and particularly how it will affect the country once Ayatollah Khamenei departs the arena, thus potentially sparking a major constitutional crisis. This issue will be examined in depth in the next chapter. At this juncture, suffice to say that the Islamic Republic, far from overcoming the clerical versus technocratic divide at the heart of Iranian statecraft, has arguably exacerbated this chronic tension by placing clerics and technocrats in close proximity.

But beyond the political system's structural tensions—which are, after all, a function of the exercise of power – the Islamic Republic has, in terms of broader culture and society, deliberately and successfully deepened the marriage between Shiism and Iranian nationalism. Of course, this merger occurred long ago and has undergone several developmental stages, including a period of forced decoupling during the Pahlavi dynasty (1925–1979). Reza Shah was keen to re-centre Iranian nationalism on the country's pre-Islamic past and set out to disenfranchise the Shia clerics and thereby undercut Shiism as a whole. Whilst his son and successor, Mohammad Reza Shah Pahlavi, was much milder in his approach, he too sought to anchor nationalism within a secular framework, which in practice amounted to the import of Western cultural values. Therefore, far from 'Persianising' Iran, the Pahlavis merely managed to impose a veneer of Westernisation, which by all credible accounts was resented by the broad mass of the people.

It is little wonder that every pillar of Iranian society abandoned the Pahlavi regime in the fateful year of 1978–1979.

By contrast, the Islamic Republic uses Shiism to mobilise and energise the public. Shia doctrine, imagery and folklore constitute the Islamic Republic's basic frame of reference and, in terms of political mobilisation, has been remarkably successful. But how do we account for the hegemonic power of this discourse? Shiism, at least in its devotional form, is of course woven into the fabric of Iranian society. But this is an insufficient explanation, especially in view of modern Iranian political history where materialistic ideologies, in particular Marxism-Leninism (and its local derivatives) made significant inroads in the second part of the twentieth century. Moreover, oppositional discourses have emerged from within the Islamic Republic, notably the reform movement, which has tried to advance Western notions of citizenship divorced from religious identity and affiliation.

But neither the loyal reformists, nor the subversive Green movement (which emerged out of the bowels of the reformist phenomenon), have been able to significantly displace, let alone overthrow, the Islamic Republic's official Shia-centric discourse. To understand the hegemonic power of this discourse, we need to examine the impact of the Iran–Iraq War (1980–1988). Whilst the Islamic Republic failed to militarily defeat Baathist Iraq, it can credibly lay claim to a moral and political victory. This is evident in the enduring legacy of the war, most visibly in the form of 'martyrs' murals and portraits, which are emblazoned on iconic buildings across the country. By contrast, in Iraq the war is long forgotten and certainly not commemorated in any significant way.

The Shia 'martyr' complex was used to maximum effect during the war for the purpose of legitimation and, more importantly, mobilisation. It helped that the homeland of Iran's enemy housed most of the important Shia shrines, notably the shrines of Ali ibn Abi Talib and Imam Hossein, in Najaf and Karbala respectively. The focus on Shia history, imagery and ideology intensified when Iran went on the offensive in June 1982, following the Iranian recapture of the border town of Khorramshahr. It was convenient to justify what amounted to the invasion of Iraq in terms of liberating the iconic Shia shrines. Hence, the battle cry of 'the path to Jerusalem passes through Karbala', became central in Iranian war propaganda.

It was the seamless amalgamation of Shia ideology and Iranian nationalism that accounted for the resounding success of Iranian wartime propaganda. In the initial phase of the war, from September 1980 to May 1982, patriotic themes dominated propaganda, with the newly established Islamic Republic rallying the people to defend their homeland against imminent Iraqi occupation. The urgency was warranted, as in the initial phase of the war, in accordance with its declared war aims, Iraq was posed to occupy large areas of the strategically important and oil-rich south-western Khuzestan province.

The thematic propaganda shift towards a focus on the defence of Shiism ran in parallel with a shift in the institutional direction of the war. In the early years, the national Iranian armed forces—comprised of the army, air force and navy—were at the forefront of repelling the Iraqi invasion and prosecuting the war. The Iranian air force in particular was instrumental in blunting the Iraqi advance and inflicting painful blows on Iraqi military and economic infrastructure. By 1978 the Iranian air force was the largest in the Middle East, indeed one of the largest in the world, and was equipped with state-of-the-art US-supplied F-4 Phantoms, F-5s and F-14 Tomcats. Although the air force leadership and large segments among the senior officers had been purged by the new revolutionary regime, the organisation was sufficiently intact to coordinate a credible air defence as well as to plan and execute sophisticated offensive missions deep inside Iraq.

From mid-1982 onwards the regular military's role was superseded by that of the Islamic Revolutionary Guard Corps (IRGC), commonly known as the Pasdaran (Guardians). Founded in May 1979 the Pasdaran was a new organisation whose initial remit of defending the Islamic revolution quickly expanded following the outbreak of war, to the point that the IRGC had by 1983 transformed into a fully-fledged tri-service military organisation. This inevitably created multi-level tensions with the regular armed forces, especially in relation to duplication of roles and a struggle for resources.

But the tensions ran even deeper to encompass ideological moorings and modes of legitimation. The regular Iranian armed forces—like major armies across the world—derive their legitimacy from the foundational concepts of the nation-states that organise and deploy them. The army exists to serve the nation, and the armed forces by extension position themselves as the bastions of nationalism. By contrast, the Pasdaran's primary role was not defined in conventional military terms of defending state sovereignty and the nation-state's territorial integrity. The IRGC foundational charter tasked it primarily with defending the Islamic revolution against internal and external threats.

As the IRGC expanded organisationally and assumed a dominant role in the prosecution of the war, the Pasdaran's chief ideologues and leading political planners set out to expand and crystallise the organisation's ideological mission. The cornerstone of that ideology was firmly rooted in the foundational values of the revolution, and to that end the Pasdaran were fully committed to the defence of the Islamic Republic and its ruling clerical class. But Pasdaran ideologues dug deeper to engineer an Iranian nationalism whose ethos departed from the specific circumstances underpinning modern Iranian nation-state formation. In other words, theirs was an ideal form of nationalism whose foundational principle is a seamless, clear-cut and perennial marriage between Iran and Shia Islam.

By contriving this ideology and its attendant modes of institutional legitimation, the Pasdaran effectively placed themselves on a par with the regular armed forces in having credible foundational concepts. In immediate terms, this political-ideological process enabled the Pasdaran to justify their transformation from a militia to a professional tri-service military organisation. In the long term, the potency of this ideological vision helped the Pasdaran to justify institutional perpetuity, to the point that Iran is currently the only country in the world with two fully independent military commands.

These processes are critically important for understanding the origins, nature and objectives of Iranian foreign policy. The IRGC is the backbone of the Iranian national security establishment and its ideological vision and resulting strategic objectives form the thrust of Iran's push for regional dominance and defiance of the United States. The Pasdaran's expansive national security role developed following the end of the Iran–Iraq War in the summer of 1988, when, contrary to widespread expectation, the IRGC successfully resisted pressure to either disband or merge with the regular armed forces. At the time, Pasdaran commanders and their allies in the political establishment successfully argued that without the IRGC, the revolution would become immediately vulnerable. This was despite the fact that the IRGC had performed poorly in the closing stages of the war, when Iraq went on the offensive by retaking the Fao Peninsula in April 1988 (originally captured by Iran in February 1986) and henceforth most of Iraqi territory that Iran had captured from June 1982 onwards.

The Pasdaran's fortunes improved following the demise of Ayatollah Khomeini and the ascension of Seyed Ali Khamenei to the leadership role. Lacking Khomeini's religious and political stature, as well as his towering charisma, the new *Valiyeh Faqih* instead sought to develop an institutional power base. The IRGC was central to this drive, not least because leading Pasdaran commanders and ideologues shared Khamenei's political and ideological outlook. This is a bond that has survived—and indeed strengthened—to the point that the IRGC high command is unflinchingly loyal to Khamenei.

This bond was arguably the main driver behind the gradual expansion of the Pasdaran's role, not just in national security terms, but also increasingly in relation to the development of an impressive economic portfolio. Today the Pasdaran exercise significant economic power, primarily through project managing some of the country's largest infrastructure projects. This is organised through the Khatam al-Anbia Construction Headquarters, the IRGC's central project management organisation. In addition, the Pasdaran either own or exercise controlling stakes in countless firms and businesses spanning the full spectrum of economic activity. This sizeable economic power notwithstanding, it is a mistake to claim (as many do) that the Pasdaran control Iran's economy. The IRGC is one significant economic player amongst many in Iran's complex and murky economy. They are not even the biggest non-governmental player; that accolade goes to the Mashhad-based Astaneh Qods Razavi, whose primary function is to manage the Imam Reza shrine but which, by extension, also manages a vast business empire employing tens of thousands of people, with an estimated annual revenue of $15 billion.

Furthermore, the regular Iranian armed forces are also involved in business activity—albeit on a smaller scale than the IRGC—without attracting any negative publicity. Chief amongst these is the ETTEKA chain of supermarkets, which originally catered to service families, but is now open to the general public. Serving and former members of the armed forces, and their immediate families, can purchase items at discounted prices. Whilst the intense focus on the Pasdaran's economic activities can be in the public interest in the framework of transparency and accountability, often the reports are exaggerated and are part of a psychological warfare campaign against the organisation. This campaign has intensified in recent years, particularly after the ascension of Hassan Rouhani to the presidency, and now forms an intrinsic feature of the power struggle between the centrist–reformist coalition and their 'principlist'—or conservative—rivals. This relationship will be explored further in the next chapter.

A full appreciation of the Pasdaran's domination of the Iranian national security state also requires an understanding of the IRGC's precise role in politics. This is a highly contentious issue and subject to widespread confusion and exaggeration. From a constitutional point of view, all armed services are barred from engaging or meddling in politics. This constitutional prohibition on political activity was reinforced by Ayatollah Khomeini's strong advice to all sections of the military, in particular the Pasdaran, to stay away from politics. Today, Pasdaran commanders—and their allies in the political establishment—would argue that the IRGC has steadfastly adhered to the guidelines of the Islamic Republic's founder. In addition, they would argue that as the primary defenders of the revolution, the Pasdaran view constitutional compliance as intrinsic to their overall mission.

The controversy starts when the Pasdaran insist on an expansive interpretation of the constitution, since the IRGC's role of defending the revolution by definition necessitates a degree of politicisation, if not actual interference in politics. Pasdaran commanders and ideologues argue that their 'intervention' in politics is limited to political analysis with a view to identifying threats to the ideological integrity and cohesion of the Islamic Republic. To that end, the IRGC regularly releases political analysis through its Political Bureau, whose chief, Yadollah Javani, is renowned for his hardline ideological approach. Additionally, IRGC commanders, including the commander in chief Major General Mohammad Ali Jaafari, regularly comment on political events, often in combative terms or, failing that, with a distinct ideological accent.

It goes without saying that this intervention produces a reaction, as members of the political class, or more accurately the reformists and centrists who are often implicitly addressed by Pasdaran commanders, hit back by advising the IRGC high command to comply with constitutional arrangements by staying clear of politics. This spat is intensifying, to the point that these confrontations have become an almost weekly occurrence as IRGC commanders and President Rouhani lock horns on a range of issues, notably the economy and foreign policy. Pasdaran commanders were perceived to favour Rouhani's main rival, Seyed Ebrahim Raissi, the powerful head of the Astaneh Qods Razavi, in the May 2017 presidential election. Major General Qasem Soleimani, the iconic commander of the IRGC's expeditionary Qods Force, met Raissi before and after the presidential elections, thus providing ammunition to the centrist–reformist camp.

But beyond these controversies and gesture politics, does the IRGC materially interfere in politics? Not surprisingly, the Pasdaran's critics are convinced they do, citing for example the disputed presidential elections of June 2009, which sparked widespread protests and rioting and counted as the worst outbreak of political instability since the 1979 revolution. These detractors trace the IRGC's overt interference in politics, and specifically vote tampering, to the June 2005 presidential elections, which catapulted the then little-known Mahmoud Ahmadinejad to the commanding height of politics. According to them, the rationale behind the Pasdaran's alleged conspiracy was simple: as a former IRGC member, Ahmadinejad was perceived as an ally who would grant the organisation favourable terms and conditions in respect of their economic activities.

In reality, Ahmadinejad did not turn out to be a solid IRGC ally, and even once accused the Pasdaran of complicity in smuggling activities.[1] Moreover, many Iranian politicians—including many reformists—were once members of the IRGC, but that does not necessarily mean they are viewed favourably by the Pasdaran high command. At any rate, the charges of brazen interference in politics, to the point of tampering with millions of votes, remain unproven. The notion of the IRGC using its paramilitary Basij wing to commandeer allied mosques as centres of electoral subversion is far-fetched, not least in view of Iran's complex political system where competing political forces provide multiple layers of oversight during elections. Under these conditions, it is unimaginable that large-scale fraud would not elicit an immediate regulatory response, let alone go undetected.

Nonetheless the IRGC's close ideological proximity to the 'principlist', or conservative, factions can be viewed as a form of political favouritism, which at minimum provides these political forces with a degree of psychological support and comfort, particularly during periods of political stress. Moreover, some of the IRGC's commanders are fearful of certain elements in the reform movement, believing that under favourable political conditions, these elements might challenge the Pasdaran's domination of the Islamic Republic's national security complex.

It is fair to say that the IRGC has weaponised an idiosyncratic conception of Shiism to spearhead an effective national security doctrine. In pure doctrinal terms—that is, stripped of its ideological content—the IRGC approach rests on creating regional strategic depth with a view to safeguarding the Iranian homeland. The ideological content of this strategy is informed by a revolutionary conception of Shiism that aspires to empower disenfranchised and oppressed Shia communities across the region.

The origin of this strategy can be traced to Iran's sponsorship of the beleaguered Lebanese Shia community in the south of Lebanon and in the Beqaa valley. This strategy predates the revolution by at least a decade as the Shah was also interested in cultivating the Lebanese Shia. It was spearheaded by the legendary Imam Musa Sadr, who was sponsored by Iran to organise the Lebanese Shia. The full extent of Musa Sadr's connection to Iran is unknown and dark rumours were circulated that the charismatic Iranian cleric of Lebanese origin was on the payroll of the SAVAK, Iran's pre-revolutionary intelligence service. It was arguably Sadr's Iranian connection—and concomitant fears of deepening Iranian influence in Lebanon—which prompted the former Libyan regime of Muammar Qaddafi to assassinate him in August 1977.

To this day the facts surrounding Musa Sadr's 'disappearance' are largely unknown. That he was officially considered 'disappeared' for more than three decades added to Sadr's legend and elevated him to almost mythical status amongst the Lebanese Shia community. In his heyday, Sadr had helped found the Amal (Hope) movement in south

Lebanon as part of a broader strategy to overcome the Lebanese Shia's political and economic marginalisation. Roughly of equal size to (if not larger than) Lebanon's other two big communities, namely the Sunni Muslims and the Maronite Christians, the Shia had been marginalised and oppressed for decades with little political weight in Beirut. Amal was the primary agency in the concerted effort to overcome these unfortunate conditions.

The charismatic Imam Musa Sadr did not live to witness the victory of the Iranian revolution, but if he had, doubtless he would have supported the movement, his connections to the Shah's regime notwithstanding. Insofar as the Iranian revolution represented the revival of Shia Islamic ethos and the reclamation of an authentic Iranian national identity, it was entirely consistent with Sadr's political philosophy. However, a speculative point of divergence rests on the clerics' seizure of power and the consolidation of *Velayat-e Faqih* as the cornerstone of the Islamic Republic. Sadr would have likely opposed this trend, but perhaps would not have done so to the same extent as leading contemporary Shia clerics, notably Ayatollah Mahmoud Taleqani.

Following the revolution, Iranian policy towards Lebanon did not initially change in a noticeable way. However, there was inevitably a greater focus on the Lebanese Shia community owing to the anti-exploitation discourse of the revolution, as expressed in the slogans centred on supporting the *mustazafeen* (dispossessed) in their struggle against the *mustakbereen* (oppressors) around the globe. But this greater focus only began to crystallise a policy shift following the Israeli invasion of Lebanon in May 1982. The Lebanese Shia community—which had initially been expected to welcome the Israelis, or at least to turn a blind eye—defied all expectations by becoming the spearhead of Lebanese sovereignty, nationalism and territorial integrity. This naturally drew Tehran's attention, initially igniting a deeply felt duty to extend a helping hand to an embattled Shia community, but gradually becoming part of a well thought-out strategy to establish highly organised and sustainable forms of Iranian influence deep inside the fabric of Lebanese Shia society. In the ensuing decades, this community-based influence branched out to penetrate wider Lebanese society as well as the Lebanese state. This policy has had such far-reaching impact, not just within Lebanon but also in the wider neighbourhood, that the Iranian investment in the Lebanese Shia community can be considered as perhaps the most successful political outreach and influence programme in the recent history of the Middle East.

The IRGC has been at the heart of this strategy from the outset. In June–July 1982, a 2,000-strong force of some of the best trained and motivated members of the Pasdaran was dispatched to Lebanon (via Syria), where it established a presence in the Beqaa valley. Although the Pasdaran rarely (if ever) engaged the Israelis directly, they were pivotal to the 'train and equip' programme that enabled mostly Shia combatants to mount a defence of their country's sovereignty in the face of Israeli aggression. Moreover, in keeping with the IRGC's ethos and constitution, the Pasdaran's role went beyond military training. Indeed, Iranian trainers and advisors played a pivotal role in helping to establish the foundational political and security/intelligence structures of what would come to be known as the Lebanese Hezbollah movement.

It was these foundational intelligence and security structures— initially embodied in the 'Islamic Jihad' group—that mounted a successful campaign against Western, notably American and French, military presence in Lebanon. Islamic Jihad inflicted heavy casualties on these forces, most dramatically in the bombing of the US Marines barracks in October 1983, which killed 270 marines, eventually forcing the Americans to beat a hasty and humiliating retreat. The events of the early 1980s in Lebanon and their immediate aftermath— notably the decade-long crisis precipitated by the seizure of Western hostages from 1982 to 1992—form much of the bad blood between Iran and the United States today.

But the IRGC's real accomplishment in Lebanon was to offer strong and sustained support to Hezbollah in the movement's effort to drive the Israelis from southern Lebanon. By the 1990s this had settled into attrition warfare, largely concentrated in an Israeli-imposed exclusion zone inside Lebanon. This zone was ostensibly protected by the Israeli-backed South Lebanon Army, but in practice Israel remained an occupying power. Hezbollah's guerrilla tactics against the Israeli Defence Forces (IDF) and their client South Lebanon Army eventually forced the Israelis to abandon the latter in

June 2000 and effectively relinquish the exclusion zone. This was a huge victory for Hezbollah and, of course, by extension the Islamic Republic of Iran.

Flush with this victory, Hezbollah went on to play a decisive role in Lebanese politics, finally overturning the institutionalised discrimination against the Shia. But this political emancipation was not without controversy, not least because many felt the Lebanese Shia had achieved political parity on the back of Hezbollah's guns. Whilst Hezbollah's victory against the Israelis was universally popular in Lebanon—and indeed across the Arab world—the fact that Hezbollah's fighting forces were better trained and equipped—and of course much better motivated—than the national Lebanese army caused deep resentment in some sections of Lebanese society.

The political divide in Lebanon deepened in May 2008 when Hezbollah resorted to using force against opposing Lebanese factions—something the Party of God had said it would never do—in order to maintain the integrity of its national security infrastructure, notably the secure communications hub. By humiliating its political opponents, and demonstrating the effectiveness of the party's armed forces in the face of inertia if not collaboration by the Lebanese armed forces, Hezbollah came to be seen as a bully by substantial sections of the Lebanese populace. However, substantial and stubborn opposition notwithstanding, Hezbollah and the Shia community's domination of Lebanese politics are not under immediate threat. Indeed, this domination appears to be sustainable, especially in view of Hezbollah's sophisticated political skills—for instance, its coalition building with sections of the Lebanese Christian community, notably the factions allied to national icon Michel Aoun.

The Hezbollah 'model', characterised by the implantation of Iranian revolutionary ideology into volatile local settings with a view to cultivating and empowering marginalised Shia communities, has since been successfully implemented elsewhere in the region. The most notable example is Iraq. Iran and the IRGC quickly stepped into the vacuum created by the ouster of Saddam Hussein in April 2003, in order to alter Iraq's strategic profile from proximate foe to tentative ally. This outcome was achieved through intervention at many levels, not least the careful cultivation of the post-Baathist Iraqi political establishment, which is dominated by Shia groups that were primarily based in Iran prior to the invasion of Iraq in March–April 2003.

As well as supporting the new Iraqi political establishment, the IRGC pursued a parallel policy of training and equipping a broad range of Shia militias in Iraq, principally to oppose the Anglo–American invasion, but also to engage indigenous political opponents, such as Baathist diehards and other Sunni-based opposition to Shia emancipation. Out of this chaotic mix, the so-called 'Special Groups' were the most important, in terms of training and organisation and the resulting lethality, but also because of their focus on fighting coalition forces. The Special Groups inflicted substantial casualties on US forces, mirroring the dramatic success of Islamic Jihad in early 1980s Lebanon.

The sweeping advance of IS in June 2014 provided the IRGC with an opportunity to transform the disparate set of militias into a relatively cohesive force. With a little help from Najaf-based Grand Ayatollah Ali Sistani—a leading *marja-e taqlid* (lit. 'source of emulation'; high-ranking Shia cleric)—who issued a *fatwa* in June 2014 urging all Iraqis to resist IS or Daesh, the Popular Mobilisation Units (PMU, or Hashd Al-Shaabi) was born. At its core, the PMU is composed of around a dozen highly trained, equipped and motivated Shia militias and Special Groups. Whilst these groups are highly autonomous in terms of their leadership, hierarchy and areas of specialisation and operation, they all share essentially the same ideology: Iranian revolutionary Shiism, spearheaded by the IRGC and presented as a discourse of 'resistance' (*moqawemat*).

In many parts of southern and central Iraq, this discourse has become hegemonic, at least in the public sphere. The proliferation of giant portraits of the late Ayatollah Khomeini and Ayatollah Khamenei in Iraq's second-largest city Basra is the clearest indication of just how deeply this discourse and its associated imagery have penetrated the political fabric of Iraqi Shia society. To think that only thirty years ago Basra was at the frontline of Baathist Iraq's war against Iran brings this dramatic geopolitical and ideological shift into sharp relief. Above all, it speaks to the strength of the Iranian revolutionary narrative and the IRGC's manipulation of it to conduct successful political and strategic outreach across the region.

Whilst the immediate rationale for creating the PMU was to push back against IS—a task to which the PMUs, in contrast to the Iraqi army, have risen, proving themselves to be highly motivated—no one is in any doubt as to the long-term function of the umbrella organisation. Insofar as the PMUs are a parallel military and security organisation, they can be considered a state within a state. This is especially true in view of the fact that the PMUs have multi-level connectivity to sensitive Iraqi institutions, and some PMU commanders also hold official functions inside the Iraqi government. By operating outside official parameters, but nonetheless observing the letter of the law (if not the spirit), the PMUs are the most effective vehicle for consolidating Shia domination of the Iraqi state.

The fight against IS provided the PMUs with an opportunity to expand their scope of operations to areas that were previously no-go zones, principally the Arab Sunni heartlands of southern and western Nineveh province, of which Mosul is the capital. The operational role of the PMUs during the campaign to liberate Mosul (October 2016—July 2017) was instructive. As the Iraqi army and specialised units of the federal police force concentrated on driving IS from Mosul, the PMUs made a pivot to the west, at first securing western routes out of the city and then fanning out further west to secure sensitive points on the northern stretch of the Iraqi–Syrian border. The strategic implications of this deep push into the bastions of Iraqi Arab Sunni nationalism and of the presence of the PMUs on the border will become clearer in the years to come. But one thing is already certain: Iranian influence in Iraq has been secured for at least a generation.

Elsewhere the 'resistance' model is being replicated in the Gulf region and in the Arabian Peninsula, albeit on a smaller scale and at a far more tentative level. In Yemen, for example, the Ansarallah movement (commonly referred to as the Houthis) consciously adopts the 'resistance' discourse and models itself on Lebanese Hezbollah. However, in Yemen's case there are important qualifying characteristics. Foremost, the Houthis are of the Zaidi Shia sect, which has important—indeed in some respects fundamental— theological, doctrinal and devotional differences from the Twelver Shias who dominate Iran, Iraq and southern Lebanon. Second, the IRGC has no formal or organised presence in Yemen, even though small numbers of IRGC Qods Force operatives may be undercover in the country. This is in stark contrast to Lebanon in the 1980s and contemporary Iraq and Syria, where the IRGC has deployed officially and in considerable numbers.

These distinctions notwithstanding, the Houthis' rhetoric places them firmly in the 'axis of resistance' camp. Moreover, the fighting prowess of the Houthis (who have withstood a ferocious Saudi- and Emirati-led military campaign since March 2015), coupled with their political and coalition-building skills (they are in alliance with former leader Ali Abdullah Saleh and sections of the military), makes them a potent and reliable ally for Iran. Furthermore, Yemen's position on the southern tip of the Arabian Peninsula, and more precisely the proximity of the Houthis' northern Yemeni heartland to the Saudi border, highlights the enormous geopolitical significance of this conflict. In short, Iran has an opportunity to replicate the Hezbollah model in Saudi Arabia's backyard, with all the potential subversive ramifications inside the Kingdom (notably in the Shia-majority Eastern Province) which that might entail.

Some analysts are keen to paint the IRGC as a rogue player in Iran's foreign policymaking process by placing the Pasdaran in opposition to the civilian policy centres, notably the foreign ministry. Seen from this perspective, the 'axis of resistance' is a subversive concept that is allegedly actively opposed by Iran's career diplomats. More careful analysis suggests that this is not the case. Whilst indeed there are tensions between the IRGC and the government on important foreign policy matters, the two are not at constant loggerheads, but are quite mutually cooperative.

Nothing proves this point better than an assessment of Syria's central role in the practical construction and logistical sustainability of the axis of resistance model. Iran has a formal alliance with Syria, dating back to the early years of the Iran–Iraq War when Syria dissented from the Arab fold by backing Iran against fellow Baathist state Iraq. This longstanding alliance constitutes Iran's only formal alliance, which speaks to Syria's critical role in Iranian diplomacy and regional positioning. At its core, the Iranian–Syrian alliance is pragmatic and driven by mutual political and strategic needs. Indeed, its origin lies in Iran's need to overcome its isolation in the Arab world and Syria's need for discounted, and in some cases free, access to oil and other essential commodities.

Needless to say, there are also political components to this alliance, not least the pull of sectarian politics. Whilst Syria's state structure is not sectarian, the minority Alawite community dominated the upper reaches of the state. The consensus amongst other Shia sects is that from theological and devotional points of view, the Alawites cannot be considered Shia Muslims, the late Imam Musa Sadr's *fatwa* to the contrary notwithstanding. Still, in terms of identity politics, the Alawites are entirely within the Shia fold. Geopolitical developments since the 1980s, notably the emergence and empowerment of Hezbollah and Iran's regional ascent, coupled with opposition from Saudi Arabia and Israel, have intensified this intra-sectarian bonding.

Syria is crucial to the sustainability of the axis of resistance, not least because it is a frontline state in the struggle against Israel and, by extension, must continually supply and support Lebanese Hezbollah. This centrality is the main reason that Iran is fully committed to the preservation of Syria's ruling elite. But in diplomatic and strategic terms, Iran's close ties to Syria remain a conventional inter-state alliance, driven by mutual interests and a mutually perceived threat environment. That this conventional alliance intersects with the IRGC-driven ideological component of Iranian foreign policy speaks to the inherent cohesion of the Iranian policymaking architecture. The Islamic Republic has mastered the art of mixing conventional diplomacy with an ideological discourse to create maximum impact in its pursuit of national prestige.

Continuity in Foreign Policy

Another major background feature is the extent of continuity between pre-revolutionary and post-revolutionary foreign policies. The Islamic Republic is often presented as a disruptive revolutionary power set on overturning the prevailing international order. This charge is usually made by critics and opponents of revolutionary Iran and naturally rests at least in part on a set of contrived and inflated allegations. But stripped of its propagandistic content, there is a level of theoretical validity in the statement, insofar as in political science revolutionary powers are considered to be by definition opposed to prevailing norms and standards.

In Iran's case, does the Islamic Republic qualify, at least in part, as a disruptive revolutionary power? There are various ways to tackle this question, one of the most effective being the deployment of a chronological approach. In the heady revolutionary decade of the 1980s, some aspects of Iran's international behaviour were problematic, at least from the point of view of the status quo. The discourse of 'exporting the revolution' carried at least an implicit threat of ouster and overthrow to various established powers in the region and beyond. However, following the conclusion of the Iran–Iraq War in the summer of 1988 and the demise of Ayatollah Khomeini a year later, the consensus amongst Iran scholars is that the radicalism of the 1980s gave way to qualified moderation and in many respects the re-appearance of familiar themes in Iranian foreign and defence policy discourse.

To establish patterns of continuity and rupture, we require a basic understanding of the goals and objectives of pre-revolutionary Iranian foreign policy. In keeping with Iran's long imperial heritage, the Pahlavi dynasty sought an expansive regional role and even dreamed of a 'new civilisation', embodied by Japanese-style economic progress implanted onto an Iranian cultural setting. The cultural setting envisaged by the Pahlavis had the veneer of pre-Islamic Persian nationalism and seemed to celebrate millennia of imperial glory, but in practice it was nothing short of thinly disguised wholesale Westernisation. In fact, in some cases the veneer was abandoned altogether, as Iran sought to openly emulate Western cultural and behavioural norms. There is consensus amongst Iran scholars and other experts that this monumental misjudgement by the Pahlavis was one of the chief causes of the Iranian revolution.

The Islamic Republic's establishment today decries the foreign policy of Pahlavi Iran for lacking depth and authenticity, which derived from the fact that the regime itself was not fully independent. There is more than a grain of truth to this charge, as the history of the Pahlavi dynasty is beset by foreign interventions. Reza Khan had come to power in 1925 at least in part because of British acquiescence. However, as an Iranian king, he sought to broaden the country's international horizons and was drawn to Nazi Germany, not just for geopolitical reasons, but also on account of genuine admiration for the achievements of the Third Reich. This shift toward Germany propelled the UK and the Soviet Union to violate Iranian neutrality in the Second World War by invading the country from the south and the north in 1941 and overthrowing Reza Shah.

The ascension of Reza Khan's son, Mohmmad Reza Pahlavi, to the throne was marked by a decade of political instability, culminating in the August 1953 coup that overthrew the democratically elected Mohammad Mossadeq. Mossadeq is the father of the Iranian oil nationalisation movement—and by extension a nationalist icon—and his overthrow in a CIA–MI6 orchestrated coup set off political and ideological ripples that continue to reverberate to the present day. The return of Mohammad Reza to the throne as a result of brazen external machination inevitably gave his entire reign a flavour of foreign dependency. Although the Shah became more confident and assertive from the mid-1960s onwards, he was never able to shake off the perception that he was an American stooge.

The Pahlavi dynasty certainly had exceptionally close ties to the United States, as evidenced by the Nixon doctrine of 1969, which essentially allowed US allies like Iran to purchase the most advanced American military equipment and weapons, barring nuclear weapons. The result was the massive expansion of the Iranian armed forces—in particular the speedy modernisation of the air force, which was to play a decisive role in the early phase of the Iran–Iraq War of the following decade. In broader strategic terms, the Shah acted as the guarantor of security in the Persian Gulf with American backing.

But beyond the close alignment with the United States, there were elements of Iranian regional policy that were both innovative and entirely in keeping with the country's vital national interests. The most striking example was Iran's intervention in 1973 in Oman's Dhofar rebellion. This was modern Iran's first deployment of an expeditionary force, a precedent that was not repeated until Iran's military intervention in the Syrian conflict forty years later. By helping to restore the political sovereignty and territorial integrity of the Omani state, Iran earned the enduring friendship of Oman. This relationship survived the revolution and has indeed strengthened over the years. It is noteworthy that Oman dissents from the Gulf Cooperation Council consensus on Iran and instead advises fellow GCC members to engage with Iran. Oman also played a leading mediatory role in the early stages of the secret bilateral nuclear negotiations between Iran and the United States.[2]

In general terms, the Pahlavi monarchy sought to turn Iran into the dominant regional power with a leading role in guaranteeing the security of shipping and commerce in the Persian Gulf. Broadly speaking, the Islamic Republic shares these same aspirations, the primary difference being ideological outlook, which affects political choices, tactics and strategy. The Islamic Republic's conception of Iran's regional role is similar to the Pahlavis', but the cultural and discursive narratives used to frame and justify this role are remarkably different, as are policymaking processes. The Pahlavi monarchy was far less institutionally dense—in the sense of a proliferation of both complementary and competing institutions—than the Islamic Republic, the result being that major policy was often crafted by the Shah and his closest advisors. By contrast, in the Islamic Republic, foreign policy and national security are conceived and developed by a wide range of institutions, whose consensual outlooks form the basis of foreign policy goals and national security requirements.

POLITICAL SOCIETY

For forty years, the Islamic Republic's political society has defied neat definitions. What kind of political system does the Islamic Republic of Iran constitute? An authentic Islamic state as defined by the principlist—or conservative—factions of the regime; an aspiring Islamic democracy as hoped for by the reformists; or a pure theocracy as claimed by the system's critics and opponents?

At first glance, the Islamic Republic could not be more different from the monarchical system that it replaced in 1979. The Pahlavi regime was ostensibly a constitutional monarchy, but in practical terms it had all the hallmarks of an absolute monarchy, in that most power was concentrated in the hands of the Shah and his inner circle.

As discussed in the previous chapter, the two systems were markedly different in institutional terms: the Islamic Republic is institutionally dense whereas the Pahlavi regime was institutionally 'light', as most decisions were taken by the monarch. Even the independence of the three branches of government (the executive, legislative and judiciary) was flimsy at best, as the Shah remained the ultimate arbiter at the national level.

Whilst the separation of powers is relatively clear-cut in the Islamic Republic, there is an intermittent debate on the independence of the judiciary. Civil society and political activists have at times accused the judiciary of being too close to the security forces, and alleged that certain judges are under the influence of intelligence agents. Typically, these accusations are made during periods of acute political stress—such as the demonstrations and riots that followed the disputed presidential elections of June 2009—when judges are under pressure to uphold law and order by cracking down on dissent.

The Islamic Republic has set up a range of organisations to regulate relations and mediate disputes between the three branches of government. At the apex sits the Expediency Discernment Council (Majmaa'e Tashkisheh Maslahateh Nezam),[1] whose role is to mediate between the three powers and resolve disputes. The EDC is a big organisation with multiple expert-led committees and policy-specific groups, including a highly regarded research arm called the Centre for Strategic Research (CSR).

Looking at the parties in control of the CSR at any given time can provide indicators of dominant political trends, or of powerful intellectual currents on the threshold of sweeping through the country's political landscape. Set up in 1989 (a year after the foundation of the EDC parent organisation), the CSR was originally in the hands of the Islamic Republic's left wing, known at the time as the Khateh Imam (Imam's Line) faction, now known as the reformists. The founding director of the CSR was Saeed Hajjarian, one of the founders and directors of the Ministry of Intelligence and Security (MOIS) in 1984. A left winger, Hajjarian used the CSR as the incubator for reformist ideas which gradually penetrated the body politic in the early to mid-1990s. Many of the leading reformist ideologues of the 1990s enjoyed stints in the CSR.

Hajjarian himself is widely regarded as one of the most influential reformist strategists who gave rise to the ideas and methods that underpinned Mohammad Khatami's landslide victory in the May 1997 presidential elections. At an intellectual level, Hajjarian coined the term 'dual sovereignty' to describe the dialectic of power in the Islamic Republic and the apparently perennial tension between elected and non-elected power centres. At a practical level, Hajjarian innovated the idea of mobilising people at the grassroots level to apply pressure on non-elected ruling elites, namely the clerics who control the commanding heights of government.

But above all, Hajjarian stayed firmly loyal to the Islamic Republic, describing his strategy as one designed to turn 'enemies' of the system into critics, and in turn to transform critics into supporters. This approach formed the parameters of the reform movement and embedded it firmly within a pro-Islamic Republic narrative to which activists, ideologues and officials formerly linked to the Khateh Imam faction could switch their focus and loyalties. It is not bold to claim that without Hajjarian's intellectual and practical input, the Islamic Republic's reform movement would never have got off the ground.

The CSR continues to be an important institution, albeit with less influence now than in the 1990s. Nevertheless, control of the CSR is a key factional battleground, with competing political currents striving hard for dominance with a view to disseminating their ideas across the Islamic Republic's body politic. President Rouhani was at one stage the CSR director and used it to diffuse centrist ideas—particularly those pertaining to foreign policy—across important institutions, including the foreign ministry and the MOIS.

The current director of the CSR is Ali Akbar Velayati, a former foreign minister and chief foreign policy advisor to Ayatollah Khamenei. A leading Khamenei stalwart, Velayati is expected to use the CSR to push Khamenei's vision both in terms of foreign and domestic policies. Velayati was elected as the head of the Islamic Azad University (IAU) Board of Trustees in early 2017, a highly important development that signified a shift away from IAU domination by loyalists to former president Rafsanjani.[2]

Since its foundation in 1982 by Rafsanjani's initiative, the IAU has transformed the higher education sector in Iran by giving millions of young people access to university-level education. Previously, admittance to the country's universities was tightly controlled through a tough examination process known as the Konkour (from the French *concours*), which ensured that only the most academically bright gained entry. Whilst the Konkour system remains in place and regulates access to the country's established universities, the IAU network gives millions of young people access to good-quality higher education at reduced meritocratic thresholds.

The IAU is one of the country's biggest organisations, boasting 400 higher education units, 70,000 lecturers and teachers, and reportedly $250 billion in assets.[3] Clearly, control over the IAU creates opportunities to influence the higher education sector as a whole, and it is thus yet another arena of factional competition. Rafsanjani was able to maintain control of the IAU over decades by appointing his loyalists in key positions, and fought off concerted campaigns by his opponents—notably Mahmoud Ahmadinejad—to wrest control of the network. However, the balance of power finally shifted to his opponents after Rafsanjani's death in January 2017.

But let us return to Hajjarian's theory of 'dual sovereignty' and the quest to give a neat definition to the character and nature of the Iranian political system. Certainly, at the very top of the system there is an apparently perennial tension between two core power centres, namely the presidency and the supreme leadership (*Velayat-e Faqih*). The presidential institution is subject to elections every four years, in which all Iranians above the age of eighteen can vote. Until January 2007, the legal voting age in Iran was fifteen—the lowest in the world.

It is important to note that the *Valiyeh Faqih* (Supreme Leader) is also indirectly elected via the Assembly of Experts (*Majlis-e-Khobregan*), which is subject to elections every eight years. The Assembly is tasked with appointing the leader and monitoring his performance to ensure consistency and compliance with the constitution. In theory, the Assembly has the power to remove the leader if his performance is deemed to be poor or consistently in violation of the law, but, needless to say, this power has never been used.

Even in terms of monitoring the performance of the leader, the Assembly of Experts is often chided for not being fit for purpose. Indeed, to date the Assembly has never publicly criticised the leadership, instead focusing on providing institutional support to the leader and demonstrating the strength of the Islamic system. These shortcomings notwithstanding, it is a mistake to underestimate the importance of the Assembly, as its core task—to appoint the Supreme Leader—is absolutely critical to the cohesion and the very sustainability of the Islamic Republic.

The current Assembly of Experts (elected in February 2016) is arguably the most important since late 1989—when the then Assembly appointed the incumbent *Valiyeh Faqih*—as it may be called upon to appoint a new leader within its electoral lifespan, which will expire in 2024. There are intermittent reports of Ayatollah Khamenei's ill health and he was verifiably hospitalised in September 2014 for prostate surgery.[4] However, many of the reports of the leader's allegedly 'serious' medical conditions—attributed to either anonymous or 'unofficial sources'[5]—are unsubstantiated propaganda efforts, designed to elicit a response from different parts of the establishment.

In this regard, it is also important to consider that Ayatollah Khamenei has access to the best medical services and that hitherto there have been no confirmed or reliable reports that he suffers from any chronic or otherwise grave medical condition. Although aging, at seventy-nine Khamenei (b. 1939) at present appears to be in relatively good health, recent hospitalisation notwithstanding. He continues to make regular public appearances and engages fully in activities related to his office. He is known to rise at dawn each day and work until the evening, often chairs hours-long meetings, and frequently delivers long speeches.

On that basis, it is not out of the question that Khamenei might comfortably live for at least another decade and continue to discharge his duties efficiently. Nevertheless, there has never been as much speculation as there is now about the potential appointment of a successor, even if it is discussed as a precautionary measure to guarantee stability and continuity. Indeed, if the Assembly of Experts appointed a successor tomorrow, it would not necessarily reflect concern about the ill health or imminent demise of the current leader. In the Islamic Republic, there is precedent for selecting a successor early, as demonstrated by the appointment of the late Grand Ayatollah Hossein-Ali Montazeri as Ayatollah Khomeini's successor in 1985. Montazeri was later stripped of this position by Ayatollah Khomeini due to his critical stance toward sensitive state policies, particularly in respect of the harsh treatment of armed dissidents in autumn 1988.

The critical role of the Assembly of Experts—which cannot justifiably be reduced to a mere perfunctory function—means that the supreme leadership of the Islamic Republic is not as unelected as the system's critics claim. However, the supreme leadership is still markedly different from the presidency, in that the latter is directly elected every four years. The differences go even deeper, as the meanings and expectations invested in these institutions by the Iranian electorate diverge significantly.

In the last couple of decades (since the electoral victory of the reformists in the May 1997 presidential election), the presidency has come to represent—at least for substantial sections of the urban middle class—a bastion of modernity. This important segment of the electorate consciously frames the country's institutions within the context of the Islamic Republic's power dialectic—in this case, between the 'elected' and 'non-elected' centres of power. The argument goes that the presidency—by virtue of being more accountable to the electorate—is more reflective of modern Iranian society and its needs and aspirations. By contrast, the 'non-elected' institutions are seen as more aligned with the traditional segments of society.

There is of course some truth in these perceptions, insofar as the clerically dominated institutions (such as the Assembly of Experts) are closer to the conservative elements in society who continue to look up to religious leaders as moral, social and political reference points. Moreover the 'non-elected' institutions, in tandem with hard power organisations—notably the Islamic Revolutionary Guards Corps (IRGC)—view themselves as the torchbearers of Iran's revolutionary ideology and position themselves accordingly. Thus, speeches given by elders in the Assembly of Experts often have very similar content to those by commanders of the Revolutionary Guards, focusing on the importance of maintaining revolutionary vigilance and protecting the ideological boundaries of the Islamic revolution.

There is increasing indication that the meaning and expectations invested in the presidency by the people have a significant impact on the behaviour and positioning of Iranian presidents. Whether by design or default, sitting presidents end up adopting an oppositional stance vis-à-vis the hardcore elements of the establishment. This phenomenon can even be traced to the period before the formal ascension of the reformists in May 1997.

It was Hashemi Rafsanjani who first brought the acute structural tensions at the very top of the Islamic Republic into sharp relief. Elected to the presidency in July 1989, Rafsanjani had reportedly played a crucial role in the appointment of Seyed Ali Khamenei to the leadership post a month earlier, following the demise of Ayatollah Khomeini in early June. He had allegedly accomplished this task by encouraging members of the Assembly of Experts to form a consensus around Khamenei. The swift deliberations of the Assembly at such a sensitive time had secured stability in a dangerously volatile situation.

Whilst the precise nature of the deliberations and the extent of Rafsanjani's influence on the proceedings are not fully known, Rafsanjani's supporters constantly refer to that epochal moment to underscore their patron's pivotal role in shaping the destiny of the Islamic Republic. For his part, Rafsanjani justified his intervention in the Assembly's deliberations on the grounds that, above all, it reflected the dying wish of the Republic's founder Ruhollah Khomeini. According to Rafsanjani's version of events, following Montazeri's dismissal as official heir in February 1989, the late Ayatollah Khomeini was quizzed by his inner circle on the resulting leadership vacuum, to which he is reported to have reacted to the effect that 'we have a future leader and that is Mr Khamenei'.

To his credit, Rafsanjani stuck to this version of events to his dying day, indeed repeating the story (as he had done on countless occasions since 1989) to a clerical audience just a few weeks before his death in January 2017. In large part, this was a reflection of the strong personal bond between him and Khamenei, which stretched back to the 1950s when both men were young revolutionaries. This personal bond survived in the face of bitter political disputes, culminating in Rafsanjani's qualified support for the Green movement in his last Friday prayers sermon at the University of Tehran in July 2009.

The extent of Rafsanjani's political downfall was underlined by the jailing of both his oldest daughter Faezeh and then his favourite son Mehdi, who was handed a ten-year sentence for financial and security-related crimes. If Rafsanjani felt bitter that his old comrade Khamenei (whose leadership he had helped to secure in those heady days of June 1989) had not intervened to spare his family from the wrath of his detractors, he certainly didn't show it. Whilst he became critical of state policies in the latter years of his life, he was nonetheless careful not to undermine the legacy of his close friendship with the Islamic Republic's second leader.

Khamenei in turn appeared to appreciate this distinction and explicitly referred to it in his personal note on Rafsanjani's demise. Whilst acknowledging significant political differences, Khamenei also fondly recalled a six-decades-long friendship for which there is no parallel or replacement in the history of the Islamic revolution. This lamentation is very real insofar as it heralds the near demise of first generation revolutionary leaders. Khamenei and Rafsanjani were the two most important survivors of the late Ayatollah Khomeini's inner circle. Once Khamenei departs the arena, the Islamic Republic will enter into wholly uncharted waters.

It is worth exploring the relationship between these two men in greater depth. Both have had a tremendous impact on modern Iranian political history and they have shaped the form and content of the Islamic Republic from its foundational moment in early 1979. Their personalities, beliefs, attitudes and leadership styles mirrored the systemic and philosophical tensions inherent in the Islamic Republic. Rafsanjani was the less ideological of the two and consistently displayed more canny political instincts. In Europe and North America, he was known as a pragmatist with whom the West could potentially do business. In reality, Rafsanjani was a cynical strategist whose greatest concern was improving the long-term viability of the revolution.

By contrast, Khamenei is an ideologue whose chief concern is the realisation of the ideals and aspirations of the revolution. To that end, he is committed to reforming Iranian society according to these ideals and to propagating these ideas across the region and, if possible, even beyond. In that regard, he has always been a more committed revolutionary than his old comrade, even though in practical terms their revolutionary credentials are on a par. Whilst by no means uncompromising, Khamenei is nevertheless more concerned with changing state and society than with consolidating power.

At important moments Rafsanjani appeared to be willing to radically change course in order to improve the prospects of the Islamic Republic. The best example of this is his first term as president (1989–1993) when he was focused on reconciling the Islamic Republic's war-battered economy with the logic and processes of capitalism and globalisation. In practical terms, this amounted to opening up the economy to foreign investment and integrating with global economic and trading bodies, including the World Trade Organization. The political current which he led, the Kargozaran (Technocrats), came to be seen as favouring a Chinese model of development, where economic liberalisation is divorced from political democratisation.

Of course, this never came to pass as the Iranian system is more complex than its Chinese counterpart, with economic arrangements and political patronage in the Islamic Republic often going hand in hand. More than two decades later, the current centrist administration led by President Hassan Rouhani continues grappling with the same problem, namely to find pathways to economic liberalisation without upsetting deeply entrenched political and ideological forces.

But the continuation of the struggle is also a mark of tribute to Rafsanjani, not least because the technocratic trend that he fostered more than a quarter of a century ago continues to play a central role in Iranian politics. Furthermore, many reformists, technocrats and centrists are keen to project Rafsanjani's heritage onto Rouhani, with a view to developing the latter's role as a symbol of the system's pragmatic face. In large measure, this is a continuation of the dialectic of power in the Islamic Republic, with 'pragmatism' and 'ideology' cast as the protagonists.

As discussed earlier, this duality is rooted in the political rivalry between Rafsanjani and Khamenei, in particular during the former's first presidential term from 1989 to 1993. During his first term, Rafsanjani had the upper hand in the power struggle with the newly installed leadership for several reasons. First and foremost, as Rafsanjani had played an important role in the ascension of Khamenei to the leadership, he felt that this 'debt' would be honoured throughout Khamenei's leadership.

Second, Khamenei clearly lacked Ayatollah Khomeini's charisma and his status as an undisputed leader of the revolution. Khomeini commanded the loyalty of the masses on a scale and intensity not matched by any modern Iranian leader. This devotion was on full display when he returned from exile on 1 February 1979 to take direct command of the revolution, and was even more so at his funeral on 3 June 1989, which drew millions of grief-stricken mourners out onto the streets of Tehran. The newly appointed leader did not command even a fraction of this mass devotion.

A related factor was the newly appointed leader's lack of religious credentials. The 1979 constitution had stipulated that the leader had to be a *marja-e taqlid* (source of emulation), the highest rank in the Shia clerical hierarchy. As a widely acknowledged *marja-e taqlid* with a sizeable following amongst rank-and-file clerics, the late Ayatollah Khomeini clearly satisfied this condition. By stark contrast, at the time of his appointment to the leadership Khamenei held the clerical rank of *hojjatol eslam wal muslimeen*, one step removed from an Ayatollah, and several levels below a Grand Ayatollah and a *marja-e taqlid*.

However, a referendum to amend the constitution (staged simultaneously with presidential elections in late July 1989) removed the criterion of high religious authority for holding the supreme leadership. This amendment effectively provided legal license for Khamenei's leadership. But in the ideological cosmos of the Islamic Republic, where religious and political authority are interlinked at multiple levels, there is a world of difference between legality and acceptance, especially by the regime's religious constituency in Qom (a site of Shia religious learning) and its satellite seminaries.

This reality has forced Khamenei's most loyal supporters to develop his religious profile, with a view to asserting a measure of religious authority in Shia clerical circles both inside and outside the country. For example, in the mid-1990s Khamenei's supporters tried to pass him off as the religious leader of non-Iranian Shias, an innovation that failed to gain any traction. Khamenei's lack of religious credentials has consistently dogged his leadership and prevented him from gaining a credible foothold in centres of Shia religious learning in Iran and Iraq.

These three factors were seized upon by Rafsanjani in his attempt to sideline Khamenei and effectively reduce the institution of *Velayat-e Faqih* to a ceremonial role. For a few years in the early 1990s, this campaign appeared to be working as Rafsanjani's core support base amongst the Kargozaran trend glorified him as the *Sardar-e Sazandagi* (Commander of Construction), in recognition of Rafsanjani's role in rebuilding the country's infrastructure in the wake of the devastating Iran–Iraq War.

But Rafsanjani and his supporters had not taken full account of two factors that worked in Khamenei's favour. First, what Khamenei lacked in religious credentials and personal charisma, he compensated for with political and managerial skills. The newly appointed leader had exceptional organisational skills in addition to ample political experience, notably having served as the country's president from 1981 to 1989. Khamenei's consistency and his cool and dispassionate approach to statecraft are two of his prominent qualities that explain his success as leader.

Second, Khamenei's ideological vigour and his proximity to the regime's Hezbollahi grassroots base meant that he commanded loyalty and support across the breadth and depth of the Islamic Republic on a scale that was unmatched by any other Iranian leader, including Rafsanjani. Whatever the truth surrounding Khamenei's appointment to the leadership—and specifically whether the appointment was tacitly approved or not by Ayatollah Khomeini on his deathbed—it was never much in doubt that the Islamic Republic's grassroots support base considered Khamenei as a natural leader. This affinity with the public and the regime's core ideological constituency gave Khamenei an unassailable advantage over Rafsanjani.

Khamenei's under-appreciated political skills were in full display in the early years of his leadership, despite the sometimes successful attempts by Rafsanjani and his supporters to foster the perception that Rafsanjani was the most powerful man in the country. The prevailing impression of Iran's political landscape, which held sway in the region and in the West, was one of Khamenei and the regime's Hezbollahi base in opposition to an all-powerful Hashemi Rafsanjani. At the time, this perception defined the perennial dialectic of power in the Islamic Republic.

The falsity of this perception was already apparent in the closing stages of Rafsanjani's first term, as the regime's core ideological constituency, in addition to its hard power institutions, such as the judiciary and the IRGC, had fully rallied around Khamenei and wholeheartedly supported him as the regime's undisputed leader. Furthermore, these institutions made it clear that they were more than ready to clip Rafsanjani's wings should he attempt to publicly challenge the supreme leadership on sensitive ideological, political and economic issues.

The support of hard power institutions for Khamenei needs to be explored further, as it speaks to the latter's vastly different leadership style vis-à-vis the Republic's founder Ayatollah Khomeini. The latter relied on his charisma and his appeal extended beyond the Islamic Republic's core constituency. Indeed, Khomeini refused to develop a leadership infrastructure that would assert authority over the system and the revolution. This was also in keeping with his humble lifestyle—Khomeini spent the final decade of his life in a simple house in Jamaran, a northern neighbourhood of Tehran.

By contrast, Khamenei has developed an elaborate and highly specialised infrastructure to support his leadership. This infrastructure is reported to directly employ hundreds of members of staff whose primary task is to enable the leader to discharge his constitutional duties. Moreover, they liaise with sensitive institutions of state in order to keep them apprised of the guidelines and opinions of the leadership. They also support the leadership in terms of public relations, for example by managing the publication and record maintenance of the leader's speeches and articles and by managing his extensive online profile.

Khamenei's relationship with the IRGC is also markedly different to Khomeini's interaction with this pivotal revolutionary organisation. In the early 1980s the IRGC was still a nascent organisation and brimming with revolutionary fervour. In structural terms, it was configured as a paramilitary organisation which did not seek to compete with the regular military across the tri-service sector. The Pasdaran had performed vital revolutionary duties in 1979 and 1980, by, for example, crushing separatist revolts on the country's fringes (notably in the Kurdish-majority areas) and suppressing hard-left organisations. It also played the lead role in crushing the armed revolt of the Mojahedin-e Khalq (MeK), an eccentric group mixing Marxism with revolutionary Shiism.

The MeK formed an alliance with the Islamic Republic's first president, Abol-Hassan Banisadr, following the latter's impeachment in June 1981. The organisation started a major terrorist campaign to destabilise and topple the clerical core of the regime. The Revolutionary Guards played a critical role in defeating this revolt, both at the street level—by confronting MeK gunmen or raiding their safe houses—and at the intelligence level—by collecting the requisite information that eventually ensured the total defeat of the MeK inside Iran by early 1983 and forced the organisation to move its surviving cadres and sympathisers to Iraq.

These effective actions by the IRGC were precisely what the late revolutionary leader Ayatollah Khomeini had envisaged. In Khomeini's vision, the Pasdaran were foremost defenders of the revolution whose main (if not exclusive) task was to protect the revolution from a wide range of counter-revolutionaries, separatists, terrorists and political subversives. Whilst the research on this issue is not conclusive, it is doubtful if Khomeini ever expected the Revolutionary Guards to develop into a permanent rival of the regular Iranian armed forces. Khomeini was also very clear on the issue of political neutrality, regularly reminding the Pasdaran of the constitutional requirement that they stay out of politics. In this respect, the late Ayatollah Khomeini was a great proponent of the clear separation of politics and the military.

Barring the 1953 coup which toppled Mossadegh, Iran is notably distinct from her Arab, Turkish and Pakistani neighbours insofar as the modern military has not played an influential role in political life. In fact, the modern Iranian armed forces are decisively apolitical, as evidenced by the army's refusal to take firm action against the revolution in 1978–79. The August 1953 coup is revealed as even more of an aberration when we consider the fact that it was driven less by internal military–politics dynamics than by the machination of foreign powers, notably an elaborate intelligence process driven by the CIA and Britain's MI6. It is also worth noting that the Islamic Republic has intensified the processes that began with the post-1953 Pahlavi regime of de-politicising the military to the greatest extent possible.

However, there are now fears that this positive tradition is being insidiously undermined, not by the regular military but by the IRGC. Critics are sure as to who to blame for this insidious phenomenon: fingers are squarely pointed at Ayatollah Khomeini's successor, Seyed Ali Khamenei. The latter's relationship with the Pasdaran is very structured, as the office of the Supreme Leader exercises oversight roles across the length and breadth of the IRGC. From the very first days of his leadership Khamenei identified the Pasdaran as one of his core support bases and developed the relationship accordingly. Initially this was no easy task; at the time Hashemi Rafsanjani was extremely popular with the Pasdaran, not least because he had served as the military's de facto commander in chief in the final year of the Iran–Iraq War. It was in that position that he played a central role in persuading Pasdaran commanders of the need to bring the war to a conclusion. His speech to the commanders of the Revolutionary Guards immediately in the wake of Khomeini's acceptance of UN Resolution 598 (which established a ceasefire in the Iran–Iraq War) was crucial in containing disquiet at the higher reaches of the Pasdaran.[6]

In the immediate aftermath of the war both Khamenei and Rafsanjani played central roles in protecting the Pasdaran from proposed disbandment or a diminution of its organisation and duties. Without this crucial political support from the upper echelons of the Islamic Republic, the fate of the Pasdaran would have been very different. Failing disbandment or integration with the regular armed forces, the Pasdaran could have been forced to come to terms with considerable restrictions on their military and security activities. Instead, under Khamenei's leadership the Revolutionary Guards steadily expanded the scope of their military activities, particularly in the ballistic missiles and aerospace sectors. Moreover, they established influence in the Iranian nuclear industry.

Another noteworthy development in the past quarter-century has been the IRGC's increased political visibility. Indeed, Revolutionary Guards commanders regularly appear on the media to comment on ideological issues, domestic politics and international political developments. In addition to appearances on the state broadcaster, Pasdaran commanders also have access to even more sympathetic media, principally in the form of online news agencies aligned with the IRGC.[7] Whilst critics of the organisation interpret this development as a clear breach of the constitution's prohibition of military interference in politics, the Pasdaran and its supporters employ an expansive reading of the constitution and argue that their foundational charter compels them to police the ideological as well as the physical boundaries of the Islamic revolution.

The sum effect of these developments has produced an iron-clad alliance between Khamenei and the high command of the IRGC. However, this nexus cannot be reduced to one of power relations and a mutual need for partnership in the face of opposition from the government, the reformists and wider civil society. It is built on a genuine ideological and emotional bond insofar as the commanders of the IRGC—and, by extension, much of the rank and file—regard Khamenei as their *Valiyeh Faqih* and undisputed ideological leader.

This speaks to Khamenei's stronger ideological commitment (vis-à-vis Rafsanjani) and his ability to attract the enduring loyalty of the most hardcore ideological elements in the system.

The institutional strength of the IRGC gives Khamenei greater confidence in containing the ambitions of successive presidents. As discussed earlier, Khamenei has successfully worked with three past presidents and at the time of writing was in the process of reigning in a buoyant Hassan Rouhani. But even once Khamenei departs the arena, the systemic tensions will persist. At its apex, the Islamic Republic is configured in a manner that produces perpetual political tension. The only ways to resolve this political conflict would be either to reduce the *Valiyeh Faqih* to a ceremonial role or to substantially strengthen the country's political society.

Network of Factions: Iran's Fragmented Political Society

To outside observers the Iranian political system is hopelessly opaque and byzantine. This may explain why the Western media and analysts have opted to simplify the situation by dividing Iranian political actors into 'moderates' and 'hardliners', or 'reformists' and 'conservatives'. Like most reductive solutions there is a kernel of truth to these simplifications, but, of course, the overall effect is a gross distortion of political reality.

On the face of it the Islamic Republic's political society could not be more different from that of the former Pahlavi regime. The latter's political society, as well as its institutional makeup, was sparse and lacking in energy and vibrancy. By contrast, the Islamic Republic offers a dynamic political society buttressed by regular elections for the Majlis (parliament) as well as the presidency. Whilst entry to these sensitive institutions is tightly controlled by the Council of Guardians (and other vetting bodies), the elections are nevertheless real and often throw up surprises that upset the establishment.

Yet, at a deeper level there is a degree of continuity between pre-revolutionary and post-revolutionary Iranian political societies, inasmuch as both lacked genuine, established and sustainable political parties. In the post-1953 Pahlavi regime (that is, following the August 1953 coup that ousted Mossadegh) there were three main political parties, all of which were tightly controlled and firmly aligned with the establishment. Prior to 1975, when the Shah adopted a single-party system, two parties played the role of incumbent and opposition. The Iran-e Novin Party (New Iran Party) played the role of ruling party, controlling both the cabinet and the Majlis. Although it had a formal structure and held regular congresses, the party was somewhat artificial, having no distinct roots or identifiable, sustainable grassroots base. It was entirely a tool of the establishment to control the political environment.

Iran-e Novin's immediate predecessor was Hezb-e Melliyoun (Party of Nationalists), which was founded in 1957 and survived for only three years before morphing into the New Iran Party. Thus, the late 1950s were the point at which the Pahlavi regime decided to initiate an establishment-aligned party system in Iran with a view to controlling the political environment by giving the impression of a vibrant political system. From the outset, the opposition party was Hezb-e Mardom (People's Party), which was founded on ostensibly liberal principles. The idea was for the People's Party to appear to be ideologically opposed to the more conservative Party of Nationalists and New Iran Party.

This two-party system was scrapped in March 1975 when the Shah decided to adopt a one-party system spearheaded by the Rastakhiz Party (Resurgence Party). In its three-and-a-half-year existence, Rastakhiz strove to create strong party structures, such as a much-touted youth wing. From the outset, the party was closely associated with the Shah's longest serving prime minister, Amir Abbas Hoveyda, who attempted to mould the party around the image of himself as the man at the forefront of Iran's development. However, like its predecessors, Rastakhiz lacked roots and a genuine base. This lack of authenticity was a major reason for the party's rapid disintegration as the Iranian revolution gained ground in 1978, and it was officially dissolved in early October of the same year.

At one level, Rastakhiz symbolised the failure to institute a multi-party system in Iran, an effort that began in 1957. More importantly (in terms of the survival of the Pahlavi regime), Rastakhiz marked the personal failure of the Shah to consolidate his political base. The decision to institute a one-party political system in Iran was a natural corollary of the Shah's growing confidence in the 1970s, as rising oil prices enabled the country to develop a credible military and, by extension, play a leading role in regional security. The Shah sought to replicate this external success in the domestic sphere by creating political tools which could enable him to shape the country's politics.

Perhaps the Shah also understood the unpopularity of his regime and its perceived cultural remoteness from the masses and sought to alleviate this problem by instituting a party that could reach alienated segments of society. But, ironically, this created even greater resentment, as Rastakhiz targeted important socio-economic groups, notably the Bazaari merchants, as part of an anti-profiteering drive. Ultimately the Shah personally lacked the political skills to manipulate the political environment in a manner conducive to regime continuity. At a deeper level, the Pahlavi regime was not institutionally dense or sophisticated enough to sustain a party system of any kind, be it an engineered multi-party 'democracy' or, more realistically, a single-party dictatorship.

However, there are deeper cultural factors at play which are worth exploring. After all, the Pahlavi regime is not entirely to blame for the failure to institute a real party system in Iran. Throughout the twentieth century and beyond, the Iranian people have been resistant to the institutionalisation of genuine political parties. 'Genuine' in this context refers to parties complying with the basic theories and standards of political science. This means organised political groups with genuine roots (that is, representing distinct socio-economic groups and interests), an active grassroots base, an identifiable and formal hierarchy and well-established mechanisms and internal governance procedures, such as congresses, rallies, conferences and related events. Very few of the political parties in the Pahlavi era or, as we shall see below, in the Islamic Republic era satisfy all these criteria.

This historical national failure has led many Iranian political scientists, sociologists, philosophers and political activists to pontificate on what deeper factors might lie behind this phenomenon. Many have focused on so-called cultural issues, and specifically on characteristics and 'pathologies' attendant to Iranian political culture. The informal consensus appears to be that Iranians find it difficult to create large organisations and sustain them indefinitely without consistent government backing and support. The same theory is applied to the private commercial sector, where there have been very few (if any) large Iranian corporate organisations. The *Bonyad* (foundation) phenomenon of post-revolutionary Iran, describing large conglomerates with vast business interests across multiple sectors, is the closest thing the Iranian economy has to Western-style corporations. The key difference is that the *Bonyads* are state-supported entities with multiple government-sanctioned exemptions and advantages, such as tax breaks.

But on closer analysis, this culture-based theory begins to fall apart. For a start, modern Iran has had at least one major genuine party, namely the Tudeh Party (Masses Party). Founded in 1941, the party was openly aligned with the former Soviet Union and sought to turn Iran into a communist state. By any standard, the Tudeh Party was a large organisation, with an extensive grassroots base of workers and a disciplined governance structure. The party even had secretive cells, principally a secret military organisation which had penetrated the higher reaches of the army. Tudeh played a key role in the events surrounding oil nationalisation from the British-controlled Anglo-Iranian Oil Company from 1951 onwards. However, the party's half-hearted support for Mossadegh irreparably damaged its reputation amongst key social groups, notably the emerging middle classes.

Following the August 1953 coup, the Tudeh Party was subjected to a harsh crackdown, with thousands of members arrested and several dozen executed. Much of the secretive and highly prized military cell was dismantled. Following the repression, most of the remaining party leadership fled to the Soviet Union or to the former Eastern Bloc countries in Europe. Although significantly weakened, the party was sufficiently coherent to attempt a comeback following the victory of the 1979 revolution. Ostensibly aligned with the left wing of the Islamic Republic, the Tudeh was still a visibly communist entity with barely concealed loyalty to the former Soviet Union.

The party was never trusted by the Islamic Republic, which set about to systematically destroy it in early 1983. The entire leadership was arrested and later forced to partake in prolonged interviews on national television. These amounted to political confessionals in which the veteran Tudeh leaders, who had hundreds of years of political experience between them, confessed to a wide range of political and intelligence-related 'crimes'. Amongst these leaders were Secretary General Noureddin Kianouri and the party's main theorist and ideologue Ehsan Tabari. Whilst both men were spared execution— unlike former navy commander Admiral Bahram Afzali, who was executed in February 1984—they both died in relative obscurity under house arrest, a decade apart: first Tabari in April 1989, followed by Kianouri in November 1999.

Although the Tudeh Party was a large, organic political organisation and managed to survive for decades under harsh conditions, it cannot be described as successful. For a start, whilst the party had an identifiable grassroots base, it did not appeal to a critical mass of Iranians. This is one reason that it never came close to seizing and holding power. Second, its close association with the former Soviet Union, which in the case of its secret military unit amounted to penetrating and spying on the Iranian military at the behest of Soviet intelligence, severely undermined its reputation. Indeed, to many Iranians the Tudeh Party is still synonymous with treachery.

Therefore, whilst Tudeh was a large and genuine political party with a progressive socio-economic and cultural agenda, its association with the geopolitical interests of a foreign power had a long-lasting impact on how Iranians perceive political parties more broadly. Whilst the experience of the Tudeh Party alone cannot explain why Iranians are averse to forming and sustaining political parties, it does at least go some way in illuminating some of the deeper psychological factors underpinning this phenomenon. In fact, Tudeh has left two legacies for public perceptions of disciplined political parties. One is the association with foreign powers; the other is indecision during critical moments of historical import. In Tudeh's case, the party's ambivalent support for former prime minister Mossadegh and its apparent unwillingness to wholeheartedly support him in August 1953 shaped public attitudes.

It is in this context that the nascent Islamic Republic set about structuring its political society. In the immediate post-revolutionary period known as the revolutionary 'spring', a multitude of groups and organisations sprung onto the political scene, free from any repression or oversight. The unregulated nature of this spontaneous explosion in political activity was also partly to blame for its relatively quick demise. Although the political space remained open until early 1981, the new authorities had started to get a grip on the situation by late 1979, and certainly after the demise of Mehdi Bazargan's provisional government.

The key challenge for the emerging establishment aligned with the revolutionary leader Ayatollah Khomeini was to contain the influence of groups which did not wholeheartedly accept Khomeini's leadership and were otherwise not fully invested in the Islamic ethos of the emerging new regime. Inevitably the key challenge came from the left, as right-wing forces were understandably considered to be either counter-revolutionaries or reactionaries.

From an organisational point of view, it was the left, and specifically militant left-wing organisations such as the Fedayian-e Khalq (Sacrificers for the People) and the Mojahedin-e Khalq (People's Holy Warriors), which had supported the revolution at the critical street level. Although these organisations inflated their role, there is no doubt that they were an important part of the revolutionary process and may have speeded up the Pahlavi regime's collapse by influencing the calculus of the Iranian armed forces. For its part, the longstanding Tudeh Party had provided intellectual support and championed the leadership of 'Imam Khomeini', throughout the revolutionary process and beyond, as the most authentic 'anti-imperialist' platform.

Much of the written history of the early years of the Iranian revolution focuses on the tough repression of the left, propagated through the state-sanctioned mobilisation of thugs, assaults on rallies, raiding of offices and safe houses and executions. Whilst these hardline approaches were features of the landscape, the real untold story is the intelligence work carried out behind the scenes to try to divide and weaken the organisations. The pre-revolutionary intelligence service SAVAK was almost immediately revived (in a diminutive form) and apparently operated under various names, including the Prime Minister's Office. This nascent intelligence agency, in conjunction with the intelligence branch of the Pasdaran, was instrumental in breaking the hard left's cohesion and consensus.

Arguably its biggest achievement was precipitating the Fedayian-e Khalq's fragmentation, a process well underway by the late 1970s, but which was exploited by the country's new intelligence establishment to support the consolidation of the new system. A new Fedayian faction known as the Aksariyat (Majority) openly sided with Ayatollah Khomeini, whilst the rest, named Aghaleeyat (Minority) by default, maintained a critical stance toward post-revolutionary political processes, and especially toward the clerics' drive to consolidate power. The so-called Majority faction justified its position on the basis of Ayatollah Khomeini's allegedly principled stance on US imperialism, international affairs generally, economic reforms and the Iran–Iraq War. But even this 'Majority' faction was not tolerated for long and by 1983 had been driven underground.

The biggest challenge to the new authorities, however, did not come from conventional hard-left groups like the Fedayian, but from the MeK, an eccentric organisation that amalgamated aspects of Marxism-Leninism with the revolutionary ethos of Shia Islam. The MeK was more organisationally coherent and ideologically resilient than conventional hard-left groups. For the authorities, the MeK was also a far more sensitive case, not least because many revolutionary leaders, including leading lights such as Hashemi Rafsanjani, were previously affiliated to the group and otherwise had extensive interactions with it in the pre-revolutionary prison system. These leaders would later justify these connections on the grounds that the MeK of the late 1960s and 1970s was markedly different to the group that sprang onto the national political scene in 1979.

Another key difference between the MeK and other hard-left groups was the former's formidable will to power. Upon realising that they could not compete with Ayatollah Khomeini at the leadership level, and by extension would not be able to dominate the new establishment, the MeK opted for the militant path, forming a militia that openly paraded on the streets and guarded their rallies and offices. A major clash was inevitable and this came about after the impeachment of the Republic's first president Banisadr (with whom the MeK had formed an alliance) in June 1981. From that point on the Islamic Republic's security and intelligence organisation set about destroying the MeK's organisation inside Iran, a task that had been largely accomplished by early 1983. However, the MeK continued to pose a considerable threat to national security, especially after relocating to Iraq where they found common cause with Saddam Hussein. They even formed a conventional army, the self-styled 'National Liberation Army of Iran', which attempted to invade Iran in an ill-fated operation dubbed Eternal Light in July 1988, following Iran's acceptance of UN Resolution 598. Following the overthrow of Saddam Hussein in April 2003, it took the new Iraqi authorities eleven years to eject this stubborn organisation from Iraqi territory.[8]

By the middle of 1981 the visible political landscape had been largely purged of non-conformist groups. Some critical groups were still tolerated, but they were not from the hard left and their impact on the ground was minimal. Arguably the best example was Nehzat-e Azadi (Liberation Movement), a moderate Islamic nationalist group to which the Republic's first PM, Mehdi Bazargan, belonged. Founded in the early 1960s, the Liberation Movement was the parent organisation of the breakaway MeK, which considered the original organisation's ideology and approach insufficiently radical.

Despite its quest for unity, cohesion and authenticity, the nascent Islamic Republic had by the early 1980s reproduced the classic left–right divide of political societies the world over. On the right sat the clerical body Jameyeh Rouhaniyat-e Mobarez (Society of Militant Clergy, or SMC) and the Hezbeh Motalefeyeh Eslami (Islamic Coalition Party), a hardcore capitalist group aligned with the big Bazaari merchants. On the left sat another clerical body, Majma'e Rouhaniyouneh Mobarez (Association of Militant Clerics, or AMC) and allied political groups such as the Sazeman-e Mojahedin-e Enghelab-e Islami (Organisation of the Mojahedin of the Islamic Revolution, or OMIR, not to be confused with the MeK).

In part to overcome these differences and to at least create a veneer of unity, the revolutionary authorities had created the Islamic Republican Party (IRP) barely a few months after the victory of the revolution. Whilst the IRP was a relatively effective organisation in its first few years of existence, by, for instance, countering Banisadr and the non-conformist groups on the left, by the early 1980s it had evolved into a fractious entity. It was failing to achieve its primary objective, which was to present political unity and propose coherent policies for adoption by different branches of government. Instead, the IRP was merely reproducing the left–right divide that existed in the wider political context. By the late 1980s it had become so dysfunctional that Ayatollah Khomeini formally ordered its dissolution in May 1987.

Throughout the 1980s the dominant political trend was the Khat-e-Imam (Imam's Line), which was aligned with the left-wing AMC. The Imam's Line can be considered the most radical faction from the time, at the forefront of revolutionary agitation in both the domestic and external arenas. For example, many of the students who stormed the American embassy in early November 1979 were affiliated with this faction. One of the most well-known students, Ebrahim Asgharzadeh, went on to develop a relatively successful political career, the highlight of which was successfully competing for the third Majlis in 1988.

The Khat-e-Imam trend was comprised of various factions, the most influential of which was OMIR. OMIR had penetrated all the important levers of political power, in particular the Majlis and the executive branch of government, which at the time was led by the left-wing Prime Minister Mir Hossein Mousavi. A nationalist with mild Mossadeghist tendencies, in economic terms Mousavi was firmly rooted in the left and championed a socialist economy where basic goods and services were subsidised. The subsidies were critically important for the poorer sections of society, which the Khat-e Imam considered as the core constituency of the revolution.

By stark contrast, the right-wing factions aligned with the SMC championed a free market economy and argued for minimal regulation and taxation. This was music to the ears of the traditional Bazaari merchants, whom the right-wing of the Islamic Republic considered to be an important constituency of the revolution. Therefore, at one level, the left–right divide in the Islamic Republic represented a struggle to prioritise different revolutionary constituencies whose socio-economic interests were not easily reconciled. After all, the rich Bazaari merchants were far removed in terms of their purchasing power (if not their actual lifestyle) from the traditional working classes and the recently urbanised slum dwellers. The only thing they had in common was a degree of religiosity and, by extension, revolutionary loyalty—and specifically fealty to the charismatic revolutionary leader Ayatollah Khomeini.

At the highest level of the system, the left–right divide was also a clash of personalities, notably a clash between Prime Minister Mousavi and President Seyed Ali Khamenei (elected in October 1981), primarily over economic policy. Khamenei was affiliated to the right wing even though he was not a hardcore capitalist in the mould of the pro-Bazaar Islamic Coalition Party. Identifying foremost with the Hezbollahi grassroots of the revolution, Khamenei prioritised social and cultural reform over economics. To him the greatest mission of the revolution was to re-order cultural priorities in line with national and Islamic standards. According to this vision, a revival of authentic values would in turn spur national growth and help to transform the country. Predictably the left argued that it was only by delivering on the revolutionary slogan of social justice, and by extension the redistribution of wealth, that the country could be truly transformed along revolutionary lines. The diving line was sharp, but the two camps had sufficient characteristics and interests in common to reside within the same system.

The Khat-e Imam remained dominant in large part because Ayatollah Khomeini appeared to be sympathetic to their position. For example, Khomeini was strongly supportive of Prime Minister Mousavi and scuppered several attempts to remove him. He also dissuaded the prime minister from resigning on at least one occasion. But Khomeini's support for the left did not necessarily translate into antipathy for the right, which in cultural and religious terms appeared to be more committed to Khomeini's vision. The late revolutionary leader was discharging his duty as the *Valiyeh Faqih* by staying above the factional divide and trying to keep a balance between opposing forces. From an institutional point of view, the left was not strong enough to compete with the right on an even playing field, which might partly explain why Khomeini sometimes intervened in their favour. Indeed, once Khomeini departed the arena, the right wing's institutional weight helped it to eclipse the left.

The power struggle of the 1980s between President Khamenei and Prime Minister Mousavi was to return more than twenty years later in explosive fashion, during the political crisis of 2009–10. But in 1989, following the death of Ayatollah Khomeini, Mousavi disappeared from the political scene, as the July 1989 amendment to the constitution abolished the role of the prime minister and invested those powers in the presidency. Mousavi's departure was the beginning of the end for the authentic left in the Islamic Republic.

The Post-1989 Political Landscape

The most important political development of the 1990s was the transformation of the Khat-e Imam trend into 'reformists'. This began as an intellectual enterprise in the Centre for Strategic Research (CSR), originally a thinktank affiliated to the presidency. Subsequently the CSR was rehoused in the Expediency Discernment Council. By the mid-1990s the bulk of the political forces once identified as the left had regrouped under the reformist banner.

Debates continue to rage as to what extent the conversion from Islamic left to 'reformist' was a genuine ideological transformation as opposed to political opportunism prompted by a shift in the balance of power and public attitudes. Certainly, by the early 1990s revolutionary fervour had subsided and the country was in the midst of recovery and reconstruction after the gruelling war with Iraq. The hardline ideology and radicalism of the Khat-e Imam no longer had traction either within the system or with the broader public. There was a widespread feeling that the revolution had moved beyond its radical phase and now needed to consolidate along more normative concepts and values, such as reconstruction and economic growth.

The shift in public attitude was reinforced by a concerted campaign by the right wing to purge the Khat-e Imam from key institutions, notably the Majlis. The elections for the fourth Majlis (April 1992) were important in this regard as swathes of left-wing candidates (many of whom were sitting MPs) were disqualified from the elections by the Council of Guardians. Amongst the disqualified candidates was the former radical and leader of the US embassy takeover Ebrahim Asgharzadeh. The institutional purge appears to have intensified soul-searching within the left and hence speeded up the process of ideological transformation.

Another important political development was the attempt by Hashemi Rafsanjani to develop an independent political base in the form of the Kargozaran (Technocrats). Although the roots of the technocratic faction go back to the revolution's first decade, it was Rafsanjani who used his personal clout, skills and connections to significantly improve the technocrat's organisational capacity and resulting standing in the political system. Like Khamenei, Rafsanjani was associated with the right wing but he was astute enough to maintain strong bridges with the left. Indeed, in the 1980s, using his position as Majlis speaker, Rafsanjani had often mediated between SMC- and AMC-affiliated factions.

What the traditional right wing and the Technocrats had in common was an exclusive focus on economic development. The Technocrats were more culturally liberal but they identified economic development—and in due course structural economic reforms— as their key platform. Neither faction had much time for political development (*toseeyeh seeyasi*), which in Iran was code for political liberalisation. The emerging reformists exploited this vacuum by developing a policy platform which focused mostly on political reforms and socio-cultural liberalisation.

Seyed Mohammad Khatami's landslide electoral victory in May 1997 took many observers by surprise, with few people at the time realising that eight years of solid intellectual and political labour had gradually paved the way for that dramatic breakthrough. The reformists controlled the executive branch of government for eight years (1997–2005) and the legislative branch for four years (2000– 04) but they singularly failed to implement their key policies, most of which revolved around structural political reforms to strengthen the democratic features of the system at the expense of its theocratic dimension, as embodied by the *Velayat-e Faqih* doctrine.

The reasons for this failure continue to be hotly debated, with most observers blaming a deeply entrenched conservative establishment reflexively opposed to reforms. Yet others blame the reformists themselves, in part because of their over-reach, but also on account of their poor political skills and failure to sufficiently cultivate powerful socio-economic constituencies. A poorly understood factor in their failure was the pushback by the Islamic Republic's security-intelligence community. It is worthwhile examining this factor at greater depth.

Political Society Versus Security Community

Part of the enigma of the Islamic Republic is that its discordant political society is balanced by a cohesive security-intelligence community.

Some of the reasons behind this cohesion were discussed in the previous chapter, notably the IRGC-led amalgamation of nationalism and Shia Islam in the context of Iran's Islamic Revolution. Therefore, the revolutionary experience—and the national-historical milieu within which it resides—is sufficiently rich and resilient to produce a sustainable moral and ideological compass.

But the Iranian security community is bigger than the IRGC. Apart from the latter, the most important organisation is the Ministry of Intelligence and Security (MOIS), which was formed in 1984. The operational reach and prowess of this large and powerful intelligence organisation will be discussed in subsequent chapters. Needless to say, the MOIS is relevant to the country's political development inasmuch as it helps to shape political outcomes. This is in violation of the ministry's foundational charter which forbade it from political meddling. However, the factious nature of the country's politics and its intermittent volatility have required a degree of MOIS intervention.

This intervention, of course, is unseen and unfolds behind the scenes. For instance, in the aftermath of the disputed presidential elections held in June 2009, the MOIS had to perform a mediating role in order to reconstitute the political landscape after months of unrest and purges. More broadly, the vicissitudes of the country's political landscape—with power regularly shifting from one group to another—necessitates a systemic counter to guarantee stability.

To illustrate the point, it is instructive to study the shift of power from the reformists to a radical wing of the conservatives/principlists led by Mahmoud Ahmadinejad in the June 2005 presidential elections. The two groups could not be more different, in terms of both their political-ideological outlook and their governance style. To press the point further, Ahmadinejad went on to develop the Islamic Republic's first fully-fledged populist trend, which attracted enormous backlash, not just from the reformists, but also from the conservatives and, in the final years of his presidency, even from elements in the establishment, who decried the former president's 'deviant' faction. These regular shifts in power and the proclivity of Iranian leaders toward grandstanding and posturing, together with a highly enthusiastic and emotionally charged electorate, are conducive to instability. In this volatile context, a cohesive security-intelligence community with the ability to make effective strategic interventions helps to restore systemic equilibrium.

To understand Iranian politics better, it is helpful to think of three constituencies and centres of power, namely political society, civil society and the security community. All three constituencies help shape the political agenda and determine political outcomes. The political society is easy to define as it is made up of avowed political actors organised along party or factional lines. These are professional politicians who compete in the political arena with a view to securing an electoral mandate. Civil society is harder to define as it is less disciplined and less transparent. In an Iranian context, it refers to a wide range of activists and concerned citizens who pursue objectives and grievances in the public arena. Most civil society activists are animated by socio-economic and cultural concerns. However, there is a growing environmental lobby in Iran which lobbies for greener policies and greater protection for national landmarks with environmental significance.[9]

Civil society activists are often perceived to be aligned with the reformists, not least because the latter set out an expansive political and socio-cultural platform that takes into account fashionable public concerns. The civil society sector can become influential at moments of political stress (such as during the post-election demonstrations in 2009) and that is one reason as to why the political establishment continually strives to co-opt civil society demands. By contrast, the security community is often at odds with civil society, detaining, interrogating and jailing activists.

Long-term political stability necessitates a degree of cooperation between all three centres of power. This requires all three actors thinking and behaving strategically, with a view to developing a shared national vision. Conversely, if these centres of power think and act in ideological terms alone—and hence prioritise parochial sectional interests over the national interest—they are likely to come into greater conflict. The prospect for sustainable political stability looks good, especially in the light of the centrist political ascendancy. In view of his national security background, Rouhani is uniquely well positioned to create strategic bonds between the Islamic Republic's political society and the country's security-intelligence establishment. Furthermore, by co-opting the reformists—and by extension a critical mass of civil society activists—Rouhani-led centrists have been able to repair the reputational damage inflicted by the 2009–10 unrest and have consequently restored the system's legitimacy.

ASYMMETRIC CAPABILITY

A major part of Iran's strategic reach and political influence across the region rests on its asymmetric capability. By extension Iran's conventional capability is relatively weak, as demonstrated by the ageing air force fleet, whose backbone is still made up of 45-year-old US-supplied F-4 Phantoms, F-5 Tigers and F-14 Tomcats.

The relative weakness of Iran's conventional forces is a direct consequence of the Islamic Republic's foreign policy, notably its decision to oppose Western and in particular US regional policies. It is the price the country pays for the more ideological aspects of its foreign policy.

But at a deeper level, what are the precise origins of this capability? As discussed earlier, Iran set out to develop modern armed forces in the 1920s following the ascension of Reza Khan to power. After many fits and starts, this ambition had been achieved by the early 1970s, as demonstrated by the flow of vast quantities of American arms and weapons systems into the country.

Indeed, at the dawn of the Iranian revolution in 1978–79 Iran possessed one of the largest and best supplied armed forces in the world. The forces were well trained and motivated, as demonstrated by Iran's successful intervention in the Omani conflict of the early to mid-1970s, in addition to the successful deterrence of Iraq throughout the 1970s.

The containment of Iraqi ambitions was a major achievement for pre-revolutionary Iran and demonstrated the country's potential as a natural regional leader and guardian of peace and stability. This containment strategy culminated in the Algiers Accord of 1975— when the Shah and former Iraqi strongman Saddam Hussein met face to face—whose cardinal clause centred on Iraq effectively relinquishing its territorial claim on the strategic Shatt Al-Arab (Arvand Roud) waterway.

Taken together, these three factors—the containment of Iraq, successful intervention in Oman and the acquisition of modern weaponry and training—were clear indicators of Iran's potential to emerge as a major military power. The pre-revolutionary regime did not seek asymmetric capabilities as it saw no pressing need for them. As long as Iran was aligned to the Western camp, and importantly to the United States, it made sense for the country to mimic Western defence and strategic doctrines.

The pre-revolutionary system aspired to Western standards and norms in every aspect of life, and the domains of defence, national security and strategic planning were no exception. From the monarchical regime's perspective, the twin aims of protecting the Iranian homeland and projecting power and influence across the region could be achieved through conventional means alone.

Therefore, the adoption of asymmetric capabilities is a clear consequence of the overthrow of the monarchical system and the emergence of a revolutionary state devoted to achieving a transformation in international relations.

The origin of asymmetric thinking in defence and strategic affairs can be situated in the revolutionary moment itself as most (if not all) of the opposition forces scrambling for the Shah's overthrow were strong critics of the country's defence and strategic posture. The depth and tenor of this opposition varied, of course, with some nationalist groups seeking an adjustment in regional policy away from Western-friendly positions, whilst hard-left groups at the other end of the spectrum agitated for the disbandment of the Iranian armed forces altogether.

But even the mainstream of the revolution, composed of the leading clerics and an assortment of religious-nationalist groups, notably the Freedom Movement (Nehzat-e-Azadi), aspired to radical changes in the defence and national security sectors. Some leading lights in the Freedom Movement, such as Ebrahim Yazdi, a close confidant of Ayatollah Khomeini who was briefly foreign minister in the immediate post-revolution period, were eager not only to cancel defence contracts with US companies but to return some of the delivered systems.[1]

The revolutionaries' distrust of the West extended to a lack of faith in the utility of Western defence equipment and arms. From a revolutionary standpoint, the Shah had assembled a formidable army in order to perform an American-assigned role of policing the Persian Gulf. This role effectively defined Iran as a 'status quo' power, a profile that was fundamentally at odds with revolutionary instincts and attendant ambition.

Luckily for the Iranian armed forces, the revolutionary instincts of Ayatollah Khomeini and the core group of clerics loyal to him did not encompass more radical tendencies. Indeed, Khomeini and his inner circle were strongly opposed to the eradication of vital national institutions. There was therefore no question of disbanding the army.

This attitude also extended to the security sector, where the dominant revolutionary core understood the critical requirement for a national intelligence service. However, in this case it was inevitable that the pre-revolutionary intelligence service, the SAVAK,[2] would have to be disbanded as it was intimately bound up with the rule of the Shah. A new service was formed immediately after the SAVAK's dissolution, its structures and functions modelled almost entirely on its predecessor.

The protection of the armed forces' institutional integrity, however, did not mean that its three services were not subject to brutal punishment. Indeed, like all modern revolutions, the Iranian revolution necessitated a purge of sensitive institutions to achieve the related aims of neutralising counter-revolutionary elements and establishing the new order.

Of the three armed services, the air force was hardest hit. Its top brass were summarily executed in the early days of the revolution. Amongst these was the air force commander Lieutenant-General Amir-Hossein Rabii, as well as the legendary fighter pilot Lieutenant-General Nader Jahanbani. The latter's execution was especially egregious as Jahanbani was not implicated in abuse of power. Many suspect that his uncompromising character and status as a role model for the air force pushed the revolutionaries to eliminate him so as to remove a potential threat.[3]

Beyond the upper echelon of the air force, many senior and even middle-ranking air force officers, and experienced fighter pilots, were forced into early retirement. This drastically reduced the operational capacity of the air force and was a major factor in Saddam Hussein's decision to launch an all-out invasion in September 1980.

The army and the navy also suffered, though not as badly. The revolutionaries were especially suspicious of the air force, as its crème de la crème, including all the combat pilots, were US-trained and many of these officers continued to maintain institutional and in some cases even personal connections with US air force personnel.

The Formative Experience of the Iran–Iraq War

When Saddam Hussein invaded Iran on 22 September 1980, he was pursuing a set of minimalist and maximalist aims. His maximalist aim was to arrest the momentum of the Iranian revolution and to set the stage for the overthrow of the nascent Islamic Republic. Iraq's declared minimalist war aim was to establish sovereignty over the entire Shatt al-Arab waterway and to 'liberate' Iran's south-western Khuzestan province, which the Iraqis called 'Arabistan'. This Iraqi war aim was legitimised on the grounds that the province's Arab population (concentrated in the provincial capital Ahvaz and in the areas close to the border) supposedly sought secession from Iran.

It was Iraq's maximalist war aims that attracted the attention of major powers. Saddam's ambition to overthrow Iran's new rulers carried with it the potential to restore the status quo ante, albeit on Iraqi terms. Despite the jingoistic bombast at home, Iraq's leaders were skilful enough to couch their war aims in diplomatic and pro status quo language on the world stage. In this endeavour they were supported by a wide range of regional and global powers, including the United States, which was still struggling to come to terms with the Iranian revolution.

The overthrow of the Shah was a traumatic experience for the United States, as it removed a reliable American ally who could secure stability in the Persian Gulf. But this disappointment soon turned to hatred following the seizure of the US embassy in Tehran in early November 1979 and the subsequent illegal detention of dozens of US diplomats. At the outbreak of the war in September 1980, American diplomats were still being held by 'students' who had stormed the embassy a year earlier.

Beyond the US, the major Western powers, including the United Kingdom, France and even West Germany, privately welcomed an Iraqi push to contain the ambitions of Iran's new revolutionary leaders, even as all countries publicly called for the cessation of hostilities. The onset of war was also an opportunity for these countries to support their arms companies by selling weapons and military equipment to both sides.

On the other side of the Iron Curtain, the former Soviet Union also implicitly welcomed conflict, albeit a short-lived one. Whilst the Soviet perception of revolutionary Iran was markedly different to that of the West, the Soviets nonetheless feared the potentially destabilising effect of Iran's ideological foreign policy. However, like the Western powers, the Soviets welcomed the opportunity to sell weapons, particularly to Iraq, which had been an informal Soviet ally since the late 1960s.

As for the regional powers, they were all fearful of the potential breadth and depth of revolutionary Iran's ambitions. The nascent Islamic Republic expounded two major themes in the foreign policy sphere which unsettled the rulers of the Persian Gulf states: anti-monarchy and revolutionary Islam. As the Gulf states were all monarchies they were naturally wary of the staunchly anti-monarchical and republican credentials of the Islamic Republic. Moreover, the type of revolutionary Islam expounded by Iran's new rulers was inimical to the conservative form of Islam promoted by the Gulf states.

Iran's new leaders viewed Islam as an inherently revolutionary force that should challenge the status quo, particularly if existing conditions were unjust, oppressive or humiliating. Arguably all three criteria applied to key Gulf States, and especially to Saudi Arabia, whose ruling regimes were based on hereditary lines of descent and whose rule necessarily implied oppressing minorities, in particular Shia Muslims. Furthermore, the Gulf states were perceived in Iran to be subservient to the United States and lacking an independent will in regional and global affairs.

Iranian propaganda targeted the Gulf states early on, a feature that intensified as the Iran–Iraq War dragged on and the Gulf states, particularly Saudi Arabia and Kuwait, stepped up their support for Iraq. However, the Gulf states' support for Iraq, which was ostensibly grounded on pan-Arab principles and took the form of financial assistance, dramatically backfired a decade later when Iraq invaded Kuwait in August 1990.

Fear of the power and reach of revolutionary Iran was one of the factors that motivated Iraq's Baathist rulers to strike at the nascent Islamic Republic with a view to fatally undermining its symbolic appeal, if not destroying it altogether. Iraq's fears centred on the Iranian revolution's appeal to its Shia majority, which was concentrated in the southern and central regions of the country. Despite constituting a clear demographic majority (by as much as 55 per cent of the population), Iraqi Shias endured a minority status and suffered greater levels of poverty and exclusion than the minority Sunni Arab population.

Despite its pan-Arab ideology and impeccable nationalist credentials, the ruling Baath party had singularly failed to integrate the Shias, particularly the tribal Shias of the deep south and the working class of the symbolic Shia cities of Najaf, Karbala and Kufa. Whilst Iraq could not be described as a sectarian state, the upper reaches of the government were overwhelmingly dominated by Arab Sunnis. Furthermore, the very top of the regime was dominated by Tikritis from Saddam Hussein's extended clan. Notwithstanding pragmatic reasons for this arrangement, to many Iraqi nationalists it signified a betrayal of the pan-Arab ideology championed by the Baath. It was precisely these vulnerabilities that Iranian revolutionary propagandists sought to exploit.

Beyond the propaganda level, the Iraqi authorities had to contend with deep-rooted ethnic, familial and structural ties between Iraqi and Iranian Shias. These are structures that centuries of Ottoman domination and decades of modern nationalist rule had failed to obliterate. The shrine cities of Najaf and Karbala (and the religious seminaries situated there) were a focal point of connectivity, as they symbolised pan-Shia unity transcending national borders.

Another acute security concern were the Shia-based political parties that were in open opposition to the Baath. The most striking example was Hizb Al-Da'wa Al-Islamiyya (Islamic Call Party), or Al-Da'wa for short, a secretive organisation founded in the late 1950s. The party's spiritual leader was Ayatollah Muhammad Baqir al-Sadr, a ground-breaking scholar and unrivalled ideologue. The latter was the author of the authoritative *Falsafatuna* (Our Philosophy) and *Iqtisaduna* (Our Economics), which set out an Islamic political philosophy and a framework for an Islamic approach to economics respectively. Both texts are considered as highly original and continue to inform Islamic political activism and economic thinking.

Moreover, Sadr's influence extends beyond the Shia world as many Sunni Muslims have been influenced by his scholarly works. This is in keeping with Al-Da'wa's original ideology that was founded in part on the politics of pan-Islam. The late 1950s and 1960s were a time of idealism and ideological optimism, not only in the Middle East but across much of the world. Moreover, this was a period before the onset of modern sectarianism in the Middle East and the neat division of Shias and Sunnis.

The Iraqi authorities' decision to execute Sadr, alongside his sister Bint al-Huda, in April 1980 sent shockwaves across the Shia clerical establishment and the masses of faithful stretching from Lebanon to India. In view of Sadr's scholarly, ideological and political stature it was a remarkably bold move that would inevitably attract long-term consequences.

In the immediate term, Sadr's execution accelerated the path to war. The Iranian revolutionary leadership interpreted the execution as a declaration of all-out war on the Iraq-based Shia clerical establishment. Since the advent of Baathist rule in Iraq from the early 1960s, contact between the Iraq-based Shia clerical hierarchy and their counterparts in Iran had been severely restricted, with movement and communications closely monitored and often disrupted by the Iraqi intelligence services. Moreover, the Baathists had cracked down on public displays of Shia identity, in particular the mourning ceremonies of Muharram (commemorating the martyrdom of Imam Hussein) which draw millions of pilgrims to Karbala and its surrounds.

But the Baathists had until early 1980 refrained from subjecting the Shia hierarchy to violence. Sadr's execution, therefore, was a sea change in perceived attitudes and intentions whose full implications were interpreted in expansive terms in Tehran. As a result, Iran stepped up propaganda with a view to stoking up unrest amongst sections of the Shia community, which in turn spurred the Iraqi authorities to undertake greater repression. A vicious circle had set in which neither side was willing or able to break.

The Iraqi authorities also capitalised on a low-level terror campaign by Al-Da'wa to justify a sweeping campaign of repression. The terror threat peaked in April 1980 in the immediate aftermath of Sadr's execution, with an assassination attempt on deputy prime minister and iconic Baathist Tariq Aziz.[4] Al-Da'wa and allied groups did not constitute a credible threat to Baathist rule in immediate terms, but they had the potential to mobilise Shia discontent in the longer term, provided they were adequately supported by Iran. This was the basis of Baathist logic, and was eventually proven right as post-revolutionary Iran went on to sponsor Al-Da'wa and other groups (some formed in Tehran) as part of a long-term strategy to displace the Baath. This investment fully paid off following the overthrow of Saddam Hussein in early 2003.

It is worth examining the long-term consequences of Sadr's execution independently of the Iran–Iraq War and broader Iranian–Iraqi relations. It could be argued that the consequences are still unfolding, as demonstrated by the sectarian conflict in Iraq. To many Iraqi Shias, Sadr's execution was a statement of intent: to obliterate the Shia clerical hierarchy and, by extension, the Shia faith.

From April 1980 onwards, the Iraqi regime declared all-out war on the Shia militant groups and political opposition more broadly. Throughout these years the illustrious Sadr family bore the brunt of brutal Baathist repression. In Iraq the family's lineage is traced to Ismail al-Sadr, who was originally Lebanese but born in Isfahan (central Iran). Ismail's father, Sadr al-Din bin Saleh, was the patriarch of the family, whose lineage is traced to Imam Musa al-Kazim (the seventh Imam of Twelver Shia Muslims) through the Sharefeddine and Noureddine families. In socio-cultural terms, the Sharefeddine and Noureddine familes are at the centre of Lebanese Shia society.

The Sadr family was therefore originally Lebanese, some of its descendants having ended up in Iran and Iraq in order to pursue theological studies and to advance the cause of Shia learning. Another prominent descendant of the family was Sayyid Musa al-Sadr (popularly known as Imam Musa Sadr) a Lebanese-Iranian cleric who returned to his ancestral homeland in 1959 to play a key role in its development in the 1960s and 1970s. This was a crucial period in Lebanese history, often celebrated as a golden age of prosperity and stability before the onset of the Lebanese Civil War in the mid-1970s. In reality, the golden age was a myth, inasmuch as the country's domination by Maronite Christians and the wide-ranging socio-economic disadvantages endured by the Shia community were a recipe for long-term instability.

Musa Sadr displayed high levels of political skill, as well as a genuine ecumenical approach to inter-communal issues and problems, and was able to negotiate an incremental improvement in the socio-economic status of the Lebanese Shia. Moreover, his organisational skills were pivotal to kickstarting large-scale community projects and advocacy at a national level. In the 1960s and 1970s Sadr helped establish or revive numerous charities and institutions, including the much-respected Jami'at al-Birr wa al-Ihsan charity group, which he revived in the early 1960s.

Sadr's biggest contribution to Shia political mobilisation in Lebanon was his co-founding the Harakat Amal (Movement of Hope), which continues to be a strong force in the Shia community and is hugely influential in Lebanese national politics. Through its partnership with Hezbollah, Amal enjoys hegemonic power over Lebanon's empowered Shia community. Today, Sadr is highly respected as a spiritual leader of the Shia community, by Amal followers and the Hezbollah leadership and rank and file alike. His portrait and posters continue to adorn walls, streets and road sides the length and breadth of the Shia communities in the south, the Beqaa valley and the southern outskirts of Beirut.

But the relationship between the two parties was not always so cordial. Amal and Hezbollah were locked in a bitter rivalry for much of the 1980s as they vied for political influence over the Shia community, in addition to fighting over land and resources. At times this dispute escalated into armed conflict, notably in 1985 during the notorious 'War of the Camps', when Amal fought Palestinian factions. Hezbollah sided with the Palestinians, a decision which brought the group into direct armed conflict with Amal. The Syrian army sided with Amal and killed dozens of Hezbollah fighters, sometimes in extra-judicial killings.

Although Hezbollah and Syria are regarded as allies today, originally the relationship was defined by bad blood and deep suspicion. The relationship was placed on a stable footing only once the Amal–Hezbollah conflict subsided in May 1988, when Hezbollah decisively defeated Amal and gained control of south Beirut. A hard-negotiated truce in January 1989 brought hostilities to a formal conclusion and from that point onward the two parties started to develop a sustainable arrangement to share power and resources in Shia-majority areas. In subsequent years Hezbollah eclipsed Amal, both politically and militarily, but the accommodation between the two sides has endured, not least because of the link to the towering figure of Imam Musa Sadr.

In keeping with ancient Shia traditions of disappearances, martyrdom and salvation, Musa Sadr 'disappeared' whilst on a trip to Libya in August 1978. Whilst it is generally assumed that he has since been killed, the precise circumstances surrounding his death remain unclear. According to some accounts the late Libyan dictator Muammar Gaddafi ordered Sadr's killing as a favour to the Palestine Liberation Organisation (PLO) leader Yasser Arafat, as Amal and the Palestinians were involved in armed clashes in south Lebanon. Other sources attribute the killing to a heated 2.5-hour exchange between Gaddafi and Sadr, which centred on theological issues and Gaddafi's violent rejection of the finer details of Shia beliefs. According to this version of events, Sadr was beaten to death for daring to openly disagree with Gaddafi.

To the Lebanese Shia this was a traumatic event which has evaded closure owing to the Libyans' refusal to disclose any useful and conclusive information as to the circumstances surrounding Musa Sadr's disappearance and probable murder. Hopes were momentarily raised during the Libyan uprising of 2011, which resulted in the overthrow and killing of Gaddafi in October 2011. However, the new Libyan rulers—and the multitude of militias who support them—have proven to be as obdurate and unhelpful in terms of disclosure as the regime which they overthrew. Thus, to some of his most devoted followers, Musa Sadr symbolises the living martyr whose suffering and uncertain fate reflect that of the community which he served so selflessly.

There is an additional layer to the Musa Sadr story which is worth exploring. Persistent but unfounded rumours tied him to the pre-revolutionary Iranian intelligence service, the SAVAK. Musa Sadr's mission in South Lebanon was viewed in some quarters as an extension of Iranian influence and Iran's desire to establish more concrete form of connectivity with co-religionists in the south of Lebanon. The SAVAK connection is unproven, and even if there is a grain of truth to it, it was probably incidental as opposed to a structured relationship. However, the notion of Musa Sadr as an agent of influence for Iran is not completely far-fetched and speaks to continuity in Iranian reginal policy. Therefore, in terms of Iranian foreign policy, the Islamic Republic's concerted drive to establish and maintain influence in Lebanon is not a radical departure from the norm, as it is often imagined.

Returning to Iraq in 1980, it was precisely this complex set of ethnic, national and religious connectivity, bounding the Shias of Lebanon, Iraq and Iran together, which worried the Baath. Under the wrong conditions—such as the unfolding revolution in neighbouring Iran—this affinity could constitute a threat to Iraqi national security. Moreover, by dint of their ideology the Baathists were propelled to push back against this transnational Shia nexus. This is for two reasons: first, the connectivity of Shia Iranian, Iraqi and Lebanese *ulama* (religious scholars) and their laymen proteges facilitated the emergence of ideologies inimical to Baathist pan-Arab nationalism. In all three countries this nexus created the setting and momentum for movements to take root that played decisive roles in each country's political destiny.

For example, in Iran, both Musa Sadr and his companion Mostafa Chamran, a physicist, political theoretician and guerrilla who was post-revolutionary Iran's first defence minister, played leading roles in the Iranian revolution. Second, the Baathists, in tandem with the professional Iraqi national security community, perceived this Shia nexus as essentially alien to Iraq, as it was Iranian-led in institutional, intellectual and even political terms. This was not just a question of ideology, but one of political and organisational direction and the great potential for the Iraqi component of this nexus to be manipulated by a foreign power: Iran.

Whilst these fears were not irrational, they spoke to the inherent fragility of the Iraqi nation-state which the Baathists were trying to hold together through iron-clad discipline and occasionally the application of brute force. Under Ottoman domination for centuries, the current territory which comprises the Iraqi nation-state was cobbled together by the British with a view to establishing a coherent polity at the heart of the Middle East. More than eighty years later, in the wake of the Anglo-American invasion of Iraq in March–April 2003, the British, alongside their American partners, attempted yet another round of nation-building in Iraq, this time arguably scoring an even poorer mark.

Thus, Iraq's anxieties and inherent structural weaknesses were major factors in the outbreak of the Iran–Iraq War. Faced with an expansionist revolutionary power next door—with access to a potentially large receptive audience inside Iraq—the Baathists feared national disintegration. Taking the fight to revolutionary Iran seemed to be the best option at the time. But with the benefit of hindsight, starting a war with Iran did not adequately address the Baathists' existential fears. Whilst the Baathists successfully suppressed the Shia political parties and movements in the short-term, they were unable to tame the long-term revolutionary potential of these forces.

The Sadr family is a prime example. They continued to be a major irritant to the Iraqi regime right up to the invasion of 2003. Indeed, Baqir al-Sadr's second cousin, Ayatollah Mohammad Sadeq al-Sadr,[5] a seminary grandee who was popular with both the tribes and the Shia streets, was assassinated by the Baathists near Najaf in February 1999. Two of his sons were killed with him, but his youngest son, Moqtada al-Sadr, went on to assume leadership over the 'Sadrist' current in post-Saddam Iraq. One of the first acts of the Sadrists following the fall of Baghdad in April 2003 was to rename the sprawling working-class eastern Baghdad district of 'Revolutionary City' as 'Sadr City'. The district would become the stronghold of the Sadrist movement and a bastion of opposition to the American occupation of Baghdad.

Relatively uneducated (in Shia seminary terms) and lacking erudition and diplomacy, Moqtada al-Sadr is an unlikely inheritor of the mantle of the legendary Baqir al-Sadr, who is widely recognised as a prodigy and scholarly authority. However, the young Moqtada followed in the footsteps of his slain father by developing the tendency into a protest movement and perennial opposition force. Unable to overthrow the new elites in Baghdad, the Sadrists instead opted to develop grassroots opposition with a view to modifying policy and winning more resources for the areas they control further south, including districts of Iraq's second city Basra.

In keeping with his martyred father's shift away from Iran-centric politics and cautious embrace of Iraqi and even Arab nationalism, Moqtada al-Sadr has sought to further distance the movement from Iran. Not only has he come to blows with pro-Iranian politicians in Baghdad but at the regional level he has undertaken provocative moves, as demonstrated by his visit to Saudi Arabia in July 2017.[6] Previously the Sadrist movement was deeply implicated in Iraq's post-war sectarian conflict, which peaked in early 2007. However, in recent years they have reached out to the Arab Sunni community, a process that accelerated following the rise of the Islamic State (IS) group. Attempts at communal outreach notwithstanding, the bulk of the embattled Arab Sunni community continues to regard the Sadrist movement with suspicion and is unlikely to embrace the mercurial Moqtada as a national leader.

The Sadrists were also at the heart of revenge attacks on former Baathist officials, former intelligence and security officers and even former Iraqi military personnel, including alleged fighter pilots during the Iran–Iraq War.[7] The execution of Saddam Hussein in late December 2006 marked a high point in the Sadrists' struggle for justice as it was fitting revenge for the execution of Muhammad Baqir al-Sadr in 1980 and the assassination of Mohammad Sadeq al-Sadr in 1999.[8] In a moment rich with vengeful symbolism, as Saddam was taken to the gallows a small group of spectators (largely made up of senior Sadrists) invoked the names of the martyred Baqir al-Sadr and Sadeq al-Sadr, in addition to pledging loyalty to Moqtada al-Sadr. But that momentous event was not the final repercussion of the violence that had been directed towards the top of the Shia clerical establishment in April 1980. On the contrary, the cycle of revenge and violence continues apace in Iraq, as demonstrated by the rise of the IS group and the continuing fragmentation of Iraq into constituent ethnic and sectarian parts.

The rise of IS and the push-back against it in some ways represent the continuation of the Iran–Iraq War, albeit fought inside Iraq's borders. The names and faces of the protagonists may have changed but the underlying forces and ethno-cultural and religious dynamics are the same. Moreover, the context is the same, namely a struggle for political and ideological hegemony and potentially even the obliteration of the other. Thus, the IS group's genocidal instincts must be analysed in the context of decades of fierce ethno-sectarian struggle marked by cycles of insurgency, repression, purges and mass killings.

The internalisation of this conflict inside Iraq's borders marks a triumph for Iran in both strategic and moral terms. It gives credence to the position of some Iranian leaders who have consistently maintained that even though Iran failed to defeat Iraq militarily by the end of the war, the Islamic Republic emerged as the ultimate victor, as demonstrated not only by the physical destruction of the Baathist regime but more importantly by the collapse of Baathist moral values and ideals.

Whilst this viewpoint conveniently forgets or glosses over the precise sequence of events which led to the downfall of Saddam Hussein (notably the application of massive military force by Iran's adversary, the United States), this perspective is not entirely devoid of merit. For a start, many of the Shia political parties and paramilitary groups now firmly entrenched in Iraq are, in ideological terms at least, an extension of the Islamic Republic in Iraq. Moreover, their most determined foe, namely the IS group and its allies, are also in many ways an extension of Iran's old Baathist adversary.

The Legacy of the Iran–Iraq War

At the southern extremity of Tehran, on the road to the city of Qom, lies Behesht-e Zahra (Zahra's Paradise),[9] a sprawling cemetery that stretches out in all directions for kilometres. Since its establishment in the late 1960s hundreds of thousands of bodies have been buried there and every year the boundaries of the cemetery expand a little further. Whilst Zahra's Paradise is the burial ground of countless ordinary Iranians from all walks of life, it has become famous as the resting place of the 'martyrs' of the Iran–Iraq War. It is also home to the thousands of people who were killed in the revolutionary struggle of the late 1970s and those killed by militant and terror groups from the early days of the revolution to the present.

Walking around the 'martyrs' section of Behesht-e Zahra, one is immediately struck by two things. First, the quiet and sereneness of the place, despite the daily flow of people (usually relatives of the 'martyrs') attending to the graves of the mostly young men who are buried on the grounds. Second, images of the these young men's faces draw attention. One cannot fail to be impressed by the sincerity reflected in these faces, which often look earnest but also exude a deceptively calm determination. In nearly all cases the portraits are accompanied by personal testimonies and wills (*shahadatnameh* or *vaseeyatnameh*) in which the fallen combatant sets out his motivation for fighting and dying, as well as his aspirations for the future of the revolution and the country. What most of these battlefield wills have in common is the centrality they place on the leadership of Ayatollah Khomeini as a key figure in the political consciousness of these young men. The leadership of the 'Imam' was critical for the transmission of revolutionary values and ideals to that generation.

Even when they waxed lyrical on real and perceived injustices in the world, often emanating from 'the Great Satan' (the USA) and lesser Western powers, and of course the Baathist tyranny of Saddam Hussein, they transmitted their disapproval and vitriol through the words of Ayatollah Khomeini, whom these combatants fittingly described as the 'Imam of the Martyrs'. Thus, the tens of thousands of young men buried at Behesht-e Zahra are a highly visible testimony to the strength—and costs—of Khomeini's charismatic leadership style. If the Iranian revolution propelled Ayatollah Khomeini to the top of international politics, it was the Iran–Iraq War that immortalised him.

By any standard, the war was an opportunity for Ayatollah Khomeini and his inner circle to consolidate their grip on power and to use it as a medium to communicate their revolutionary values and aspirations to the rest of the world. But it is important not to be too cynical about this process. Power consolidation was certainly a key factor, but revolutionary ethos and the pursuit of revolutionary goals was an equally important if not superior consideration. The sincerity etched in the faces of Iran's 'martyrs' is in part a reflection of the revolutionary convictions of their leaders. Thus, Behesht-e Zahra is arguably the best place to study the sociology and anthropology of 1980s Iran, as it combines in one place the themes of martyrdom, sacrifice, struggle, leadership, politics and the quest for transformation. At that level, Zahra's Paradise is a powerful affirmation of Iran as a revolutionary power, and a clear-eyed one at that, if the coherent testimonies of the fallen combatants is any measure to go by.

The strategic value of the sacrifices of the combatants of the Iran–Iraq War was not lost on Iran's leaders. The martyrs' quarter of the cemetery is awash with revolutionary slogans and grand statements attributed to revolutionary leaders, Ayatollah Khomeini and his successor Ayatollah Khamenei. One banner reads: 'The martyrs are the symbol of Iran's power.' This slogan is both a revolutionary statement and the embodiment of a deeply held belief in the efficacy, indeed necessity, of asymmetric power. At one level, of course, it is a statement of the obvious, namely that Iran was able to withstand a ferocious assault by a far better equipped and much better supported adversary through revolutionary fervour and the willingness by a critical mass of young people to make the ultimate sacrifice in the service of revolutionary goals and ideals.

But it is the concerted attempt to transform the sacrifice of the fallen into strategic blocks of power which defines Iran's management of the legacy of the Iran–Iraq War. In the years since the war's ending, massive efforts have been expended to document its every aspect, from specific battles and their strategic and political context, to broader strategy and tactics, and, of course, the lives and dying wishes of the 'martyrs', in particular senior officers and notable army and Islamic Revolutionary Guards Corps (IRGC) commanders. Countless books have been produced and several big organisations are tasked with documenting and publicising the war efforts, all with the intention of keeping it firmly in the public consciousness.

This effort is discernible even at street level, as demonstrated by the murals and portraits of the 'martyrs' adorning the walls of buildings and public places in every city, town and village in Iran. In addition, roads are usually named after 'martyrs', often local lads on the streets where they used to live or nearby. In terms of public broadcasting, not a week goes by that the national broadcaster does not showcase a new documentary or special programme dedicated to telling stories from the war. The Iran–Iraq War may have ended thirty years ago, but the Islamic Republic has succeeded in keeping its reality, dramas and combatants readily accessible to all Iranians by way of murals and broadcasts.

Of course, there is a more cynical dimension to this exercise in constant public remembrance. Both state and society continue to draw benefits from the blood of the martyrs. Every few months the remains of slain soldiers are recovered from the former front lines and paraded in Tehran, other major cities, or wherever the dead combatants hailed from. The parades and commemorations are state-sponsored and are primarily designed to keep the memory of the 'martyrs' alive and keep the spirit of the Iran–Iraq War in the public domain.

At a societal level, millions of Iranians are connected to combatants who were killed, maimed or otherwise directly suffered as a result of war. The people closest to these combatants, for example their sons and daughters, qualify for a wide range of benefits, including lower barriers to entering prestigious universities. Families of fallen soldiers also have access to essential commodities at subsidised prices. There is a wide range of benefits and millions of people are invested in them. It is clearly in this community's material interests to keep the memory of the war alive and to pay lip service to revolutionary values, all the while enjoying an economic advantage over the rest of society.

Cynicism aside, both the Iranian state and society learnt important lessons from the Iran–Iraq War. These lessons continue to shape foreign and domestic policies, in addition to public attitudes to a wide range of global, regional and domestic affairs. The war has defined contemporary Iran, and in that respect was an epochal event, whose far-reaching effects will continue to influence the country's evolution well into the twenty-first century.

So, what are these key lessons? The most important in terms of foreign policy is the loss of faith in the international community, which did not take major steps to stop the Iran–Iraq War when Saddam invaded in September 1980. On the contrary, leading world powers were happy for the Iraqis to advance into Iran and to accomplish some of their war aims, if not to score a decisive victory. The international community only got serious about ending the war when Iran went on the offensive following the liberation of Khorramshahr in May 1982.[10] The first serious attempt at ending the conflict, namely UN Security Council Resolution 598, adopted in July 1987, came about at a time when Iran still held a decisive advantage, the disastrous Karbala offensives of late 1986 and early 1987 notwithstanding.[11]

More importantly, the world was silent in the face of Iraqi war crimes, notably the liberal use of chemical weapons throughout the war, particularly toward its conclusion. Iranian combatants were routinely subjected to chemical weapons, particularly after 1984. Moreover, Iraq's regaining of the military initiative in the spring of 1988 would not have been possible without the use of chemical weapons. The retaking of the Al-Faw Peninsula in April 1988 and the Majnoon Island in June would have arguably failed had the Iraqis not used chemical weapons. The efficacy of chemical warfare lies not only in the mass casualties it produces, but equally in the fear and chaos it sows amongst an army. Iranian combatants who had hitherto displayed high levels of motivation started to retreat in panic in the spring and summer of 1988 as Iraq sought to regain lost territory.

The world paid some attention to Iraqi war crimes when the town of Halabja was attacked with chemical weapons in March 1988, resulting in at least 5,000 Iraqi Kurdish civilian deaths. The sight of dead bodies, including babies, frothing at the mouth and apparently frozen in time brought into sharp relief the horrors of chemical warfare. Despite this attempted genocide and yet another example of an egregious war crime, the Iraqi regime got away with barely a slap on the wrist. Not only did the major powers fail to condemn Iraq, but there was in fact a half-hearted attempt to implicate Iran in the attack.

The Iraqi regime attacked Halabja primarily in response to a perception that the town's residents had welcomed Iranian soldiers who were undertaking a large-scale operation in the area. Code named Zafar-7, the operation's ultimate objective was the capture of the Iraqi Kurdish city of Sulaymaniyah. Iranian forces came very close to capturing Sulaymaniyah—in addition to the strategic Darbandikhan dam—but Iranian forces, spearheaded by the army's 55th parachute division and the 84th infantry division, were forced to retreat in the face of a relentless chemical weapons artillery and rockets barrage.

Chemical weapons had a profound impact on the morale and psychology of the Pasdaran, who had been at the forefront of offensives since 1982. The IRGC combined unconventional tactics (such as human wave attacks) with a revolutionary fervour, both of which were a radical departure from the doctrines and strategy of the regular armed forces, who preferred to fight the war on conventional terms alone. The liberal use of chemical weapons removed the Pasdaran's tactical advantages by exposing combatants to poisonous gasses which either killed on the spot or at the very least produced immediate incapacitation. The efficacy and lethality of these weapons also removed the Pasdaran's psychological advantage, namely their high morale and willingness to take extreme risks, thus depriving Iran of a crucial advantage in the war. The result was that by the end of 1987 the Pasdaran had lost the ability to launch major offensives designed to alter the strategic course of the war.

It is no surprise that the greatest impact of the war was felt by the Pasdaran and allied forces (such as the Basij). The exposure to unconventional warfare and weapons of mass destruction had a profound psychological impact which Pasdaran commanders and strategists were determined to exploit for strategic purposes. The immediate conclusion that was drawn was that Iran had failed to win the war because it lacked adequate unconventional and asymmetric capabilities of its own. While the development and deployment of chemical weapons was not a viable option (as Ayatollah Khomeini had ruled it out by allegedly issuing a *fatwa* to that effect), less controversial asymmetric capability was judged to be both morally acceptable and within technical reach.

Another big lesson from the Iran–Iraq War was the necessity to be strong and self-sufficient in the defence arena in the face of an indifferent, indeed hypocritical, diplomatic world. The Iran–Iraq War brought into sharp relief the worst aspects of diplomacy and international relations, with double standards and callous indifference trumping the moral urgency to adequately address aggression and war crimes. The major powers backed Iraq and turned a blind eye to its transgressions, as part of a wider effort to contain revolutionary Iran. These were hard lessons which the Iranians absorbed at the deepest levels of their military, diplomatic and intelligence services.

Post-War Deterrence

Just after midday on 12 November 2011, a massive explosion ripped through the Shahid Modaress missile base near the village of Beed

Kaneh north-west of Tehran, killing seventeen members of the aerospace division of the Revolutionary Guards. Amongst the dead was Brigadier-General Hassan Tehrani Moghaddam (posthumously promoted to the rank of major-general),[12] the head of the missile unit of the aerospace division. The explosion was a massive blow to the IRGC and immediately raised suspicions of possible Israeli or American sabotage. The timing was significant as it occurred at the height of a concerted campaign by American and Israeli intelligence services to recruit, demoralise or even assassinate leading Iranian nuclear scientists. Targeting Iran's ballistic missile force with a spectacular act of sabotage was thought to be entirely in keeping with the US–Israeli modus operandi to disrupt Iran's deterrent capability.

For twenty-eight years Tehrani Moghaddam had been at the heart of the Iranian missile programme. In fact, he is universally recognised as the founder of Iran's modern missile programme, having established the Pasdaran's missile command centre in October 1983. Prior to this date Iran had no indigenous missile technology and did not possess a single ballistic missile. As discussed earlier, the focus of the pre-revolutionary government had been on the development of conventional capabilities and no effort had been expended on developing strategic capability centred on ballistic missiles and related technology.

Thus, the life, personality and career of Hassan Tehrani Moghaddam has defined Iran's ballistic missile programme. Born to a devout family in Tehran, in many ways Tehrani Moghaddam typifies the profile of the young men who flocked to join the newly founded Pasdaran after the victory of the revolution. These were fairly well educated young men—often fresh out of university or in the middle of their studies, which were interrupted by the revolution—and hailing from devout middle-class or lower-middle-class families. Whilst the Pasdran also absorbed its fair share of people from working-class or even rural backgrounds, these recruits stayed at low levels and rarely succeeded in breaking through into command positions. By contrast, middle-class and lower-middle-class recruits formed the bulk of the Pasdaran's commanders, strategists and managers.

Whilst these young men were massively affected by the revolutionary environment, they were not necessarily doctrinaire in ideological terms. Their devotion was first and foremost to the 'Imam', that is, the charismatic leadership of Ayatollah Khomeini. In view of their middle-class and lower-middle-class backgrounds, most of these men had nationalist instincts. However, the religiosity of their families—combined with the prevailing mood music of the revolution—easily enabled them to combine Iranian nationalism with Shia Islam. Thus, the foundational ideology of the IRGC was in large measure determined by the type of men it initially attracted into its ranks.

Moghaddam joined the IRGC in 1980 and was thrown into the deep end by the outbreak of the Iran–Iraq War on 22 September 1980. He had immediately stood out as an exceptional commander and pioneer, initially because of his work on artillery and his determination to establish the IRGC's first artillery units. The Pasdaran had begun life as a militia and a security force for leading personalities—or a glorified bodyguard service. The immediate revolutionary chaos of 1979, with key peripheral regions (notably Kurdish-majority areas and the Turkmen-majority area of Gonbad-e-Kavus) in open revolt against the central government, the Pasdaran were pressed into action to help quell these uprisings. But it was only the outbreak of the Iran–Iraq War that began the process of transforming the IRGC from a paramilitary to a military organisation.

In the first two years of the war the Pasdaran remained a light infantry force lacking heavy weapons. Disputes and recriminations continue to this day about the regular military's reluctance to supply even light weapons to Pasdaran combatants in the southern Khuzestan front. Thus, in the face of a broad range of obstacles, notably institutional resistance from the regular military, it was left to pioneers like Moghaddam to develop the Revolutionary Guards' capabilities. The first priority was to acquire heavy weaponry with a view to forming mechanised divisions, equipped with tanks, armoured personnel carriers and related hardware. The acquisition of artillery capability, with a view to softening Iraqi defences in preparation of lightning infantry attacks by the Pasdaran and Basij forces, was pursued in tandem. The IRGC's development of artillery-based capabilities, complete with a research centre in the provincial capital Ahvaz (Khuzestan province), can be considered as the first major step toward acquiring full military status.

The precise circumstances behind the establishment of a missile command centre in October 1983 still remain unclear. What is beyond dispute is that Moghaddam was at the centre of the effort and steadfastly pursued this ambition, continually pitching strategists and budget holders for resources and funds. Without his towering personality, pioneering spirit and dogged persistence, the missile programme would have been delayed for years at least, and might not have begun on solid foundations. We can speculate on the motivations for setting up the command centre and beginning wide-scale research activities in earnest on missile-related issues.

The initial motivation may have been kindled by exposure to missiles in the opening years of the Iran–Iraq War. Unlike Iran, Iraq possessed a missile arsenal supplied by the Soviet Union. Iraq first acquired this capability in 1976 and the war with Iran allowed the Iraqis to gain valuable operational experience by using existing stockpiles. Iraq's strong defence partnership with the Soviet Union meant that depleted stocks could be quickly replenished. However, Iraq's stockpile was limited to Scud missiles and the 9K52 Luna-M (more popularly known by its Nato reporting name of Frog-7). The latter was used extensively in the early years of the war, often targeting the important Khuzestani city of Dezful, home to the large Vahdati air force base, Iran's most forward air base in the war. In October 1982 Dezful became the first Iranian city struck by Scud-Bs, whose original Soviet name was R-17.

In the latter years of the war the Iraqis requested better and longer-range missiles from the Soviet Union, notably the TR-1 Temp (Nato reporting name: SS-12 Scaleboard), but these requests were refused, presumably because the Soviets did not wish to see an escalation of the war. Unperturbed, the Iraqis set about improving existing Scud-C stockpiles with a view to striking the Iranian capital Tehran. The Scud-C had a potential range of 500–600 km, but it was notoriously inaccurate and carried a much-reduced warhead. It was basically the Scud-B but with greater range. The Iraqi version of the Scud-C (the Al-Hussein) had even poorer accuracy and carried a warhead of just under 500 kg, but it surpassed the 500 miles range, thus enabling the targeting of Tehran. The Al-Hussein was used extensively in the last and most intense phase of the 'war of the cities'[13] from late February to late April 1988. In this period just over 200 modified Scud-Cs were fired at the Iranian capital, resulting in more than 2,000 deaths.

Initially Iran had no reply to Iraq's firing of Frog-7 and Scud-B missiles. The IRGC missile command centre was set up to address this critical shortcoming. This effort was also informed—indeed given greater urgency—by the realisation that Iran could not rely on the air force to respond to Iraqi missile strikes. Whilst the Iranian air force had established full parity—and even partial air superiority—in the early stage of the war, this modest advantage had been eroded by 1983. This was largely due to the fact that Iran could not replace lost planes and faced great difficulty in sourcing spare parts for the remaining fleet. By contrast, Iraq faced no barriers in quickly replacing lost planes, either from France or from the former Soviet Union.

Iran's first acquisition of ballistic missiles probably occurred in January 1985 when several Scud-Bs and their launchers were purchased from Libya. Although the Libyans were staunch Arab nationalists, and unlike Syria had not dissented from the Arab fold by opposing Iraq, they were nonetheless keen to maintain friendly relations with Tehran. A shared animosity toward the USA contributed to a strategic convergence between Tehran and Tripoli. The Libyans were directly approached by Tehrani Moghaddam's team at the missile command centre in Ahvaz and most probably sent advisors to Iran to assist the team in the use and deployment of the missiles.

Iran first used ballistic missiles in the war on 12 March 1985 to strike the Iraqi city of Kirkuk. The missile was probably a Scud-B and it was most likely launched from the central front areas. This was a test for what followed two days later, when Iran struck Baghdad with Scud-Bs, and again on 15 March. Altogether a dozen Scud-Bs were fired at the Iraqi capital, causing mass casualties, with up to 100 reported killed. This was a major strategic development in the war as it changed the calculations of the Baathist regime. Hitherto, Iraq had sole possession of ballistic missiles and launched them periodically, fully intending to cause civilian casualties with a view to sabotaging Iranian morale. From March 1985 onwards Iraq no longer enjoyed an unassailable advantage in this arena.

In terms of indigenous research and development, the Libyan acquisition began Iran's quest to develop and deploy locally made missiles. While there is no evidence that any reverse engineering was performed on the first dispatched missiles (indeed most were quickly fired at Iraq to create equilibrium in the 'war of the cities'), they were undoubtedly subjected to exhaustive scrutiny by Moghaddam's team at the Ahvaz-based missile command centre. What is clear from publicly available information—including extensive media interviews given by Moghaddam's original colleagues—was the Iranian intention to develop an indigenous capability from the very outset. By contrast, Iraq only developed this objective ten years after first acquiring ballistic missiles in 1976.

It is worth noting that the American intelligence community had under-estimated Iran's expansive ambition in this arena. A Central Intelligence Agency (CIA) document produced in mid-1986 gets the basic facts about Iran's and Iraq's ballistic missile capabilities right, and moreover accurately analyses their short- to mid-term intentions, but fails to predict the scope of Iran's programme in the decades ahead.[14]

In view of Iran's expansive ambitions, Moghaddam's team sought diversification from the very outset. Thus, in addition to the Libyan acquisition, dozens of Hwasong-5 missiles were purchased from North Korea, probably in late summer 1985. The Hwasong-5 was essentially a modified version of the Scud-B, with a longer range and higher-quality explosives. By establishing a production line for a local version of Hwasong-5 (probably in early 1988), Moghaddam started Iran's indigenous ballistic missile industry in earnest. Iran's slightly modified version of Hwasong-5 was called Shahab-1. The latter was continually tested, produced and reproduced from the late 1980s to 1994, with a view to achieving greater modification and improvement.

In keeping with the essential features of the Scud-B, and the modifications effected on it by the North Korean variant of Hwasong-5, Shahab-1 had a probable range of 350–400 km and a high explosive payload of between 600 and 750 kg. The Shahab family of ballistic missiles thus form the foundation of Iran's ballistic missiles programme. There are three verifiable versions, with Shahab-3 (including its B, C and D variants), with a range of up to 2,000 km, being the most advanced and up-to-date missile.[15] Shahab-4 was a civilian spin-off of the Shahab-3 and designed to be Iran's first space launch vehicle, but the project went nowhere. Alleged existence of the Shahab-5 and Shahab-6, with the latter alleged to be a full-fledged ICBM capable of reaching the eastern seaboard of the US, is pure disinformation, often emanating from Israeli sources.

The Shahab family of missiles combine a mix of reverse engineering, modification and authentic indigenous technology. Whilst they are based on North Korean (and ultimately Soviet) designs, Iran can claim these missiles as its own due to the time and effort expended on their local modification. Moreover, the Shahab family set the foundation for spin-offs which in due course became established models. For example, Shahab-3 eventually morphed into Ghadr-101, which in turn developed into the Ghadr-110, a medium-range ballistic missile whose chief hallmark was that it was propelled by a mix of liquid fuel and solid fuel. Ghadr-110 has a range of up to 2,000 km, bringing all of the Middle East, including Israel, within range.[16]

In tandem with continually modifying the Shahab family (and its spin-offs), the IRGC's missile command centre (which by the late 1990s had been subsumed under the Pasdaran's aerospace division), had started work on solid-fuel ballistic missiles. These have a clear advantage over liquid-fuel missiles in terms of survivability and military utility.[17] The Fateh-110, and the first modified version Fateh-110A (test fired in September 2002), ranks as Iran's first achievement in the domain of solid-fuel ballistic missiles. Four modified versions were unveiled over the next decade, the latest version of which has a range of 300 km.

The Fateh-110 (and its variants) in turn set the foundation for other solid-fuel rockets, notably the Zelzal, whose first variant was a heavy artillery rocket, but whose latest version, Zelzal-3 is considered a full-fledged solid-propellant ballistic missile. The latest modified version, Zelzal-3B, has a range of 250 km and is ideal for striking rear enemy formations in a dynamic battle scenario.

In terms of the future trajectory of the ballistic missile programme Iran is continually developing and testing modified versions of existing stockpiles with a view to improving the range and accuracy of its missiles. This is a vital process in the research and development cycle, inasmuch as continual testing and modification create new pathways for indigenous military technology. It is instructive that the Shahab family has morphed into the Sejjil, with two verified models, notably Sejjil-1 and Sejjil-2. These are advanced solid-propellant ballistic missiles, which may be setting the foundation for the development of Intercontinental Ballistic Missile (ICBM) capability. The Sejjil-1 is a medium-range missile capable of hitting targets 2,400 km away, thus bringing US and Nato bases in Eastern Europe within range. Sejjil-2 reportedly has a better navigation system, bigger warhead and lower detection rate, but that comes at the cost of a lower range, reportedly of just 2,000 km.[18]

In terms of assessing the efficacy of Iran's ballistic missile deterrence, one of the key questions is the size of the Iranian arsenal. Conservative Western defence estimates put the number of ballistic missiles in Iran's arsenal in the mid to high hundreds, with the bulk comprised of the Shahab family. But these estimates were credibly challenged in October 2015 when the IRGC dramatically unveiled an underground missile base where rows of launchers and missiles were visible.[19] The Pasdaran's claims to operate several of these vast underground facilities are credible and raise the spectre of missile bases and bunkers across the country, possibly housing thousands of ballistic missiles, rockets and long-range artillery. The deterrent value of this potentially huge inventory, in addition to its offensive capability, is considerable insofar as it enables Iran to deploy the 'swarming' effect by launching hundreds of missiles at a range of targets simultaneously.

The IRGC has already deployed the 'swarming' effect in real operational conditions when it hit Mojahedin-e Khalq bases in Iraq with dozens of short-range ballistic missiles (possibly up to seventy) back in April 2001. More recently, in June 2017, the IRGC fired six Zolfaghar (modified version of Fateh-110) solid-propellant ballistic missiles at Islamic State targets in Syria's eastern Deir ez-Zor province. This was in retaliation for twin terrorist attacks on the Iranian parliament and the mausoleum of the late Ayatollah Khomeini, which were claimed by the IS group. The IRGC attack apparently achieved mixed results as not all of the missiles hit the intended targets.

The landmark nuclear accord (JCPOA) has failed to arrest the momentum of Iran's missile testing. Indeed, the Iranians claim that the two issues are strictly separate, a position which the Europeans appear to sympathise with. On this issue, there appears to be a Euro–Atlantic split, insofar as Europe (with the possible exception of the UK) regards Iran's ballistic missile programme as part of a legitimate defensive strategy, whereas the US strongly objects to it on the grounds that it threatens its allies Israel and Saudi Arabia.

For their part, IRGC commanders are adamant that they will follow the path of Hassan Tehrani Moghaddam, the father of Iran's ballistic missile programme. This is a programme that was founded at a moment of strategic panic, approximating an existential crisis, as Iraq attacked Iranian population centres with relative impunity, with the intention of sabotaging morale, sowing chaos and destroying public confidence in the Islamic Republic. But the programme also reflected national ambition, underpinned by revolutionary zeal, notably a desire to acquire capabilities which would enable Iran to challenge status quo powers, in particular the United States, whose military presence in the region is inimical to Iranian national security interests.

Short of invading Iran, the United States has few options in terms of arresting Iran's momentum in the ballistic missile sphere. The Trump administration is keen to change the terms of the JCPOA (as announced by Donald Trump in mid-October 2017) with a view to linking it to curbs on Iran's missile programme. Another idea that is being mooted is negotiating a separate deal (linked to the JCPOA) which addresses wider US strategic and security concerns, including the missile programme. This will be a non-starter, not just for the IRGC but indeed for the Islamic Republic as a whole, as the missile programme is deeper rooted and more emotive than the nuclear programme. Giving up the missile programme is tantamount to betraying the legacy of the Iran-Iraq War.

IRAQ
PROXIMATE THREAT OR STRATEGIC ALLY?

Iraq has loomed large in Iranian strategic thinking for millennia. Ancient Iranian empires had to raise armies in the lands now constituting modern Iraq in order to secure their grip on Asia Minor. The Sassanid Empire built its most majestic cities—including its capital city Ctesiphon, or Tisfun—and its most robust garrison towns in Mesopotamia. Consequently, many modern Iraqi villages, towns and cities, including the capital city Baghdad, have Persian names. Modern Iraq's most westerly province, Anbar, is Persian for 'warehouse', as 300 years before the advent of Islam, the province was controlled by a local tribe allied to the Iranian Sassanid Empire.[1]

The rise of Islam in the seventh century AD proved fatal to the Sassanid Empire, the last great pre-Islamic Iranian power. Its demise unfolded on Mesopotamian soil, beginning with the epic battle of al-Qadisiyyah in 636 AD. Victory by the Muslim armies there was followed by another victory at the battle of Nahavand five years later, which effectively sealed the fate of the Sassanid Empire. These ancient battles—and the ethno-political narratives which define them— are important in that they continue to shape views and perceptions on both sides. It is no coincidence that Saddam Hussein dubbed his September 1980 invasion of Iran 'Qadisiyyah Saddam' in an attempt to both appropriate and recreate history.

Following the Muslim conquest of Iran and the re-emergence of local Iranian states several centuries later, the ancient land of Mesopotamia once again loomed large in Iranian strategic consciousness. By that point countless Iranians had made their home in Mesopotamia, not least because it was at one stage both the seat of Islamic political power and a great centre of learning. The demise of the Umayyad Caliphate, followed by the advent of the Abbasid Caliphate in the middle of the eighth century AD, had seen the transfer of political power from Damascus to Baghdad. Thus Baghdad, and its satellite towns and villages, attracted many Iranians with the means and vision to travel with a view to accessing knowledge and power. These Iranians added to a substantial pre-existing Iranian heritage on Mesopotamian lands, both in genetic and cultural terms.

Iraq is the heartland of Shia Islam insofar as the majority of the battles, events, trials and tribulations that defined Shiism—and more importantly set it apart from the orthodox Sunni sect—unfolded on Mesopotamian soil. Most of the infallible Imams of the Twelver Shia sect were killed in Iraq. This includes Imam Ali (the cousin and son-in-law of the Prophet Muhammad) and his son Imam Hossein. Hossein's martyrdom at the battle of Karbala in 680 AD marked the foundational moment of Shiism as it defined the fatalistic, grief-stricken and martyrdom-seeking aspects of the sect.

However, despite this history, the majority of the inhabitants of southern and central Iraq are thought not to have practised Twelver Shiism until well into the sixteenth century.[2] Indeed, for close to a thousand years Shia communities in southern and central Mesopotamia constituted a minority—albeit a substantial one—and there was relatively peaceful coexistence with Sunni Muslims. This mirrored the reality in neighbouring Iran, where Sunni Islam was in the ascendance until the early sixteenth century. The transformational event in both countries was the advent of the Turkic Safavid dynasty, which came to power in Iran in the early sixteenth century and set about converting the entire country to the Twelver Shia creed.

Longstanding ethno-cultural connections, not to mention strategic connectivity born out of geographic proximity, inevitably focused Safavid attention on Iraq. This became a strategic urgency—indeed an existential issue—in view of the Safavids' deadly rivalry with the

Ottoman Empire. Thus, the Ottoman–Safavid wars were as much religious-ideological wars as they were strategic contests for territory and resources. The quest for strategic depth unfolded on Iraqi soil as control of Mesopotamia was seen by the Ottomans as central to establishing enduring hegemony in West Asia. For the Safavids—who despite their Azeri-Turkic and Caucasian origins had by the middle of the sixteenth century fully embraced Iranian nationalism—the struggle was more existential, as full control of the southern and eastern regions of Mesopotamia would enable the Ottomans to launch an invasion of the Iranian heartland to the east.[3] The memory of al-Qadisiyyah weighed heavily on the Safavid strategic consciousness.

In hindsight, and with the benefit of 500 years of political and strategic developments, the addition of Shiism as a marker, if not an independent category, of strategic rivalry between Iran and Iraq is what has made this difficult relationship so central to the balance of power in the entire Near East. The close association between modern Shiism and Safavid power inevitably contrived close bonds between Iranian nationalism and Twelver Shia Islam. By contrast, modern Iraq's Ottoman heritage and its struggle to come to terms with its substantial Shia population meant that Iraq was destined to play the role of counterweight to Iran.

The rise of ideologies and identity politics in the second half of the twentieth century transformed a traditional rivalry and long-term balance of power dynamics into a bitter enmity. Nationalists of different stripes came to power in Iraq from 1958 onwards, starting with Brigadier-General Abd al-Karim Qasim's coup against the Iraqi monarchy. This was followed by the so-called 'Ramadan Revolution' in February 1963, which propelled the Baath party to power. The Baath espoused a militant strain of Arab nationalism, which was by definition inimical to Iranian power, if not to the very concept of the Iranian nation-state. The Arab nationalist core of the Baath was supplemented by a strong strain of Iraqi nationalism, particularly after Saddam Hussein and the 'Tikriti' clique came to the fore in July 1968 following the second and decisive Baathist takeover of the state. Thus, by the early 1970s Iraq had transformed into a seat of Arab and Iraqi nationalisms whose hostile outlook towards Iran challenged the existing strategic balance of power.

The Baathists were forced to be pragmatic in the 1970s (as demonstrated by the 1975 Algiers Accord) as a relatively strong Iran allied to the United States made large-scale hostilities unthinkable. Thus, the underlying enmity between the two states did not escalate beyond limited border clashes. However, the Iranian revolution changed that calculus—not only did it temporarily weaken Iran, but equally importantly it destroyed the alliance with the United States. Additionally, the emergence of an ideological state in Iran gave rise to a doctrinal layer to the conflict, as 'Khomeinism' was a potent counter to the Arab nationalist creed of the Baath. War was inevitable.

The Second Gulf War: A Game Changer?

The fall of Saddam Hussein and the subsequent rise of Shia power in Iraq have been widely interpreted as heralding the beginning of Iran's strategic leap in the region. The logic behind this assertion is trenchant enough. After all, as discussed earlier Baathism was by definition inimical toward Iran. All forms of Arab nationalism that emerged in the latter half of the twentieth century adopted twin enemies in the form of Iran and Israel. But in the case of Baathism—which came to power in Iraq and Syria—most of the antipathy was directed towards Iran. In the case of the Iraqi Baath, this hostility was underpinned by a parochial narrative based on Mesopotamian history, in addition to a strategic calculation rooted in conventional inter-state rivalry.

Proponents of this hypothesis argue that prior to the overthrow of the Baath in 2003, Iraq had been an effective counterweight to Iran, consuming much of Iran's strategic energy and blocking the Islamic Republic's concerted effort to join up its influence architecture in the Levant. Indeed, the removal of the Baath has given Iran a direct land route to its allies in Syria and Lebanon and allegedly given rise to an ambitious project to create a permanent land corridor from the Western Iranian border (adjoining Iraq) all the way to the Eastern Mediterranean coast.[4] If it comes to fruition, this land corridor would come to symbolise Iran's strategic depth at the heart of the Middle East and an enduring presence (albeit by proxy) on the Eastern bank of the Mediterranean Sea.

The strategic advantage gained by the overthrow of Saddam came on the heels of the overthrow of another Iranian adversary, this time on the country's eastern borders, namely the Taliban in Afghanistan. The 11 September 2001 terrorist attacks in New York and Washington, DC had at first rattled the Iranian leadership, who feared that the US might misuse the attacks to apply even greater pressure on Iran. It is worth remembering that since the mid-1980s Iran has topped the list of the US State Department's state sponsors of terrorism.[5] Hitherto, some of the most spectacular terrorist attacks on US targets around the world had been blamed on pro-Iranian groups, most recently the June 1996 attack on the Khobar Towers in Saudi Arabia, which killed nineteen US servicemen. After 9/11, there was a sigh of relief in Tehran when very early on US attention was fully focused on neighbouring Afghanistan, where the Taliban were accused of sheltering the terrorist network that had allegedly planned the attacks on the US.

Therefore, from the perspective of strategic opportunism, Iran's regional surge effectively began with the 9/11 attacks, which had been planned and executed by the Islamic Republic's ideological enemies in al-Qaeda. Much has been made of Iran's alleged 'collaboration' with the US in the effort to topple the Taliban after 9/11. These claims, whilst containing some truth, consciously ignore the fact that Iran had an Afghanistan policy long before the US developed an interest in toppling the Taliban. Starting with the Soviet invasion of Afghanistan in late 1979, the Islamic Republic immediately set up outreach programmes to local resistance groups. By the mid-1980s Iran had developed strong ties with the heart of the Afghan resistance, in part led by Ahmad Shah Massoud, who as a Tajik shared ethno-linguistic ties with the Iranians. But Iran's closest allies were the Shia Hazara groups, which by the mi-1980s had coalesced to form Hezb-e Vahdat (Unity Party).

Post-1979, Iranian policy in Afghanistan was designed primarily to counter Pakistani influence, and the 'jihad' to drive out the Soviets was a secondary consideration. This strategic rivalry came into sharp relief following the withdrawal of Soviet forces from Afghanistan in early 1989. Almost immediately, Iran's policy toward the embattled Najibullah regime in Kabul softened, out of fear of the consequences should the Mujahideen overrun Kabul. The bulk of the Mujahideen had strong ties to Pakistan and some groups, notably Gulbuddin Hekmatyar's Hezb-e Islami (HI, Islamic Party), were considered extensions of Pakistan's Inter-Services Intelligence (ISI) agency. Unlike Iran, Pakistan had a comprehensive Afghanistan strategy underpinned by strong ties to the Pashtuns of southern Afghanistan, bordering Pakistan.

Comprising Afghanistan's largest ethno-linguistic group, the Pashtuns had formed the ruling elite since Afghanistan's independence in 1919. In view of the significant Pashtun population in Pakistan, concentrated in a region known administratively as the Federally Administered Tribal Areas (FATA), Pakistani policy favoured strong Pashtun domination in neighbouring Afghanistan. However, due to its progressive socialist ethos, the Najibullah regime was anathema to Pakistan. What the Pakistanis desired above all was a conservative Islamic system in Kabul that took Pakistan's security and strategic interests in the country into full consideration. This Pakistani policy had little to do with Iran and everything to do with India, inasmuch as Afghanistan constituted Pakistan's strategic depth in the event of armed conflict with India.

The Najibullah regime finally fell in April 1992 after putting up more than three years of stiff resistance to a wide range of Mujahideen groups, most of which had benefited from covert CIA support in the 1980s and continued to be generously supplied by the CIA's ally, Pakistan's powerful ISI. As anticipated in Tehran, the victorious Mujahideen groups immediately descended into inter-group fighting, reducing much of Kabul to ruin. The Shia-majority areas of Western Kabul were badly hit, primarily by Hekmatyar's HI, which targeted these areas for a mix of political and sectarian reasons. Whilst Iran continued to maintain ties with some Mujahideen groups, notably with Ahmad Shah Massoud and Burhanuddin Rabbani, the Islamic Republic was powerless to prevent the deliberate wide-scale targeting of Shia civilians in Western Kabul.

The rise of the Taliban in 1994 was immediately interpreted in Tehran as the latest manifestation of Pakistan's comprehensive Afghanistan strategy. Having lost faith in the traditional Mujihadeen groups' ability to restore stability in Kabul, Pakistan now seemed fully invested in the new Taliban force. This was despite the fact that many of the Taliban's early territorial gains were at the expense of Hekmatyar's HI, hitherto

Pakistan's most reliable ally in Afghanistan. Whilst the Taliban had much in common with the HI—both were primarily Pashtun-based groups and espoused ultra-conservatism—the sectarianism of the former was more pronounced than in HI.

The Taliban focused much energy on damaging Iran-linked Shia groups with a view to minimising Iranian influence in Afghan affairs. In March 1995 the Taliban struck their first blow against Iran by luring the leader of Hezb-e Vahdat, Abdul Ali Mazari, into a trap in order to 'arrest' the 49-year old Afghan Shia leader. In reality it was a death trap and Mazari's body was found the next day in Ghazni. The shocking nature of the kidnapping and murder was a clear statement of intent on the part of the Taliban in respect of the pro-Iranian Shia Islamic groups. Not only would these groups not be allowed a role in the new order but they could expect to be subjected to arbitrary violence. More broadly, in terms of Afghanistan's Shia population as a whole, whilst the Taliban did not specifically target Shia civilians uninvolved in the country's multiple conflicts, it was nevertheless clear they would crack down on manifestations of Shia culture and identity.

With the Taliban closing in on Kabul, Iran increased support to Ahmad Shah Massoud, having been encouraged by Massoud's airlift to Herat in February 1995, which saved the strategic western city from a determined Taliban offensive. But despite stiff resistance from Massoud and allied forces, the Taliban pressed ahead, relying on practical and financial support from Pakistan and Saudi Arabia respectively. Following the Taliban's capture of Kabul in late September 1996, Iran once again stepped up support to Massoud, who was now leading the newly formed United Front (aka Northern Alliance). But any hope Iran, India and Russia may have had of Massoud-led forces liberating Kabul was dashed as the Taliban insidiously pressed northward, moving ever closer to the heartlands of the Northern Alliance.

The Taliban struck another blow at Iran in August 1998 when a renegade faction—most likely working in conjunction with the Pakistani sectarian group Sipah-e Sahaba—attacked the Iranian consulate in the northern town of Mazar-i-Sharif, killing ten Iranian diplomats and a journalist. The Iranians were reportedly killed in execution style. The massacre caused a huge outcry in Iran and initially led to fears of a military response, as Iran amassed nearly 100,000 soldiers on the border. Whilst Iran refrained from a military response, behind the scenes it stepped up support to the Taliban's myriad opponents. This incident above all created a strong desire for revenge and strengthened Iranian resolve to help topple the Taliban.

Thus, when the US-led coalition commenced military action against the Taliban in early October 2001, Iran tacitly approved of the operation. The degree of cooperation with the US is subject to debate and is at any rate unlikely to have been as extensive as it has been made out to be. The US reached out to the Northern Alliance with a view to employing them as the coalition's boots on the ground. There would have been overlap with pre-existing Iranian operations in support of the same alliance. As the Taliban's grip on power loosened in the autumn of 2001 all key regional stakeholders, including Iran, Pakistan, India, Russia and even China, stepped in to varying degrees in order to influence the outcome of the conflict. Equally, all parties were keen to influence the post-Taliban political order.

For Iran, the outcome of the conflict—or at least of its initial phase of intense US bombings—was satisfactory inasmuch as the Taliban had been ousted from power. Without the US-led intervention, the struggle against the Taliban would have taken many more years (possibly more than a decade) to achieve even the minimal desired outcome. It was only forceful and unequivocal US intervention that was able to neutralise—at least temporarily—Pakistan's considerable strategic advantage. Of course, in the ensuing years the Pakistanis adapted their approach and tactics to meet the requirement of the new political reality in Kabul and before long they had re-established most of their previous influence. The longevity of the Taliban-led insurgency and the growing lethality of Taliban-linked special operations groups, such as the Haqqani network, are in large measure due to Pakistani support and direction.

The most important aspect of the limited Iranian–US engagement in Afghanistan in autumn 2001 is the lasting sense of Iranian betrayal following former US president George W. Bush's characterisation of Iran as a 'rogue' state comprising an 'axis of evil', alongside Iraq and North Korea, in his State of the Union speech in January 2002. To the Iranians, this reaffirmed an earlier suspicion that the US could never be trusted, and that the Americans would be happy to exploit

Iran's position and capabilities for short-term gain and then stab the country in the back once US objectives had been met. Whilst Iranian expectations from the US may have been too high—more than two decades of enmity could not be overcome by limited cooperation in Afghanistan—the shock and hurt of Bush's 'axis of evil' speech were profound and had lasting consequences.

In early 2002 US attention focused on Iraq as the post-9/11 strategic momentum claimed another state—this time one that was wholly uninvolved in the terrorist atrocity. By the summer of 2002 it was clear that both the US and the UK were intent on invading Iraq and that the UN process for the verified elimination of Iraq's weapons of mass destruction was merely a fig leaf for what was essentially—in legal terms at least—an illegitimate war. It is important to consider the question of Iran's attitude to the unfolding war. Did the Islamic Republic, as it was widely suspected from the beginning, tacitly welcome an invasion, even though officially Iran was strongly opposed to military action by the US and the UK?

It is worth noting that despite the strengthening hurricane that was coming their way Iraq's Baathist leaders kept up their anti-Iranian rhetoric to the bitter end. Indeed, a war of words broke out in late August/early September 2002 between Iraq's then vice president Taha Yassin Ramadan and Iranian officials over Iran's commitment (or lack thereof) to the Palestinian cause.[6] Iranian officials politely reminded Ramadan to stay focused on the catastrophe that was about to engulf his country. The point here is that the enmity between Baathist Iraq and Islamic Iran was so intractable and profound that not even the imminent threat of large-scale US military intervention could reduce its intensity, even temporarily.

It is fair to say that despite the genuine excitement at the prospect of the removal of the Baathists, Iranian leaders would have been ambivalent towards the US military intervention. Tensions between Iran and the US were running high in the aftermath of the Afghan intervention, especially after Bush's infamous 'axis of evil' speech. Iranian leaders would have been anxious about the possibility of further US military interventions following the invasion and occupation of Iraq. Above all, they would have been fearful of a direct US military threat to Iran. At any rate, the presence of tens of thousands of US troops next door would not be considered an attractive proposition by any Iranian government, let alone by clerical leaders deeply sceptical of US power.

The one element that could have swayed attitudes in Tehran would have been the anti-Saddam Shia-based opposition groups that had based themselves in Iran since the early days of the Iran–Iraq War. By 2002 many of these groups, in particular SCIRI and al-Da'awa, had developed sophisticated international lobbying arms and were active in Western capitals, including London and Washington, DC. These groups were committed to the overthrow of the Baath, some of them apparently at any cost. All the major exiled Shia-based groups were supportive of the impending Anglo-American military intervention and they would have made their views very clear to their Iranian hosts and patrons. In view of these groups' informational role—they supplied useful intelligence both on Iraq and on Western countries in which they maintained offices—Iranian leaders and officials would have taken their views and aspirations into consideration.

Iran–Iraq Relations Post-1988

Understanding Iran's attitude toward the US-led intervention in Iraq in 2003, the subsequent occupation, and Iran's current policy in Iraq requires a survey of the important issues and developments in Iran–Iraq relations following the end of the war in August 1988. UNSC Resolution 598 came into force in late July 1988 and by early August both sides were committed to a formal ceasefire. But this was only a ceasefire, not a satisfactory conclusion to the conflict, let alone a formal peace treaty. Thus, in the summer of 1988 Iran and Iraq had entered into a tense period of no war and no peace. Much of the international community, in tandem with significant constituencies in both countries, did not believe the cessation of hostilities would prove sustainable.

The end of hostilities was greeted very differently in the two countries. In Iraq most people were relieved and a significant segment of the population—presumably those aligned with the ruling Baath party—were jubilant at the sight of Iran's qualified capitulation. The final months of the war had seen Iraq regain the advantage, primarily owing to the liberal use of chemical weapons, which had a devastating impact on the morale and combat capability of Iranian forces. Moreover, Iraqi advances had finally forced the Iranian leadership to accept UNSC Resolution 598 which had been adopted a year earlier in the summer of 1987. Initially Iran had objected to the resolution on the ground that it had not identified Iraq as the aggressor and hence made no provisions for compensation or reparations.

The Iraqi leadership made much out of Iran's belated acceptance of Resolution 598, arguing that it was a sign of Iraq's 'victory' in the war. Saddam glorified the day of Iran's acceptance as the 'Day of Days' and a marker of Iraq's 'victory'. Significant numbers of Iraqis were in agreement, as demonstrated by the jubilant crowds in Baghdad. Propaganda aside, in real terms the end of the war could not be construed as an Iraqi 'victory' as Iraq had not achieved any of its original war aims. In fact, the war had bankrupted Iraq and created a highly militarised society which would struggle to adapt to peace. Indeed, Iraq was beset by structural socio-economic problems almost immediately and within two years it had found itself in deep conflict with much of the international community following the invasion of Kuwait in August 1990.

Meanwhile in Iran, the immediate post-war mood could not be more different. There was a pervasive sense of demoralisation and of loss, with many Revolutionary Guards and allied Basij paramilitaries wanting to continue the fight. After all, Iran's wartime mantra had been 'war until victory' and many of the combatants struggled to come to terms with its abrupt end. Had it not been for the towering and charismatic leadership of Ayatollah Khomeini, Iranian military commanders might have had to contend with mutinies and other post-conflict disorders involving the lower ranks. As for the general population, there was a sense of relief, not least because the final months of the war had witnessed the most intense phase of the 'war of the cities', when Tehran and other major urban centres were hit by hundreds of ballistic missiles and scores of devastating air raids. But there was also disappointment and a sense of loss, as everybody understood that Iran had effectively been forced to accept UNSC Resolution 598.

After the war had ended, the Islamic Republic feared a loss of legitimacy and even potential instability. Therefore the authorities were on their guard to deal with any security-related issues. These fears had been heightened by a desperate and suicidal military operation by the Mojahedin-e Khalq (MeK) in the final days of the war. In open violation of Resolution 598, the MeK and its Iraqi patrons had invaded Iranian territory from the central front with a view to occupying Iran's Kermanshah (Bakhtaran) province. The MeK's aim was to use Kermanshah as the launch-pad for an assault on Tehran and the overthrow of the Islamic Republic. It was a wildly forlorn hope underpinned by multiple profound miscalculations bordering on the delusional.

Predictably, the MeK force was routed and more than 1,200 of its fighters were killed in what the organisation dubbed Operation Foroghe Javidan (Eternal Light). In Iran the counter-offensive was known as Mersad (named after a Quranic term denoting 'entrapment'), a fitting name as the MeK force was lured deep into Kermanshah province before it was destroyed in the Chahar Zabar gorge. The Islamic Revolutionary Guards Corps (IRGC) led the assault, supported by both air force fighter jets and the army's aviation units (Havanirouz) comprised of attack helicopters. The Mersad operation was a rare example of almost perfect coordination between the army and the Revolutionary Guards, which yielded a dramatically successful result. Unfortunately for Iran it had come right at the end of the war; had this level of coordination existed earlier, Iran might have achieved better war results.

The army commander leading Operation Mersad and overseeing the seamless coordination between the army and the IRGC was Colonel Ali Sayyad Shirazi. Only a captain at the point of the revolution's victory, Sayyad Shirazi belonged to a small cadre of army officers who were fiercely dedicated to the revolution and actively assisted the revolutionaries. He was rewarded for this effort as he quickly climbed up the ranks, particularly after the outbreak of the Iran–Iraq War.[7] Sayyad Shirzai played a leading role in the reorganisation of the army, particularly at the doctrinal level. He helped establish the Agheedati-Seeyasi (Political-Ideological) departments, which were a brazen attempt at introducing ideology into the army's ranks and thus aligning the armed forces with the ruling establishment. This was a tortuous effort and, in its initial phases at least, bred considerable resentment. However, it is a testament to Sayyad Shirazi's leadership qualities that he was able to introduce these reforms whilst at the same time improving the combat capability of the army.

The Iranian armed forces were demoralised in the early phase of the revolution as they were subjected to widespread purges, which included the execution of senior officers. Although the army was not as badly hit as the air force, when war broke out in September 1980 the army was demoralised and disorganised to the point of struggling to put up adequate resistance to invading Iraqi forces. Whilst morale gradually improved and the army began to partake in operations from 1981 onwards, their role was always secondary to that of the IRGC and the allied Basij forces. The sensitivity and controversy surrounding these issues continue to this day, as former army commanders struggle to rehabilitate the army's reputation.

By the time Colonel Sayyad Shirazi had been appointed as army commander in 1984, efforts were well under way to improve combat coordination with the IRGC, particularly during major offensives. Some modest gains were achieved, particularly during the Valfajr-8 offensive of February 1986, during which Iran seized the strategic Al-Faw Peninsula. However, this was not replicated on a consistent basis, as demonstrated later in the year and in early 1987 during the disastrous Karbala offensives.

In terms of introducing ideology and attempting to change the doctrinal concepts of the armed forces, Sayyad Shirazi's equivalent in the air force was Colonel Abbas Babai, who at the time of his death in October 1987 was head of the air force's operational command. Like Sayyad Shirzai, Babai was a stalwart revolutionary who had some background in anti-Shah activities in the air force prior to the revolution. Like all Iranian air force fighter pilots of his generation, Babai had been trained in the United States in the late 1960s and early 1970s. He was known by both his peers and his American instructors as exceptionally pious but also highly capable. It was this mixture of religiosity, ideological commitment, technical ability and leadership qualities which enabled officers like Sayyad Shirazi and Babai to define the development of post-revolutionary Iranian armed forces.

Sayyad Shirazi's role in crushing the MeK's last incursion into Iran was to cost him his life eleven years later, when he was gunned down outside his home in April 1999 by an MeK terrorist posing as a road sweeper. MeK terrorist operations in Iran were planned and rehearsed in their Iraqi bases that had survived the Iran–Iraq War. This was surprising inasmuch as the MeK army (self-styled as the 'National Liberation Army') was an outgrowth of the Iran–Iraq War and its entire existence and raison d'être was bound up with the war. MeK leaders had defied expectations by clinging on to their Iraqi patrons and keeping most (if not all) of their wartime privileges. The rationale of the Baath for keeping the MeK in place was simple: as long as Tehran continued to give sanctuary, arms and money to Shia-led Iraqi opposition groups, Iraq would reciprocate in kind.

The trouble for Iran was that the MeK was more than just an opposition group. In strict security terms, the group was a mere irritant to Iran as its rhetoric far outweighed its capabilities. However, the group elicited strong emotions in Iran due to the fact it had killed thousands of Iranian leaders, officials and ordinary supporters of the Islamic Republic. Moreover, the group's unflinching commitment to the overthrow of the ruling system—coupled with its cult-like organisational discipline and ethos—made the Iranian security services extremely nervous. The fear at that time was that, should the Western powers decide to adopt the MeK as a client and direct political and financial support to it, in tandem with applying extreme pressure on Iran, the situation could potentially become dangerous.

Therefore, targeting the MeK inside its Iraqi heartland was a key priority for the Iranian intelligence services. The IRGC was keen to target the group militarily but this was deemed to be politically unacceptable—in terms of the potential risks, namely an Iraqi response—so soon after the cessation of hostilities. Through 1989 and 1990 Iraq was still regarded as stronger than Iran, at least in military terms. Whilst the Iraqis kept the MeK in check during this immediate post-war period, by preventing the group from attacking Iranian forces across the border, both sides knew it was only a matter of time before rival opposition groups based in the two countries resumed their activities in earnest. This would inevitably impact adversely on bilateral relations with the potential of even reigniting large-scale fighting.

It was only after the Gulf War of 1991, which resulted in the significant downgrading of Iraqi military power, that Iran gained the confidence to attack MeK bases in Iraq. The first major attack occurred in April 1992 when eight F4 Phantoms attacked the MeK headquarters in Iraq at Camp Ashraf, situated in the eastern Diyala province. Although one Phantom was shot down, the raid achieved the desired effect of undermining the MeK's sense of invulnerability inside Iraq's borders. The raid was also a strong message to Iraq that Iran would not tolerate the MeK presence in the long term and henceforth would be taking active measures to disrupt their activities and organisation in Iraq.[8]

The Iraqis, of course, had grievances of their own in terms of dissidents as a wide range of Shia-led Iraqi opposition groups were based in Iran. But unlike the Iranian MeK these Iraqi groups did not have large sprawling camps that could be struck with air raids or missile strikes. Unable to launch attacks inside Iranian territory, the Iraqis gave the green light to the MeK to restart attacks inside Iran. Thus, by the middle of 1992 the tacit post-war understanding of not sponsoring terror attacks on each other's territory had broken down. However, every cross-border activity by the MeK carried the risk of immediate reprisals as Iranian intelligence and military forces struck at MeK positions inside Iraq. This was a reflection of the significant improvement in Iranian intelligence capability, which had by the early 1990s thoroughly penetrated the MeK organisation in Iraq and was thus able to accurately track cross-border activity. The outside world got a glimpse into the extent of this penetration after an MeK member was revealed to have been an agent of Iranian intelligence in early 1995, more than eighteen months after he had been declared dead by the organisation following a cross-border raid into Iran. Mohammad Edalatian's appearance on Iranian television,[9] during which he claimed he had shot dead three of his comrades before fleeing across the border, was clear evidence of the exceptionally high skills and capabilities of the Iranian intelligence services.

The Iranian intelligence services usually responded to cross-border attacks by organising hit-and-run guerrilla attacks on MeK personnel, often when they were travelling on the highway from Baghdad to Diyala. There were two prominent incidents of this kind in the spring and summer of 1995, which claimed the lives of six senior MeK personnel. The sophistication of these attacks, characterised by targeted assassinations focusing on key MeK leaders and operatives, suggested superior intelligence and the deployment of highly trained teams with the ability to conduct special operations deep inside Iraqi territory. MeK terrorist attacks deep inside Iranian territory, particularly in the major cities, often invited a military response. This usually took the form of Katyusha strikes on the Ashraf camp, and other MeK bases, by the IRGC. On a few occasions the Iranian air force conducted air strikes on MeK bases, as, for instance, in May 1993 and September 1997.

Following the election of the reformist Mohammad Khatami to the presidency in May 1997, the MeK stepped up terror attacks with a view to discrediting the reformist administration. Such was the level of penetration of the MeK organisation that most such planned attacks were foiled at the border before the MeK teams could establish themselves in urban centres in order to launch attacks on pre-designated targets. On the few occasions that attacks took place— often taking the form of inaccurate mortar strikes on symbolic targets in Tehran[10]—the IRGC would respond forcefully and with increasing confidence. For instance, in April 2001 the IRGC launched dozens of short-range ballistic missiles at MeK bases across the border in response to persistent low-level terrorist attacks. This dramatic escalation was as much a message to Iraq as it was to the MeK in that it underlined the IRGC's resolve to attack locations in Iraq with significant force. The message was received in Baghdad, and in time MeK terrorism tapered off significantly.

The Gulf War of 1991 had a major impact on the regional balance of power, as it clipped Iraq's wings following the conclusion of the Iran–Iraq War in 1988. As discussed earlier, the end of the war brought a sense of triumph to Iraq, which could legitimately boast of having successfully contained revolutionary Iran's ambitions. However, what was left unsaid by Iraqi officials and propagandists was that this half-victory could not have been achieved without the financial generosity of the Gulf states, in particular Saudi Arabia and Kuwait. Iraq had emerged from the war heavily indebted and with a badly deformed economy that could not adapt to peace. This was a major factor behind Saddam's decision to invade Kuwait in August 1990, thus inviting an overwhelming diplomatic and subsequently military response from the major world powers.

The Kuwait War also rebalanced Iran–Iraq relations insofar as it removed Iraq's advantage following the ending of the Iran–Iraq War two years earlier. The ceasefire of August 1988 was transformed into a partial peace agreement in September 1990 as Iraq withdrew from the pockets of Iranian territory that it still occupied. Moreover, Saddam acceded to many Iranian demands (most of which were enshrined in the 1975 Algiers Accord), including shared ownership of the Shat Al-Arab (Arvand Rood). This dramatic climb-down by Iraq was designed to alleviate pressure on the eastern front (by placing Iran–Iraq relations on a stable footing) so that Iraq could meet the threat from the US-led armies assembling in Saudi Arabia.

The overture to Iran intensified during the combat phase of the crisis (January–February 1991) as Saddam ordered sections of the Iraqi air force to seek shelter in Iran with a view to escaping allied bombing. It was yet another miscalculation by the Iraqi leader as following the conclusion of the war Iran refused to return the Iraqi fighter jets on the grounds that they constituted war reparations for Iraq's commencement of the Iran–Iraq War more than a decade earlier. The seized fleet was significant, numbering some 160 fighter jets and a few military transport planes, some of which (particularly the SU-24s) could be immediately integrated into the Iranian air force. In fact, Iran subsequently tried to operationalise all the planes, which were mostly of Soviet origin but did in fact contain two dozen French supplied Mirage F1s.

Iran's attitude toward the Kuwaiti invasion of August 1990 was defined above all by vindication. Kuwait after all had been Iraq's foremost supporter, transferring up to 20 billion dollars in loans and grants to Iraq in order to sustain the Iraqi war machine. In view of its substantial Shia minority (comprising up to 35 per cent of the population), Kuwait was fearful of Iranian subversion. Iraq's invasion of Iran in September 1980 was greeted with quiet approval in Kuwait and much hope and resources were invested in an Iraqi victory. Kuwait stepped up its financial support of Iraq following Iran's successful Valfajr-8 offensive of February 1986, which wrested control of the strategic Al-Faw Peninsula from Iraq. The positioning of Iranian Pasdaran at the southern tip of the Al-Faw Peninsula brought Iranian forces within 10 miles of the Kuwaiti border. Kuwait and Saudi Arabia

115

were reasonably satisfied with the outcome of the war, as neither side desired an outright Iraqi victory. Both states hoped for successful containment of the Iranian revolution, which they felt had been achieved by August 1988.

Iraq's increasingly aggressive behaviour beginning in the spring of 1990 was a huge shock to both Kuwait and Saudi Arabia, two states that potentially had the most to lose in the event of a major regional war involving the Western powers. When the moment of reckoning came on 2 August 1990, neither state was prepared for the profound shock and displacement that ensued, with the Kuwaiti royal family hastily fleeing across the border to Saudi Arabia. Whilst officially Iran condemned the occupation, privately Iranian officials—and indeed the population as a whole—could barely hide their sense of vindication and a feeling that karma had come calling on Kuwait's rulers. During the war, Iranian leaders had repeatedly warned the leadership of the Persian Gulf countries about the expansionist nature of the Baathist regime and the inherent malice of Saddam Hussein, but these warnings fell on deaf ears. Now that these predictions had been proven true, Iran was anxious to reap the full strategic dividend.

Iran accepted Saddam's overtures in September 1990, which enabled the two sides to partially de-militarise the border, in addition to exchanging the bulk of their prisoners of war. In Iran the released prisoners of war were branded as *Azadegan* (the Liberated) and celebrated as heroes of the war and the revolution. The *Azadegan* occupied a place in the Islamic Republic's hierarchy for those who had made sacrifices for the revolution and the state: on the most exalted end of the spectrum stood the 'martyrs' (*Shaheedan*), followed by the permanently maimed and injured (*Janbazan*) and finally the *Azadegan*. These three categories were not only important in propaganda terms, but they also carried tangible material implications, as direct and indirect association with these groups brought a range of financial and other material benefits.

The outcome of Operation Desert Storm in early 1991 was clearly beneficial to Iran as it destroyed much of Iraq's military capability and led to the Baathist regime's regional and international isolation. Moreover, it placed burdensome restrictions on Iraq, embodied by the northern and southern 'no-fly' zones, thus severely curtailing Iraq's ability to exercise full sovereignty within its borders. These restrictions all but removed Iraq's ability to project power across the region. The principal beneficiary of these developments was Iran, which following the conclusion of hostilities emerged as the foremost power in the Persian Gulf. Thus, the origin of Iran's strategic leap can be traced to the First Gulf War and the strategic strangulation of Iraq.

But Iran's relief at the containment of Iraq was balanced by fears and apprehension centred on the forceful entry of the US, and to a lesser extent UK, into the region. More than twenty-seven years after the invasion of Kuwait, this Western military presence has proven remarkably durable. For example, the United States continues to station thousands of troops in Kuwait alone and in addition to the military deployment there is a strong US presence (comprised of up to 20,000 civilians) in the country, which lies on Iran's doorstep. Whilst the regular deployment of American and British warships to the Persian Gulf began in earnest in the latter half of the Iran–Iraq War, following Operation Desert Storm this had become a permanent presence. As will be explained later, this enduring Western military deployment dominates Iran's threat perception.

However, the proximity of American and British forces to Iran's borders, and the inevitability of limited engagement with these forces, notably in the Persian Gulf arena, created a degree of familiarity that Iran would use to its advantage during and after the Second Gulf War of 2003. Moreover, at the diplomatic level Iran was involved in the attempts to keep Iraq strategically embattled, principally through the enforcement of the northern and southern no-fly zones.

Therefore, in the diplomatic domain there was a slight degree of convergence with the UK/US position on Iraq, to the extent that all parties agreed that Saddam's Iraq had to be kept in check. These developments, which unfolded over twelve years, essentially prepared Iran for the military, security and diplomatic repercussions which would follow the Anglo-American invasion of Iraq in March/April 2003. Whilst Iran's attitude to the invasion was not clear-cut—and there was still much uncertainty in Tehran as to the real intentions of the US administration—at least Iran was in a position to adequately meet the crisis.

Iran's Response to the Anglo-American Invasion of Iraq

The United States' 'shock and awe' military tactics deployed against an enfeebled Iraqi regime engineered the quick collapse of Baathist power. To the Iranians, there was more than a degree of embarrassment as US military might had achieved in three weeks what Iran had failed to achieve in eight years. There were, of course, multiple mitigating factors, not least that the Iraq of 2003 was considerably weaker than the Iraq of the 1980s. Moreover, the Islamic Republic has consistently argued (correctly, for the most part) that it had not only been fighting Iraq during the war, but had had to contend with most of the regional states in addition to the major powers, including, at different points, both world superpowers.

The Iranian military and security establishment's first priority was to place their Iraqi Shia allies in positions where they could influence the immediate post-invasion environment. The Ministry of Intelligence and Security (MOIS) had ascertained by July 2002 that an invasion of Iraq was inevitable. This deduction had been made on the basis of Western diplomatic intelligence which the MOIS had been able to access. Thus, Iranian planning for the invasion had begun in earnest by the middle of the summer. The Iraqi Shia opposition groups, in particular the Supreme Council for the Islamic Revolution in Iraq (SCIR), now known as the Supreme Islamic Council of Iraq (SICI), were instructed to gather intelligence on the plans and intentions of the British and American governments. The modest SCIRI office in north-west London was crucial to this effort, not least because both UK and Iranian intelligence exercised influence over it. Thus, the SCIRI office also acted as an informal centre for the exchange of secret messages between the two governments.

More broadly, SCIRI was central to the Iranian effort of reaching out to sympathetic Shia constituencies in the Iraqi south. SCIRI's armed wing, the Badr Corps (which was still considered as an extension of the IRGC), was positioned along the Iran–Iraq border and during the invasion in late March 2003, several thousand of its combatants crossed the border into Iraq, the bulk of them from the northern sector where they were given free and unhindered access to Patriotic Union of Kurdistan (PUK) *peshmerga*. The PUK was a longstanding Iranian ally and was used to coordinating with Iranian forces, dating back from the days of the Iran–Iraq War. The IRGC, MOIS and other military and security bodies also regularly called on the PUK in that period to gauge the mood in Iraqi Kurdistan just prior to the invasion. Iran's overriding concern in Iraqi Kurdistan converged with that of the UK and US: all sides wanted the region to remain calm and stable in the face of the tornado that was about to hit the rest of Iraq.

A major unknown factor as far as the Iranians were concerned was the position and behaviour of the 'Sadrists'. Since the assassination of Ayatollah Sadeq al-Sadr in February 1999 the Sadrists had gone underground and the whereabouts of the slain Ayatollah's youngest son, Muqtada al-Sadr, were not known. The Iranians knew that Muqtada al-Sadr controlled a large network and that under the right conditions he could transform that network into a large social and political movement. But for four years, the Iranians had been wary of approaching Muqtada through intermediaries for fear that his network was penetrated by Iraqi intelligence. These fears preceded Muqtada's leadership of the movement, as even his father was suspected by the Iranians of having covert links to Iraqi intelligence. The belief in Tehran was that Sadeq al-Sadr's extensive social and charitable activities would not have been tolerated had he not been connected at some level to the Iraqi security establishment.

In the event, true to form, the Sadrists proved to be volatile in the early days of the occupation. On 10 April 2003, a Sadrist mob attacked and killed Abdul-Majid al-Khoei, the son of the hugely influential Grand Ayatollah Abu al-Qasim al-Khoei and the head of the London-based eponymous al-Khoei foundation. Al-Khoei had made the fatal mistake of returning to Najaf at a hugely uncertain moment. Moreover, he had made the fatal error of walking with Haydar al-Killidar al-Rufayee, the gatekeeper of the Imam Ali shrine in Najaf under Baathist rule. The latter was almost certainly an Iraqi intelligence agent, and at any rate he was widely resented by the Shia faithful for implementing Baathist policies in respect of the shrine and the wider Shia estate. Al-Killidar al-Rufayee died on the same day: both men had been brutally stabbed to death. Muqtada al-Sadr was immediately implicated in the assassinations, especially as he had reportedly failed to intervene to help a gravely wounded al-Khoei.

Although Abdul-Majid al-Khoei was no friend of the Islamic Republic (the MOIS regarded him as an Anglophile with connections to British intelligence), his brutal murder sent shockwaves throughout the Shia establishment. The Iranian intelligence community feared that if left unchecked—or disengaged—Muqtada al-Sadr and his followers could cause major instability in Kufa, Najaf and further south. It was at that point that a decision was made to engage Muqtada. He was invited to Iran in June and reportedly spent most of the summer in Qom and Tehran, where he was extensively courted by different components of the Iranian establishment.

Broadly speaking, Iran adopted a two-pronged approach to undermining and ultimately defeating Anglo-American strategic objectives in Iraq. At one level, SCIRI and Al-Daawa were encouraged to work closely with the Americans with a view to defining the post-Baathist political order. At another level, Muqtada al-Sadr and the Shia 'street' were utilised to push back against the occupation. In due course 'special' groups were formed from within the ranks of the Sadrists to oppose the occupation at a military level. From the start the Iranians were much more exercised by the British presence in Basra and the south generally than by the American presence in Baghdad and the rest of the country. At one level this was the continuation of the volatile Anglo–Iranian relationship and reflected Iran's deep mistrust of the UK. But at a more pragmatic level, the Iranians had identified the UK military presence in Basra and the surrounding region as the Achilles heel of the occupation and accordingly mobilised and directed resources to test the limits of that vulnerability.

Constant harassment of UK forces—coupled with the local population's deep antipathy toward the British military presence—eventually forced the British to scale back their local ambitions. The siege of UK bases in Basra throughout 2007 had a major adverse impact on the morale of UK commanders and helped to drive a wedge between them and their American counterparts who favoured a tougher approach toward insurgent groups linked to Muqtada al-Sadr's Mahdi Army. The two British bases in Basra—one centred at the airport and the other located in the heart of the city at Basra Palace—were subjected to a constant barrage of mortar and rocket fire.

The low-level attrition warfare against British forces waged by the Mahdi Army and an assortment of allied or associated groups was the single biggest factor behind the British decision to withdraw the bulk of their forces from Iraq by the end of 2008. Both during and after the Mahdi Army-led attacks, a debate had raged in British military and intelligence circles as to what extent Iran was involved in the anti-British campaign in the south. British Prime Minister Tony Blair was convinced that 'elements' of the Iranian 'regime' (as Blair put it) were behind the arming and financing of Iraqi insurgent groups.

It is almost a certainty that the Qods Force was centrally involved with the higher-end Mahdi Army-linked groups, arranging for training and in some cases even providing strategic direction. The Quds Force was also well placed to arrange for the Mahdi Army to access the experience and skill-set of Lebanese Hezbollah, which had gained vital guerrilla warfare experience fighting Israeli occupation forces in southern Lebanon. The capture of Hezbollah operative Ali Musa Daqduq by US troops in Basra (who were acting in part on UK-supplied intelligence) appeared to lend credence to this hypothesis. US officials believed Daqduq was behind the highly sophisticated attack on US forces in Karbala on 20 January 2007. That attack cost the lives of five US soldiers, four of whom were kidnapped and subsequently shot execution-style. The assailants were dressed as US soldiers and were clearly acting on specific intelligence and appeared to have significant inside help from the local security forces. The attack in late January 2007 was arguably the most sophisticated attack on US forces during the occupation.

Whilst alleged Iranian support to insurgent groups in the south had a decisive role in forcing the British out of Iraq, the effect on US forces further north was more mixed. The Islamic Republic could not allow the US to succeed in its aims in Iraq as that would have made Iran immediately vulnerable to a wide range of US pressure, including the threat of a limited military strike. Utilising the political Shia groups under its influence, in addition to influencing the Najaf-based Marjayeeat's views on the US-led occupation, constituted the political dimension of the pushback against US plans. Although the Marjayeeat was not directly under Iranian influence, the grand *marja* (source of emulation), Grand Ayatollah Ali al-Sistani, was Iranian-born and thus sympathetic to the position and goals of his native country. Although officially divorced from politics, Ayatollah Sistani nonetheless played the most important role in guiding Iraq's Shia community toward a political path that ensured full Shia political emancipation on Iraqi (as opposed to American) terms. As far as Iran was concerned, this was a positive outcome.

The US military and political authorities in Iraq were more forthright than their British counterparts in accusing Iran of aiding the insurgency and specifically targeting US troops. The introduction of 'Explosively Formed Penetrators' (EFP) into the insurgency, and their utilisation specifically by Shia groups perceived to be aligned to Iran, was a game-changer insofar as it made both British and US soldiers on patrol much more vulnerable to roadside bombs. A sophisticated form of Improvised Explosive Device (IED), the EFP's hallmark was the deep penetration of armour, which caused devastation to British and American troops. The Americans believed that the Qods Force had transferred the technology to Iraq and that it oversaw its local production and distribution. It was a bold charge, not least because the EFP was responsible for hundreds of US military casualties, hence necessitating a forceful US response. On occasion, senior US commanders hinted at conducting limited strikes on Qods Force facilities inside Iran, but these never materialised, presumably because US leaders and diplomats were wary of the possible political consequences.

By the time the bulk of US forces had left Iraq by the end of 2011, the IRGC, as well as the broader Iranian defence and security establishment, must have felt satisfied. The Iranian strategy of conducting complex political and guerrilla campaigns in Iraq had forced a partial US retreat. The US had failed to remake Iraq in its own image and any illusions about nation-building were abandoned once the extent of local resistance became clear. But from the Iranian perspective, the struggle for Iraq was a perennial quest, and it entered a new phase once the US withdrew. Iran, after all, has to live with Iraq next door whereas the US could just walk away.

The Future of Iran–Iraq Relations

Looking back at the events of the past fifteen years, it is easy to understand why Iranian strategists feel satisfied that they have succeeded in altering Iraq's strategic profile from that of proximate enemy to friend and even potential ally. Whilst the US did not exactly leave Iraq on Iran's terms, the fact that the Americans failed to achieve even modest goals is considered as a partial victory in Tehran. Following the US withdrawal from Iraq in December 2011, Tehran continued to consolidate its influence in Baghdad, primarily by shoring up the position of then Iraqi prime minister Nouri al-Maliki, who was widely seen to be close to Iran.

The sudden loss of US influence as a result of the military withdrawal allowed Iran to press home its advantage and to bring several issues to a resolution. Foremost was the case of the Mojahedin-e Khalq (MeK), who doggedly refused to leave Iraq even though they had been disarmed soon after Saddam's downfall. The US decision to grant the Fourth Geneva Convention, which covers the protection of civilians in times of war, to MeK members following their surrender and disarmament was perceived in Tehran as a desire by the US to use the group as a bargaining chip. The fact that the Americans continued to protect the MeK in the face of objections from successive Iraqi governments (who demanded their immediate expulsion) was at minimum indicative of a tacit understanding between the MeK and the US military in Iraq.

However, toward the end of the US military presence the Iraqi government got bolder in confronting MeK members confined to their former headquarters at Camp Ashraf. In July 2009, Iraqi security personnel forcibly entered the camp to establish a police outpost and in the ensuing clashes eleven MeK members were killed. A similar clash occurred in April 2011 during which thirty-four MeK members were killed and several hundred were wounded. Following the withdrawal of US forces in December 2011 pressure continued to mount on MeK leaders but they still obstinately refused to leave Ashraf, even in the face of a potential calamity. The coup de grace was delivered on 1 September 2013 when an Iraqi militant group (ostensibly acting as an official security body) stormed the camp, liquidating fifty-two MeK commanders and senior members. This operation was almost certainly commissioned and directed by the Qods Force. Following this deadly assault, the MeK finally surrendered the camp, bringing a three-decades-long presence in Iraq to a close.[11]

On another front, the rise of the Islamic State (IS) group and its sweeping offensive in north-western Iraq in June 2014 gave Iran the opportunity to deepen its military and security cooperation with Iraq. The IRGC Qods Force and other Iranian military units were at the forefront of combating IS in Iraq from 2014 through to 2017. This effort was largely independent of a US-led campaign against the IS group, thus underscoring the delicate balance of power in Iraq, as both the US and Iran continue to jostle for influence. The rise of IS also gave the US the opportunity to return to Iraq in a military capacity, albeit in a largely advisory role. Nevertheless, US boots on the ground translate into political influence, and consequently some of Iran's post-2011 gains were eroded.

Looking ahead, Iran is set to regain the strategic advantage over the US, as demonstrated by the rise of the Popular Mobilisation Units (PMU). Formed in the immediate aftermath of the IS offensive in June 2014—and enjoying the blessing of the Najaf-based Marjayeeat—the PMU have emerged as the most effective component of the Iraqi security forces. They were at the forefront of the ground offensives against IS, often fighting the hardest battles in remote corners of the western Anbar province, and offering countless 'martyrs' to the cause.

The PMU have kept up the momentum by helping Iraq overcome other security and sovereignty-related challenges, notably against Kurdish secessionists, who held an advisory independence referendum on 25 September 2017 which the Iraqi supreme court had ruled illegal. The PMU were at the forefront of the Iraqi effort to retake Kirkuk and other disputed areas in mid-October, thus successfully asserting Iraqi sovereignty against a potent centrifugal force. The fact that this contribution came on the heels of the PMU effort against the IS group has helped raise the militias' national prestige and increased Iraqi leaders' determination to enhance their interoperability with the wider Iraqi defence and security sectors.

Whilst the extent of Iranian influence on the PMU is disputed, there is no doubt that certain key components of the umbrella force, notably Asaib ahl al-Haq, Kata'ib Hezbollah and Harakat Hezbollah al-Nujaba, are funded, trained and partially directed by the Qods Force. What is also beyond dispute is the fact that the PMU are there to stay, at least for the foreseeable future. The ejection of IS from Iraq is not tantamount to threat eradication, as the causes of Arab Sunni discontent have not been adequately addressed. Therefore, to meet the militant and terrorist threats emanating from that deep well of discontent, Iraq will continue to require an ideologically motivated force that can match the opposition's zeal and ferocity.

The rise of the PMU—and their ideological and organisational links to Iranian-aligned groups in neighbouring Syria and further afield in Lebanon—is a clear indication of Iraq's transformation into Iran's strategic depth. Influence in Baghdad is now central to Iranian regional power projection and strategic consolidation. Specifically, in terms of bilateral ties, the sustainability of Iraq as Iran's strategic depth necessitates a weak but united Iraq.

SYRIA
MISSION ACCOMPLISHED?

As the eight-year Syrian conflict seemingly draws to a close, Iran can convincingly claim to have played a leading role in the preservation of the Syrian state, the ruling Baath party and the presidency of Bashar al-Assad. The survival of this state also ensures the continuing control of the commanding heights of the government by a narrow clique of Alawites. Whilst Syria cannot be described as a sectarian state—insofar as Sunni Muslims and other religious groups are fairly represented at most levels of the bureaucracy—the domination of the upper reaches of the government and the army by Alawites was one of the major causes of the civil war.

As Syria represents Iran's sole formal ally, its survival is central to Iranian foreign policy. Beginning in 1980, Iran and Syria have steadily developed an iron-clad alliance based on shared values, perceptions and policies. At the centre of this alliance is a deep enmity toward Israel, and by extension a strong desire to contain American influence in the region. Moreover, the alliance between the two countries has allowed them to dominate Lebanese politics since the mid-1980s, thus denying both the US and its traditional Arab allies (notably Saudi Arabia) the opportunity to exclusively determine the course of events in the Arab world's most politically and culturally diverse society.

Had the Syrian regime been brought down by the pressure of what was initially a popular rebellion and subsequently became a full-fledged armed insurrection, there is little doubt that the successor regime would have changed Syria's strategic profile beyond recognition. The alliance with Hezbollah would have been severed, which in practical terms means that Iran would have been denied the opportunity to use Syrian territory to ferry arms and supplies to its Lebanese allies. Moreover, under a new Sunni-led regime, Syria would have likely pivoted toward Saudi Arabia and the conservative Gulf states, thus denying Iran the opportunity to project influence beyond its immediate neighbourhood. In short, the fall of Syria would have represented a strategic disaster for the Islamic Republic of Iran. US General James Mattis was right when he claimed that the fall of Bashar al-Assad would constitute the biggest blow to Iran since the ending of the Iran–Iraq War.[1]

While the Iranians might not have predicted a protracted proxy war in Syria (such as the one that has unfolded in recent years), they likely anticipated some degree of prolonged internal strife. In view of Syria's centrality to Iran's strategic posture, Iranian military and intelligence organisations would have kept a close eye on the country's politics. In addition to formal intelligence cooperation, Iran maintains an independent intelligence gathering capability in country. This is composed of sympathetic Syrians (who spy for Iran without the knowledge of their government) as well as Iranians who either reside in the country or travel there for business or religious reasons (e.g. pilgrimage to the Sayyidah Zaynab Shrine).

More broadly, Iran would have learnt important lessons from the last major uprising in Syria, notably the Muslim Brotherhood revolt that began in 1976 and culminated with the siege of Hama in February 1982. Although that conflict resulted in the routing of the Islamists, Hafez al-Assad's victory was not conclusive enough to settle the issues once and for all. At any rate, a myriad of underlying issues, notably a sectarian imbalance at the upper reaches of the state and the authoritarian rule of the Baath Party, were bound to lead to some form of conflict in the future. What is surprising is that it took thirty years for the conflict to resurface, this time in a more widespread and ferocious form.

As a side note, it is worth remembering that the Syrian Muslim Brotherhood are alleged to have approached Iran in the early 1980s (before the conflict subsided) with a view to eliciting Iranian support. The Syrian Muslim Brothers were reportedly rebuffed by Mehdi Karroubi, who at the time was the head of the Martyrs Foundation (Bonyad-e Shaheed) and a close confidant of the late Ayatollah Khomeini. Karroubi emerged as one of the leaders of the opposition Green movement following the disputed presidential elections and currently languishes under house arrest.

The context for the Muslim Brothers' attempt at gaining Iran's support was their misunderstanding of the nature of the Iranian revolution. The Syrian Brotherhood had come to believe that owing to the 'Islamic' nature of the revolution, and the Iranian leaders' professed desire to 'export' revolutionary ideals across the region, the Islamic Republic would look favourably on any Islamic movement. The leaders of the Brotherhood had failed to realise that even at that early stage (barely a few years after the victory of the revolution), Iranian leaders prioritised the national interest over abstract ideals. Moreover, both the Syrian Muslim Brotherhood and the movement's Egyptian core did not fully appreciate the significance of the mild sectarian undertones of the Iranian revolution. Although officially committed to Muslim unity, the leaders of the revolution framed this unity in the language and imagery of Twelver Shia Islam.

By the time the Syrian civil war broke out in late 2011 (following the suppression of largely peaceful protests in Sunni-majority areas), Iran's conception of its revolution was firmly anchored in a symbiotic relationship between Shia Islam and Iranian nationalism. Moreover, on a practical level, and following decades of intermittent interaction, the Islamic Republic's relationship with moderate Sunni Islamic movements was strained at best. The only exception was the Palestinian Hamas, which is an offshoot of the Egyptian Muslim Brotherhood.[2] However, even that relationship almost broke down after Hamas sided with the Syrian opposition.

Understanding Iran's commitment to Syria requires an analysis of the various components of this relationship, ranging from national interest, sectarian politics and ideology. This chapter sets out to explore all these themes against the backdrop of both domestic developments and Iran's relationship with the wider world. It also looks at the costs of Iran's intervention, considering human and financial aspects as well as the domestic political cost. Iran's interventions in the Arab world generally, and the costly Syrian intervention more specifically, have been the subject of public concern for years. This concern was evident in the protest movement that emerged suddenly in the closing days of 2017 when protesters beseeched Iranian leaders to 'abandon' Syria and to 'think' about the people instead. The fact that Iran pursues this costly intervention in the face of visible public opposition is testament to just how committed Iranian leaders are to their interventionist regional policy.

Syria and Iran's National Security Doctrine

Syria is central to Iran's national security doctrine. Not only is it Iran's only formal ally, but it is an Arab ally at that, which multiplies its utility to Tehran. One of the enduring lessons of the Iranian revolution in relation to foreign policy has been that a pro-Arab shift in Iran's attitude and policies does not necessarily equate to closer relations with the Arab world.

The Shah's regime was relatively distant from Arab causes; Iran had neither a coherent policy on the Palestinian issue nor a significant outreach programme to the region's Arab Shias. There was a slight shift in the 1970s as the Shah took a stronger interest in Lebanese affairs, but in general Iran remained aloof from Arab affairs. This detachment was reinforced by Iran's relatively good relations with Israel, as demonstrated by the presence of an Israeli diplomatic mission in Tehran.

The head of that mission was the legendary Israeli diplomat Uri Lubrani,[3] who served in that position for a five-year period beginning in 1973. Lubrani is credited with forecasting the downfall of the Shah, even though neither the Israeli nor the US government appears to have heeded his warnings. The presence of the Israeli diplomatic mission in Tehran was a potent reminder of the Shah's fundamental instincts regarding foreign policy. In addition to close alignment with the United States, the Shah sought friendly relations with Israel primarily as a means of balancing the Arab powers in the region. Foremost among these were Iraq, Saudi Arabia and Egypt.

Iraq, of course, constituted Iran's most proximate security-military threat and the Shah (as well as the current regime) sought to balance it with the lowest possible costs. In regard to Saudi Arabia, although relations were hardly as frosty as they are today, the two countries were even then natural rivals, which in the Shah's view necessitated a careful balancing act. In the 1970s, one feature of the Iranian–Saudi rivalry (in addition to longstanding geo-sectarian fissures) was a competition between the two states to garner American support and sympathy. Needless to say, this aspect of the rivalry disappeared following the revolution.

As for Egypt, despite rapidly improving relations in the 1970s (as demonstrated by the Shah's close bond with the Egyptian leader Anwar el-Sadat), imperial Iran viewed the country as a perennial rival for regional influence, if not as a threat. It is noteworthy that Sadat's predecessor, Gamal Abdel Nasser, had an anti-Iranian mindset and pioneered trends in the Arab world whose consequences continue to unfold. One such innovation was Nasser's misnaming of the Persian Gulf as 'the Arabian Gulf', a highly provocative move which flies in the face of both historical and legal facts. Nasser may have initiated this change, but the mantle was taken on by the rich Arabs of the Persian Gulf, who put big money behind the project. By approaching media companies, publishers, universities and education institutes the world over, the Gulf-led pan-Arab effort soon began paying dividends as more and more international organisations started to use the name 'the Arabian Gulf'. Even the seemingly incorruptible British Broadcasting Corporation caved into Arab pressure by adopting the supposedly neutral—if not painfully bland—term 'the Gulf'.

The Shah's pro-Israel policy was more reflective of vulnerability to outsider influence than an ability to influence the outside. It was at least in part informed by Israel's 'alliance of the periphery'[4] doctrine, by which the Jewish state sought to cultivate non-Arab powers on the region's periphery with a view to defeating the blockade and enmity of the region's Arab core. The three primary countries identified as central to this strategy were Iran, Turkey and Ethiopia. Iran was arguably the most important country to this idiosyncratic Israeli doctrine, because of deeply held perceptions of commonality in the face of Arab hostility and potential reciprocity in the security and military sectors. The Shah and his foreign policy establishment were no doubt influenced by these Israeli notions.

By the late 1970s, Iran and Israel had already set down the foundations of a credible security and military partnership. The pre-revolutionary Iranian intelligence community—spearheaded by the SAVAK[5]—had extensive ties to its Israeli counterparts and the SAVAK was reportedly trained from the outset by Mossad and other Israeli intelligence services. There was less cooperation in the military sector, but the very fact that the Iranian armed forces were largely trained and equipped by the US (which was also a major supplier of arms to Israel) pointed to favourable foundational settings for an Iranian–Israeli military partnership. It is easy to imagine that had the revolution not succeeded, Iran and Israel would have gone much further in their cooperation in the security and military sectors. At any rate, there is little doubt that imperial Iran would not have interfered in the Israeli–Palestinian conflict by sponsoring Palestinian groups.

The Shah, though, was searching for potential Arab allies, albeit haphazardly. The warming relations with Sadat's Egypt were the most promising sign, but it is doubtful this could have developed into a close conventional partnership, let alone a formal alliance. The relationship was based on a personal bond rather than a careful appraisal of the two countries' potential for alignment in the all-important military and security sectors. In geopolitical terms, Iran and Egypt were of roughly equal weight, a pertinent fact which pointed more toward rivalry than cooperation. Moreover, in view of Egypt's perception of itself as the cultural and intellectual vanguard of the Arab world, it was only a matter of time before relations worsened, even if the Shah had not been overthrown.

In the post-revolutionary period Iranian–Egyptian relations have been volatile, and at times hostile, in part reflecting the two states' competition for influence in regional flashpoints, notably the Israeli–Palestinian conflict. In keeping with Iran's other sensitive relations (for example, with Saudi Arabia and the UK), the introduction of an ideological dimension has greatly complicated Iranian–Egyptian relations. From an Egyptian point of view, revolutionary Iran posed a double ideological threat, foremost because of its Shia orientation, but also its more general sponsorship of political Islam. In this regard, the Egyptian establishment has been deeply worried by potential alignment between the Islamic Republic and the Muslim Brotherhood movement.

When Iranian revolutionaries seized power in 1979 they were determined to radically reshape Iran's foreign policy. The pivot towards the West, and the US in particular, had come at the expense of insufficient engagement with the non-Western world, in particular big Asian powers like India and China. In the decades after the revolution, the Islamic Republic expended considerable effort to developing ties to both of these powers, in particular with China.

In the Arab world, the radical shift in Iran's worldview did not produce a favourable response by the country's immediate neighbours, nor the more distant Arab countries in the Levant and North Africa. Whilst the Persian Gulf states, notably Saudi Arabia and the United Arab Emirates (UAE), were wary of the Shah's ambitions, they had come to regard imperial Iran as a reliable and stable status quo power. To that extent, both Saudi Arabia and the UAE were confident that the Shah would not attempt to overturn the balance of power in the region.

Moreover, the rivalry between the Kingdom of Saudi Arabia and the imperial state of Iran had been a conventional one based on an age-old balance of power doctrine. There was no ideological dimension to this rivalry, and in conceptual terms imperial Iran was founded on the Western nation-state model. Indeed, if there was an ideological angle to the rivalry, it hailed from the Saudi side, as the Saudi state is founded on the Wahhabi creed. By contrast, whilst Twelver Shiism was the state religion of imperial Iran, neither of the Pahlavi kings saw themselves as true defenders of the faith, whether at home or abroad. The second Pahlavi king developed some interest in Shia communities in Iraq and Lebanon toward the tail end of his reign, but not to the extent of interfering in the internal affairs of sovereign states.

By all credible accounts, the Persian Gulf states were unsettled by the fall of the Shah and fearful of the consequences. This fear intensified in the months after the victory of the revolution as it became evident that some revolutionary leaders were eager to 'export' the revolution, albeit via non-military means. The Persian Gulf states had reason to be anxious as their regimes, like the deposed Shah's, were based on monarchical principles of dynastic succession. Moreover, the 'Islamic' nature of the Iranian revolution was worrisome to the Gulf Sheikhdoms inasmuch as it threatened to mobilise their own populations on the basis of Islamic identity. In that early period, the Gulf Sheikhdoms were not so worried about the potential sectarian dimension of the revolution's message. This came later, after the outbreak of the Iran–Iraq War in September 1980.

Further afield, none of the Arab North African states were particularly welcoming of the advent of revolutionary Iran. Whilst 'radical' (or anti-Western) states such as Libya and Algeria welcomed the downfall of the Shah, they did not exactly embrace his successors either. Egypt, of course, was hostile to the revolution, as demonstrated by its granting sanctuary to the terminally ill Shah in March 1980. Following his death in July of the same year the Shah was buried at the Al-Rifa'i mosque in Cairo. This was a provocative move on Egypt's part that was bound to raise the ire of the Islamic Republic. The resulting enmity proved so deep that Iran openly celebrated the assassination of Anwar Sadat in October 1981 at the hands of Islamic militants. Sadat's assassin, the renegade army officer Khalid Islambouli, was commemorated on an Iranian stamp as the 'execution' agent of the 'traitor' Sadat, following his own execution by firing squad in April 1982.

With neighbouring Iraq openly hostile, and potentially belligerent, the nascent Islamic Republic sorely needed an Arab ally, or, failing that, a friend. This estrangement from the Arab world provides a new framework for understanding the origins of the Iranian–Syrian alliance. On the face of it, Syria was a less-than-ideal candidate for a potential Iranian ally. For a start, Syria was militantly secular and an ideological compatriot of the Baathist regime in Iraq. The notion that Syria could develop strong ties with a revolutionary Islamic power in Tehran at first seemed fanciful. But on closer inspection, Syria was the right choice all along.

Apart from its ruling Alawite complexion, Syria was more of a rival to the Baathist regime in Baghdad than an ideological ally. The shock of the Camp David Accords of 1978 briefly brought the two Baathist states together, as demonstrated by plans for full union, but this proved short-lived. Following the seizure of power by Saddam Hussein in July 1979, and the ouster of Ahmed Hassan al-Bakr, the plan collapsed as a vengeful Saddam crushed pro-Syrian elements in the Iraqi Baath Party. From that point onward Syria and Iraq became bitter enemies, a state of affairs that became irreversible once Syria sided with Iran following the outbreak of war.

In addition to its rivalry with Iraq, Syria was an attractive proposition to Iran on account of its ambitions of hegemony in neighbouring Lebanon. Indeed, most Syrians tend to regard Lebanon as a natural extension of Syria, dismissing Lebanese sovereignty as an irritant imposed by the colonial French. From the outset, revolutionary Iran sought to establish influence in Lebanon, not only in view of the latter's substantial Shia population, but also because of its strategic location, in addition to its reputation as the testing ground for the region's radical politics and ideologies. To secure access to Lebanon, Iran needed to be on friendly terms with Syria.

Therefore, in addition to breaking Iran's isolation in the Arab world, Syria provided concrete practical help in both balancing Iraq and enabling access to Lebanon. These three features constituted the foundation of the Iranian–Syrian alliance, a close strategic bond that has lasted for almost forty years. Indeed, this is one of the most remarkable and enduring alliances in modern international relations. It has shaped the balance of power in the region, in conventional terms and ideologically. The Iranian–Syrian alliance is the foundation for the ideologically inspired 'axis of resistance', which self-identifies as a counter to US, Israeli and Saudi influence.

Conventional Aspects of Iranian Intervention

It is fair to say that the outbreak of protests and demonstrations in Syria in March 2011 caught Iranian leaders and officials by surprise. The Iranian leadership had earlier welcomed the chain of revolts that began in Tunisia in December 2010, and which quickly spread to Egypt, Bahrain and Libya. The downfall of the Tunisian dictator, Zine El Abidine Ben Ali, in mid-January 2011 was much celebrated in the Iranian press. After all, the overthrow of a secular and pro-Western dictatorship was nothing to be feared in Tehran.

By extension, there was much excitement when the revolt, dubbed the 'Arab Spring' by the Western media, spread to Egypt in late January 2011. The Islamic Republic and the Egyptian regime led by Hosni Mubarak had been locking horns since the early 1980s. Throughout this period, the Egyptian regime had consistently accused Iran of supporting Islamic militants out to overthrow Mubarak. Certainly, on the face of it at least, Iran's glorification of Sadat's assassin, and broader rhetorical support for Egyptian Islamic militants, lent credence to Egyptian accusations. But as to the extent (if any existed) to which Iran lent practical support to Egyptian militants, there is little by way of evidence.

What is relatively clear is Iran's inability to develop strong ties to the largest group opposed to the Egyptian regime: the Muslim Brotherhood. Although the Egyptian Brothers had initially welcomed the Iranian revolution, and sections of the movement even supported Iran during the war with Iraq, they grew increasingly disappointed with the Islamic Republic's qualified embrace of nationalism and apparent inability to eschew Shia paradigms of resistance and power projection. The result was that by the time of the Egyptian 'revolution' in early 2011, Iran's ties to the Muslim Brotherhood were at their weakest point for decades.

That didn't stop Iran from framing the rapid political changes in Tunisia and Egypt as part of an 'Islamic awakening' and a natural extension of Iran's Islamic revolution more than thirty years earlier. The term 'Islamic awakening' has a long and deep history in the Islamic Republic. The leader Ayatollah Khamenei had employed the term consistently in his speeches throughout the 1990s and beyond to describe deep-rooted societal and political changes in Muslim-majority states in the Middle East, North Africa, and even parts of Asia.[6]

The implication was clear: people in countries like Egypt and Tunisia had rebelled not just because of desperate economic conditions, but more importantly because they sought to assert their 'authentic' Islamic identity in the face of the intrusive—and in some cases oppressive—cultural mores of Westernised elites. The expectation was of a decisive shift toward political Islam, which would in turn significantly impact these countries' foreign policies. In Egypt's case, a dramatic shift in foreign policy could prove to be of enormous significance, potentially leading to the renegotiation or even abandonment of the Camp David Accords, which since the late 1970s have defined Egypt's regional posture.

In the event, Iranian expectations were only partially realised, reflecting the 'partial' nature of the so-called revolutions in Tunisia and Egypt. Whilst Islamists in both countries were immediately empowered, and went on to win elections and form governments, their power and influence was constrained by a set of constitutional, political and deep state resistance, in addition to lobbying by Western powers. In Tunisia's case, the Islamists were pressured into sharing power and relinquishing many of their foundational values in the process. As for Egypt, it took a soft coup in July 2013 to overthrow the democratically elected president Mohamed Morsi and the emerging Muslim Brotherhood establishment.

Whilst Iran was more than happy to brand the political upheavals in Egypt and Tunisia, and to a lesser extent Libya, as part of an Islamic awakening, it was decidedly silent on the outbreak of street protests in Syria. By contrast, Iran had welcomed the Bahraini uprising which began in January 2011 (and which was suppressed with the help of a Saudi-led intervention) and also framed it as part of the broader Islamic awakening sweeping the region. But Bahrain was a special case, as it had a clear communal and sectarian dimension and touched directly on Iranian regional policy. Iran's position toward Bahrain, including the 2011 uprising and its aftermath, will be examined in the next chapter.

Iran's initial deathly silence on the Syrian protests had more than a whiff of hypocrisy about it. It smacked of double standards and predictably was maximally exploited by both the Arab and Western press. The persistence of the Syrian protesters finally forced the Islamic Republic to stake out a clear position on the uprising. The Syrian case was exceptional, argued Iranian leaders and officials, as the protests were either instigated or manipulated by foreign powers (the United States and 'reactionary' Arab states) and were clearly aimed at toppling a 'progressive' state. 'Progressive' in this case was a reference to Syria's strategic profile as a resistance state with an impeccable anti-Israeli track record.

By the summer of 2011 it was dawning on Iranian leaders and strategists that the Syrian uprising was not going to go away. In fact, it was morphing into an armed rebellion, in part because of a harsh government crackdown and simultaneous extensive foreign sponsorship of emerging opposition and armed groups. At around this time there was a realisation in Tehran that the uprising, and the emerging armed rebellion, had the potential to topple the Syrian state.

This scenario posed a massive challenge to Iran's national security doctrine of strategic depth. Absent a reliable Syrian ally, Iran would be deprived of significant influence beyond its immediate neighbourhood. In view of the scale of this challenge, it was hardly surprising that the Iranians would mobilise all their resources to contain the threat.

Whilst Iran had been advising the Syrian government on counter-protest methods and information warfare management from the beginning of the uprising, it was only in the summer of 2011 that significant resources were dedicated to the task of stabilising Syria. It was also around this time that the Islamic Revolutionary Guards Corps (IRGC) Qods Force was formally deployed to Syria. However, these units did not engage in combat until early 2012.

Iran was well placed to provide the Syrians with counter-protests and anti-riot training and advice. The Iranian security forces had had to contend with major protests and riots following the disputed presidential elections of June 2009. Prior to that, there had been a series of student-led protests, beginning in July 1999 and culminating in 2003. In fact, the Islamic Republic had had to deal with street protest movements and mass rioting from its inception. Whilst the last major immediate post-revolutionary protest took place in June 1981 (during the final stage of the transition to clerical rule), and was reportedly attended by hundreds of thousands of mostly Mojahedin-e Khalq supporters, the Islamic Republic learnt early on of the importance of developing specialised counter-protests and anti-riot security forces.

This was one of the enduring lessons of the Iranian revolution, during which the Shah's regime struggled to contain intensifying street protests. The main reason for this was that the country lacked dedicated counter-protests security forces. In their absence, the Shah had to deploy the army, which was neither trained nor motivated to counter street protesters. Every over-reaction and mistake by soldiers (who were often conscripts) galvanised further street protests in an intensifying revolutionary cycle. The Jaleh Square massacre on 8 September 1978 is often considered the point of no return in terms of containing street protests and demonstrations. Iran's revolutionary leaders were determined to learn from the Shah's mistake and thus prevent another revolutionary scenario from taking hold.

The investment in counter-protests and riot police resources paid off in the early 1990s, when the country was hit by a series of events born of economic-related unrest. The most important was the uprising in parts of Mashhad in late May 1992, when protesters and rioters attacked government buildings and even reportedly took over police stations. A similar event took place in April 1995 in Eslamshahr, just over 10 km away from Tehran. Speedy deployment of specialised security forces, which included elements of the IRGC, prevented the unrest from spreading to the capital.

The same forces and expertise were deployed more recently against protesters and rioters, following the sudden outbreak of unrest across Iranian provincial centres in late December 2017 and early January 2018. By deploying minimal lethal force, the Iranian security establishment has mastered the art of containing street-level unrest. Of course, in very serious situations the authorities will deploy the IRGC and the Basij auxiliary force. Both forces were deployed extensively during the 2009–2010 post-election unrest, when large crowds of people posed a threat to the orderly control of the Iranian capital.

In the Syrian context, based on the experience of the late 1970s and early 1980s, IRGC planners would have known that the demonstrations and protests would quickly intensify into an armed rebellion. This was inevitable, not just in view of the nature of the Syrian regime, and broader political culture which informed the actions of the protesters, but equally on account of the reaction of foreign powers to the uprising. Syria was not short of enemies, and it was inevitable that these powers would extend significant support to the emerging rebels.

Iran is often accused of exacerbating the Syrian crisis and even speeding up the transition from protests and demonstrations to armed rebellion. This is unfair, not least because it takes no account of recent Syrian history and the country's political culture. In fact, a case can be made that had Iran not intervened in the early phase of the unrest, by providing expert advice to the Syrian government, then the situation could have spiralled out of control much earlier.

Indeed, even by December 2011, when armed rebellion was well underway across much of southern and central Syria, as well as areas close to the capital Damascus, the Iranians were confident that the situation was 'under control'.[7] This was both a reflection of self-confidence, in terms of being able to help the Syrians contain the uprising, and a misreading of several key features of the rebellion. Specifically, Iran under-estimated two central features of the conflict. First, although foreign sponsorship of the rebellion was inevitable, the Iranians had not fully appreciated that several Gulf Arab states, Turkey, and at least one European power (France) would pull out all the stops to overthrow the Syrian regime. Second, Iran did not fully account for the dominating role of jihadist groups in the conflict.

Based on a careful appraisal of the last uprising in the late 1970s and early 1980s, Iran assumed that the Syrian Muslim Brotherhood would stay at the forefront of the rebellion. This assumption was correct in the early phase of the rebellion, where the Muslim Brotherhood not only organised street protests, but actively promoted them overseas through its extensive organisation in the Gulf states and Europe. The Muslim Brotherhood was also behind the formation of many of the embryonic armed groups. But from early 2012 onwards the increasing radicalisation of the conflict created a favourable climate for full-fledged jihadist groups, often with only tenuous connections to the Muslim Brotherhood.

The emergence of the Nusra Front in early 2012 marked the entry of al-Qaeda into the Syrian conflict. At that point the IRGC Qods Force made a strategic miscalculation by not fully appreciating the significance of this arrival. Iranian military and security planners in Syria reckoned that al-Qaeda would remain an essentially 'terrorist' force in Syria, by conducting spectacular terrorist attacks and the occasional hit-and-run assaults on Syrian forces. The notion that the Nusra Front might develop into a credible quasi-military force with control over significant swathes of territory was entirely lost on Qods Force planners and analysts in early 2012. In addition, the Qods Force misread the strategic intentions of al-Qaeda's Syrian chapter. Based on previous tactical cooperation with al-Qaeda, the Qods Force believed that the jihadist group would refrain from attacking Iranian or Iran-aligned targets (such as Hezbollah) inside Syria. This assumption proved to be entirely false.

In fact, the Nusra Front and its multiple incarnations, including the contemporaneous Hay'at Tahrir al-Sham, have proved to be the most effective fighting forces amongst the myriad rebel groups. They have also been the most durable, as demonstrated by their control over Idlib province. The flip side of the coin was that the emergence of the Nusra Front, and later on the Islamic State (IS) group, radicalised the armed Syrian opposition to the extent of adversely impacting the strategic calculus of the Western powers. Whilst leading Western nations such as France, and to a lesser extent the UK and the US, sought Assad's removal, they were loath to see him replaced by jihadists with a global outlook.

At a deeper level, the emergence of a jihadist-terrorist nexus in Syria enabled Iran to develop a counter-terror narrative, which it could then incorporate into its broader propaganda on the Syrian intervention. It was a clever move as it met two immediate objectives: to placate public opinion at home, and to narrow the divide with Western powers over the nature of the conflict in Syria. The notion of fighting jihadist terrorists appealed strongly to the Iranian public as Iranian propaganda had projected the intervention as a means to keep the terror threat at bay and prevent it from reaching Iranian borders. As for the Western powers, this was the first time the Islamic Republic had found common cause with the West over terrorism.

Although al-Qaeda was far from an Iranian ally, and certainly at an ideological level the two sides were bitter foes, Iran had tried to manage the threat through complex, often non-kinetic means. This sometimes took the form of limited tactical cooperation.[8] The net result was respite from terrorism as the al-Qaeda leadership directed its members and sympathisers to avoid targeting Iran. At the same time, in terms of propaganda, Iranian rhetoric on global jihadist terrorism, as embodied by al-Qaeda and its affiliates, was markedly different from Western counter-terrorism discourse. Whilst condemning terrorist atrocities around the world, the Islamic Republic also took care to berate US foreign policy and Israeli actions, which it described as the causal roots of global terrorism.

Regarding Syria, however, Iranian rhetoric on counter-terrorism was remarkably similar to Western rhetoric, insofar as both sides described the emergence of jihadist groups on the Syrian landscape as a threat not only to Syrian sovereignty but also to the security of the region and beyond. Yet, Iran and the West diverged on how they framed the jihadist threat, in terms of both the causal roots of the

Syrian conflict and its eventual resolution. Whereas the West saw the emergence of the jihadists as a reaction to the brutal crackdown of the Syrian government, the Iranians argued that it was precisely the potential for jihadist violence that necessitated a harsh crackdown in the first place.

In terms of conflict resolution, the West was careful to distinguish jihadists from non-jihadist rebels, even though the distinction was often blurred. By contrast, Iran took the opportunity to conflate all the rebels with the jihadists with a view to framing the entire conflict as a fight by Syria and her allies against terrorism and the *takfiri* trend (groups which declare some Muslims to be non-believers). Iran's approach was not purely based on propaganda, as many of the non-jihadist rebels were of a strict Islamist bent and actively cooperated with the Nusra Front. In this area, the definition of 'jihadist', at least in the Syrian context, was key.

The Western definition appears to be based on threat proximity, thus disqualifying groups who are exclusively focused on overthrowing the Syrian state. This definition ignores the fact that many of these groups actively describe themselves as 'jihadist', insofar as that term accurately describes the conceptual and ideological foundation of their struggle against the Syrian state. By contrast, the Iranian definition takes a much closer look at the content of these groups' beliefs, which in many cases are informed by sectarianism and related bigotry. This is not to ignore the non-jihadist, indeed non-Islamist, dimension of the revolt. But whilst groups like the Free Syrian Army—some of whose factions can be described as non-Islamist—were in a relatively strong position at the beginning of the conflict, it is widely accepted that the non-Islamist component of the rebellion had been reduced to the point of irrelevance by the summer of 2013.

Another conventional aspect of Iran's intervention—and one which has been arguably the most successful—is Iran's skilful coalition-building in the conflict. The deployment of Lebanese Hezbollah, and subsequently the mobilisation of Shia-led militias comprised of Iraqis, Afghans and Pakistanis, was part of this strategy, although admittedly there was an ideological or non-conventional aspect to this deployment as well. Nevertheless, the partnership with Lebanese Hezbollah in particular demonstrated Iran's belief that the response of the Syrian state to the rebellion—as the rebels drew in extensive regional support both in terms of funding and manpower—had to be to reciprocate in kind. This meant drawing in regional fighters with a view to balancing the conflict.

But the most striking aspect of Iranian coalition building has been the partnership with the Russian Federation. Even before the Syrian conflict, Iran and Russia had been close partners, as they shared similar interests and views on a wide range of regional and international issues. These ranged from international terrorism and the conflict in Nagorno-Karabakh, to establishing the legal status of the Caspian Sea. The latter became a pressing issue following the collapse of the Soviet Union, as the littoral states were forced to draw up a legal regime to manage and distribute the Caspian Sea's resources.

In the Syrian context, both Iran and Russia shared a strong interest in preserving the status quo. This necessitated pushing back against the Gulf Arab states, Turkey and the Western powers, who had formed a loose coalition to apply pressure on the Syrian government to cave in to the rebellion's main demands. Both Russia and Iran understood that regime change in Syria could prove to be potentially catastrophic for their regional standing and interests. In this regard, Iran obviously had more to lose as the collapse of its only formal ally was tantamount to near-complete regional isolation. In contrast to Iran, the Russians were also concerned about their global standing, as another Western-led regional regime change would inevitably equate to a loss of Russian influence and prestige. The Russians had stood by and watched something very similar unfold in Libya, and were consequently determined to prevent its recurrence in Syria.

Unconventional Aspects of Iranian Intervention

Qasem Soleimani spearheads Iran's regional strategy of influence-building and penetration through non-state actors and aligned communities. In recent years, his has been the most visible face amongst Iranian leaders and commanders. Soleimani's posters and portraits appear in remote communities and towns from Iraq to Lebanon. Moreover, he is celebrated as a hero by pro-Iranian groups from as far afield as Bahrain and Eastern Saudi Arabia to Yemen. At

143

home, Soleimani is a popular figure who appeals to a rising sense of Iranian nationalism. His embrace of social media by proxy has further endeared him to a younger generation proud of Iran's growing self-confidence on the regional stage.

Major-General Soleimani is the commander of the Qods Force, the expeditionary force of the Revolutionary Guards. In many ways Soleimani has defined the Qods Force since being appointed its commander in late 1997.[9] But his involvement with the unit goes back much further, probably to its foundation at some point in the mid-1980s. Indeed, Soleimani was deeply involved in special operations during the Iran–Iraq War. As a result of these operations, which often involved deep penetration behind enemy lines, Soleimani would have cultivated strong links to Iraqi Kurdish and Shia leaders. These connections formed the basis of his empire building across the region.

Soleimani's story is also one about the broader odyssey of the IRGC and its gradual transformation from a paramilitary force to a full-fledged military organisation with considerable political and economic outreach. Born in the remote village of Qanat-e-Malek in the south-eastern Kerman province, Soleimani hailed from a poor and devout family. He reportedly worked as a brick layer and a contractor for a local utility company in Kerman before the Iranian revolution changed his fortunes beyond recognition. Soleimani was amongst the crop of young men who joined the Revolutionary Guards at its foundational moment and went on to forge long and successful careers in the organisation.

Having formally taken over the reins of the Qods Force in late 1997, Soleimani set about expanding its operations in addition to creating new fields of specialisation. Following the end of the Iran–Iraq War, the 2nd Qods Corps (as the organisation is formally identified in the IRGC order of battle), continued to operate inside Iraq, primarily in an intelligence capacity. Occasionally the Qods Force partook in special operations, often in tandem with its local Kurdish and Shia partners. In addition to Iraq, the Qods Force was also deployed in neighbouring Afghanistan, where it operated both independently and alongside trusted local partners. It played an important role in the downfall of the Taliban in late 2001, principally by not impeding US efforts at toppling the movement.

In the early 1990s, the Qods Force expanded beyond the region for the first time, with small deployments in Sudan and Bosnia and Herzegovina. The deployment in Sudan was designed to shore up the Islamist-leaning government of Omar al-Bashir, who at the time was on friendly terms with Tehran. The burgeoning relationship was underscored by a visit of then Iranian president Hashemi Rafsanjani to Khartoum in 1991, during which the two sides agreed to step up their political, economic and security cooperation. For Iran, the connection to Sudan was strategically important for two reasons. First, it was a direct challenge to Iran's bitter rival Egypt and a means by which to apply direct pressure on Cairo. Second, Sudan offered a stronghold from where the Islamic Republic could build influence across the African continent. Following Rafsanjani's visit, both the IRGC and the Ministry of Intelligence and Security (MOIS) established a formal presence in Khartoum.

The Qods Force soon followed suit by providing military 'advisory' services to Sudanese forces fighting the Christian-led Sudan People's Liberation Army (SPLA) in the south. The SPLA'S connections to Israel made it a natural enemy of the Qods Force, which was determined to contain Israeli influence in that remote corner of Eastern Africa. More importantly, the Qods Force wanted to help Khartoum contain the rebellion in the south with a view to establishing a permanent presence in the country. Sudan's relative estrangement from the West, and its hostility towards the US, made it a natural ally in the eyes of the Qods Force and the wider IRGC establishment. Moreover, Sudan's appeal to Islamic militants across the region (and beyond), on account of its leaders roots in the Muslim Brotherhood, made it an attractive location to intelligence services. The opportunity to both spy on and make connections with Sunni Islamic militants in part explained the presence of the MOIS, the Qods Force and the broader IRGC in Khartoum.[10]

Further afield, the outbreak of the Yugoslav Wars in the early 1990s provided the Qods Force with the opportunity to expand into the heart of Europe. The context for this intervention was the desperate predicament of Bosnia's Muslim population (known as Bosniaks) who were at risk of extermination during the country's bitter civil war, which pitted Serbs, Croats and Bosniaks against each other. The Qods

Force, alongside specialised units of the MOIS, was operating inside Bosnia as early as 1993. Apart from assisting local forces militarily, the Qods Force operatives also helped in arranging arms shipments to Bosniak military forces. There were credible reports that Iranian arms shipments to Bosnia had the tacit approval of the Clinton administration.[11]

Therefore, by the time Qasem Soleimani formally took over the reins of the Qods Force, the clandestine organisation was already a full-fledged expeditionary force with extensive combat and special operations experience in at least four different countries. Soleimani spent the next two decades building on this experience by expanding special operations missions, in addition to creating new specialisms. For example, prior to his formal takeover, the Qods Force had no presence in the West. As it was an expeditionary military force, the Qods Force was only deployed to combat-centred operational settings. Yet, beginning in early 1998, Soleimani and his team set about creating clandestine operational cells in Western Europe and North America. These cells were tasked with collecting operationally useful information, such as extensive surveillance of buildings, institutions and individuals of interest to the Qods Force and the broader IRGC establishment.

There were plenty of hiccups along the way, not least institutional resistance from established intelligence organisations. Since 1984 all collection activities in Western Europe, North America and Australia had been the exclusive domain of the MOIS. By the late 1990s there was widespread acceptance in the Iranian intelligence community that the MOIS was the only organisation with the experience and requisite expertise to operate effectively in Western operational environments. Soleimani's plan to set up collection activities in this arena inevitably touched off resistance by the MOIS leadership.

There were valid arguments against Qods Force activity in the West, particularly in the United States. First and foremost, the operational environment in the West, especially in the Anglo-Saxon countries, was much tougher. Second, the Qods Force was not strictly speaking a collection agency. Its intelligence teams specialised in long-term surveillance optimised for kinetic activities. This type of activity would hardly be tolerated by Western states, and the potential diplomatic fallout was immense.

The MOIS leadership was concerned that Qods Force activity would endanger its own operations in the West. In stark contrast to the Qods Force, the MOIS focuses on the patient and long-term study of Western political systems, in particular their foreign and defence establishments. Whilst Western governments do not turn a blind eye to MOIS activity, by the same token they rarely make it impossible for the latter to operate within their jurisdictions. The MOIS leadership's specific fear centred on over-reaction by Western counter-intelligence agencies who might knowingly or unknowingly conflate Qods Force operations with those of the MOIS. Clearly, Western governments will not stand for aggressive intelligence-led kinetic activities on their soil. Thus, the MOIS feared losing the ability to operate in key countries, notably Germany, France, the UK and the US, as a result of heavy-handed action by these countries' counter-intelligence forces.

These fears were partially realised, in that the Qods Force's known record in Western countries is far from satisfactory. The most notorious case centred on an alleged plot in 2011 to assassinate the Saudi ambassador to the United States, Adel al-Jubeir. According to the US prosecutors, elements in the Qods Force had masterminded the plan, which involved subcontracting the kinetic side of the operation to a Mexico-based drugs cartel. The plot as set out by US authorities had many questionable features, not least the hapless Iranian at the centre of the plot, Mansour Arbabsiar. By all credible accounts, Arbabsiar was as far removed from competent covert activity as is possible.

Whilst Qods Force involvement in the alleged plot to assassinate al-Jubeir has not been established beyond reasonable doubt, there is little doubt that the Qods Force has been involved in similar—albeit less extreme and sensational—operations in the West. Insufficient knowledge of target countries (notably a lack of deep knowledge on target country counter-intelligence capabilities), coupled with questionable methods and tradecraft, in addition to impatient planning, guidance and expectations, has defined Qods Force operations in the West. As a result, Qods Force operations are relatively easy to detect and disrupt. A recent case of disruption took place in Germany in January 2018, when federal prosecutors (tipped off by German counter-intelligence) ordered raids against ten suspected Qods Force operatives.[12]

It is precisely for these reasons that the MOIS had been opposed from the outset to Qods Force activity in the West. However, in the Middle East and Afghanistan, the Qods Force could operate free from domestic institutional constraints, that is, opposition from the MOIS. In fact, the two organisations had worked closely together to frustrate US plans in occupied Iraq and Afghanistan. Once the Syrian uprising escalated into an armed rebellion, there was an acute understanding in Tehran that the MOIS and the Qods Force would have to work together in order to contain and defeat the threat.

To Qasem Soleimani and his inner circle in the Qods Force, the Syrian conflict presented an opportunity to elevate Iran's strategic standing in the region. At a personal level, it is easy to imagine that Soleimani saw the conflict as a chance to redress the imbalance in the conceptual foundations of Iranian foreign policy by once again prioritising revolutionary values at the expense of pragmatism. Like other veteran IRGC commanders, Soleimani's worldview is primarily shaped by the experience of the Iran–Iraq War. Men like Soleimani fought the war on unconventional terms, driven in large measure by the messianic force of the Islamic revolution. Many had thought that messianic force had long been extinguished. Soleimani was to prove them wrong.

IRGC propaganda has framed the Syrian conflict, and specifically Iran's role in it, in religious terms. Iranian or Iran-aligned combatants sent to Syria are described as *Modafeaan-e Haram* (Defenders of the Shrine), a reference to the Sayyidah Zaynab Mosque in the southern districts of Damascus. The mosque is a pilgrimage site for Shia Muslims as it contains the grave of Zaynab, the daughter of Imam Ali and the granddaughter of Prophet Muhammad. The term 'Defenders of the Shrine' immediately implies that the mosque is under threat by *takfiris*, hell-bent on erasing symbols of Shia identity. By extension, the entire Shia existence in Syria, and potentially the broader Levant, is conceived of as at risk of annihilation at the hands of jihadists and *takfiris*.

This religious framing of the conflict has been key to Iran's success at assembling an international fighting coalition in Syria. Besides Lebanese Hezbollah, a wide of range of Shia-led armed groups have been mobilised to fight on the side of the Syrian government. These fighters come from a diverse set of countries, including Iraq,

Afghanistan and Pakistan. At the practical level, the Qods Force is responsible for the recruitment, training and deployment of these disparate armed groups, which are usually organised and deployed along national lines. For example, the Afghan fighters are organised as the 'Fatemiyoun'[13] division, whilst the Pakistanis are assembled in the 'Zeinabiyoun'[14] division. The Iraqis are often from established armed groups and militias, including the Asaeb Ahl al-Haq, Kataeb Seyyed al-Shohada, Kataeb Hezbollah and Harakat al-Nojaba.[15] Apart from its religious significance, the deployment of foreign fighters signals Iran's intention to counter the regionalisation and internationalisation drive of the Syrian rebels and jihadists. Indeed, foreign fighters have featured heavily in the propaganda and actual membership of jihadist groups.

The mobilisation of Shia-led groups from across the region (and beyond) has led to accusations that Iran has actively fuelled the sectarian dimension of the conflict. By 2014 the sectarian dimension of the Syrian conflict was so acute that it appeared Iran and Saudi Arabia were engaged in a region-wide geo-sectarian conflict whose central locus was Syria. The rise of the Islamic State (IS) group in 2013 was crucial to this sectarian radicalisation. The state-building ambition of the IS group, coupled with its ultra-Salafi ideology, inevitably sharpened the sectarian edge of the conflict and took proxy warfare to a new level.

To Soleimani and the Qods Force leadership, the rise of the IS group was a propaganda coup which at face value appeared to validate their contention that the foreign-backed Syrian rebels were out to annihilate Shias. At a practical level, it was an opportunity for the Qods Force to expand its operations and to fight the IS group on both sides of the Iraqi–Syrian border. This process intensified following the IS group's sweeping advance across north-western Iraq in June 2014. Soleimani's Qods Force, in tandem with the broader IRGC establishment, effectively took charge of Iraq's resistance against IS, primarily through the mobilisation of Shia-led militias. Indeed, the Qods Force was in many ways the mastermind behind the formal creation of the umbrella militia coalition known as the Popular Mobilisation Units.

The religious dimension of the conflict has allowed the Islamic Republic to recreate the ambience of the Iran–Iraq War, albeit at a much more limited level. Iran's 'martyrs' in Syria—which now number just over 2,000—are celebrated in much the same way as the martyrs of the 'sacred defence', that is, the gruelling eight-year war with Iraq. More specifically, the Syrian conflict has produced iconic martyrs who have revived the martyrdom doctrine underpinning the unconventional aspect of Iran's strategic posture. The most iconic 'martyr' of all was 25-year-old Mohsen Hojaji,[16] who was captured by the IS group on the Iraq–Syria border in August 2017 and was subsequently beheaded. Pictures depicting a defiant and seemingly relaxed Hojaji in captivity (apparently moments before his grisly demise) have made him the poster child of Iran's military effort in the region.

Soleimani can take much of the credit for the re-energisation of the unconventional aspect of Iran's strategic posture. Through his leadership and idiosyncratic approach to special operations doctrine, Soleimani has created a small military empire which relies more on local allies than on deployed Iranian forces to project power. To that end, Soleimani's personal connections with local commanders and leaders have been critical. These connections are longstanding; for instance, Soleimani's relationships with Iraqi and Kurdish tribal leaders and militia commanders stretch back to the mid-1980s. Soleimani's personal network is the key to his success and one reason as to why the Qods Force has succeeded in spearheading Iran's small empire-building project at relatively low cost.

The key question revolves around the sustainability of Soleimani's enterprise. In terms of blood and treasure, the Qods Force's operations are sustainable, not least as the Islamic Republic is willing to make much greater sacrifices to protect its vital interests in the region. Seen from this perspective, the issue of sustainability is centred more on the durability of the regional balance of power, and the reliability and loyalty of Iran's allies and clients in relation to the region's volatile strategic architecture. Much depends on the eventual outcome of the Syrian conflict, and the extent to which Iran can maintain and consolidate its influence in the face of stiff opposition from friend and foe alike.

Rationalisation of Syrian Intervention

Certainly, hitherto Iran has been one of the winners in the Syrian conflict. Not only has the Islamic Republic helped to save its ally, the Syrian regime, from collapse, but by directly inserting itself in the conflict it has hugely boosted its influence in the country and the wider region. The human cost (just over 2,000 combatants killed) is significant but more than bearable. Meanwhile, the financial cost, which according to the highest estimates is circa $5 billion annually,[17] is painful but not unbearable, at least for the foreseeable future. At any rate, the financial cost does not take into account the potential financial gains, as Iran is now in a strong position to demand economic and commercial concessions from the Syrian government.[18]

The war has also helped Iran to raise its diplomatic standing internationally. This has been achieved through close cooperation with the Russian Federation, which forcefully entered the war in late September 2015. The Russian air campaign against Syrian rebels is credited with shortening the war, thus potentially saving Iran much blood and treasure. The culmination of Russo–Iranian military cooperation occurred at the battle for Aleppo in late 2016 as the Russian air force prepared the ground for a series of successful ground offensives by the Syrian Arab Army and allied pro-Iranian militias.

Military cooperation prepared the ground for joint diplomatic ventures in the closing phase of the conflict. Iran is a key player in the parallel Astana peace process led by Russia. The relative success of Astana, coupled with the Syrian government's increasing military momentum on the ground, has emboldened the Russians to convene a peace congress in the Black Sea resort of Sochi. By inviting all key participants, including the Kurds, the Russians aim to produce a lasting post-conflict settlement, as demonstrated by plans to draft a new post-conflict Syrian constitution. As Russia's closest partner in Syria, Iran is expected to play a key role in this process. Seen from this perspective, Iran's gains in Syria appear to be secure, at least in the short- to mid-term.

But Syria also presents a wide range of uncertainties, which could potentially undermine Iranian plans to secure a long-term foothold in the country. For a start, the main conflict has not yet fully concluded. Whilst the Syrian government is closing in on the last major rebel redoubts, as demonstrated by the offensive to retake Idlib province, sporadic guerrilla-style fighting is expected to continue for the foreseeable future.

Moreover, there are three unresolved secondary conflicts in Syria, all of which impact on Iran's position in the country. First, the empowerment of PKK-aligned Syrian Kurds is bound to cause intermittent conflict with Turkey, in addition to drawing the ire of the Syrian state. The Syrian Kurdish People's Protection Units (YPG) has created a proto-state in the form of 'Rojava',[19] a fact on the ground which to varying degrees poses a threat to the interests of Turkey, Syria, Iran and Russia. Any plans to uproot Rojava must take account of strong US military support for the Syrian Kurdish entity, as demonstrated by the deployment of 2,000 American military personnel to eastern Syria.

Second, the Islamic State group, whilst dispossessed of much of the territory it used to hold, has not been fully dislodged from Syrian territory. In fact, IS continues to maintain a strong presence on the Iraq–Syria border, and specifically within Syrian and Iraqi communities in close proximity to the border. The presence of IS is not a direct threat to Iran but indirectly presents an opportunity for the US to maintain a near-permanent presence in Syria, ostensibly to combat IS and allied groups.

Third, al-Qaeda (in the form of the Nusra Front and its latest incarnations) and allied groups have set down deep roots in Syria, which are likely to endure for years, if not a whole generation. Whilst the Nusra Front is in the process of being dislodged from its stronghold in Idlib province, the group is sufficiently resilient, both in organisational and ideological terms, to survive as a guerrilla movement for years. The prospects of non-IS jihadist groups in north-west Syria look favourable in light of Turkey's continuing hostility toward the Syrian government. Turkey has joined Russia and Iran to search for a lasting solution as part of the Astana process, but nevertheless appears committed to consolidating its zone of influence in north-western Syria, ostensibly to contain the territorial ambitions of the YPG.

Beyond Syria's political and operational environment, Iran faces a challenge at home on the issue of fully justifying and validating its Syria policy. Domestic dissatisfaction with foreign policy, and specifically with the intervention in Syria, flared up in the protests and riots that gripped the nation's provincial towns in late December 2017 and early January 2018. Slogans at the protests indicate a deep cultural divide between the protesters and the state. It was not only the cost of this foreign policy which protesters were objecting to, but the very principle of supporting 'Arab' causes in Lebanon, the Palestinian territories and Syria. The rejection of Arab causes is encapsulated by the slogan of: 'We are Aryans; we don't worship Arabs'.[20]

Other slogans included: 'Leave Syria alone, think of us instead' and the now iconic 'Neither Gaza nor Lebanon, I sacrifice my life for Iran'. The latter slogan also featured in the 2009–2010 protests[21] and is thus an established opposition mantra to the country's foreign policy. These slogans indicate that quite apart from objecting to the costs of the country's foreign policy, at a deeper level the protesters are rejecting the foundational concepts of this policy.

Whilst the protesters by no means represent the majority opinion in the country, the periodic unrest does raise questions about the sustainability of the Islamic Republic's foreign policy. The question is not yet acute as the protest movement which erupted in late December 2017 has nowhere near the critical mass necessary to threaten the foundations of the Islamic Republic. However, in the current trajectory, with the reformist movement effectively moribund, periodic unrest and uprisings cannot be ruled out. In due course these mini-uprisings may sufficiently scale up to create the conditions for a major political shift, if not full-fledged regime change. It remains to be seen if the Islamic Republic's national security and foreign policy establishment is sufficiently resilient to withstand these changes.

IRAN AND THE GULF
AN UNEASY EQUILIBRIUM

Historically the Persian Gulf region has been critical to Iran, not only in terms of immediate power projection, but also in terms of internal defence and security. As the country's most effective gateway to the outside world, the Persian Gulf is central to Iran's national security.

In the ancient world, the Persian Gulf was the most effective route for the armies of the Achaemenid Empire both to project power in the immediate strategic environment and to keep potential threats at bay. The Achaemenids and later the Sassanids would treat the Gulf as the main access point to North Africa, in addition to keeping a watchful eye on the Arabian Peninsula, which the ancient Persian empires never fully occupied.

In later centuries, and by a turn of fate, the Persian Gulf would prove to be Iran's main vulnerability in the face of predations by European empires, notably the Portuguese and the British. The latter proved to be particularly inimical to Iranian interests in the Gulf, perennially clashing with Iran's inherent aspiration to be the dominant force in the region.

Specifically, it was Britain's complex relationship with the Arabs on the southern side of the Gulf that eventually dismantled much of Iran's complex web of influence and territorial extension, some of which dated back millennia. Indeed, the roots of Iran's modern-day legal and political issues with two of the small Gulf states—Bahrain and the United Arab Emirates—can be directly traced to the conscious decisions and default positions of the British Empire.

The Gulf region is also important culturally as it constitutes Iran's primary interface with the 'Arab' world. The proximity to the heart of the Arab world—Saudi Arabia is just over 50 km away at the narrowest point of the Gulf—has ensured a high degree of interaction between Iranians and Arabs. Whilst the most visible manifestation of this is expressed in trade and commerce, there are also important political and demographic dimensions to this longstanding contact.

The demographic dimension is evident in the rich diversity and cross-pollination of peoples and cultures that exists on both sides of the Gulf. Indeed, there are large Iranian (or Iranian-origin) communities in Oman, the UAE and Bahrain. Conversely, there is a significant Arab minority on the Iranian side of the Gulf, from Bandar Abbas, close to the Strait of Hormuz, to Bushehr on the northern reaches of the Gulf.

This demographic and cultural mix has often balanced political and sectarian tensions and served a practical purpose in terms of building bridges between Iran and the sheikhdoms of the Persian Gulf. The practical bonds are vividly illustrated by the hundreds of thousands of Iranians who reside in the United Arab Emirates (mostly in Dubai), and whose relatively advantaged position in the economic hierarchy has created an equilibrium—albeit an uneasy one—in Iran's fraught relations with the UAE.

The political, strategic and cultural sensitivity of the body of water separating the Iranian plateaux from the Arabian Peninsula is encapsulated by a more-than-five-decades-long wrangle over the precise naming of the Gulf. The correct historical and legal name is the Persian Gulf, but this designation has been challenged since the mid-1960s by the Arab states, who rather predictably call it the 'Arabian Gulf'.

Iranians are especially sensitive to this misnaming, as they see it, to the extent that they have set up private and governmental organisations dedicated to 'defending' the name of the Persian Gulf.[1] These organisations have taken it upon themselves to contact media groups, publishing houses, universities—or indeed any organisation seen to be using either the term 'Arabian Gulf' or the more neutral term 'the Gulf'—with a view to persuading them to use the 'correct' historical and legal designation.

There is even a Persian Gulf National Day in Iran, celebrated on 30 April annually and named after the climax of the Persian–Portuguese War in 1622, when the Safavids expelled the Portuguese from the Strait of Hormuz. Iran's sensitivity and intense focus on the Persian Gulf are in part an attempt to raise awareness of historical heritage and to generate pride in Iran's historical achievements in the area. But ultimately, it is a political movement which seeks to impose a form of ownership, or failing that political dominance, on this sensitive body of water.

In this instance, Iranian actions are a direct reaction to Arab attempts to achieve the opposite, that is, to divest Iran of historical agency and to undermine Iran's political position in the Gulf. These are the political objectives which back in 1964 first motivated the Egyptian leader Gamal Abdel Nasser to introduce the change of the Persian Gulf's name. As an icon of Arab nationalism, and a self-styled symbol of progressive politics, Nasser was then by far the most influential leader in the Arab world. A cultural movement started by him was bound to gain traction and to resonate widely with Arab establishments and peoples alike.

The spat over the naming of the Gulf speaks to the deep cultural and ethnic fissures between the Arab world and Iran. Moreover, the fact that the locus of this identity conflict is concentrated on the Gulf helps brings the strategic dimension of this rivalry into sharp relief. After all, the Persian Gulf is one of the most sensitive geopolitical hotspots on the planet; a confluence of multiple political, environmental, security and sectarian challenges. Furthermore, the Strait of Hormuz is the exit point for 20 per cent of the world's oil supply. The requirement by global powers to secure the flow of oil has predictably attracted a near-permanent Western naval presence in the Persian Gulf.

The militarisation of the Persian Gulf, beginning in the mid-1980s and intensifying following the two Gulf Wars in 1991 and 2003, has constituted the most severe strategic setback for the Islamic Republic. Not only does this prevent Iran from realising its full strategic potential, but more worryingly for the Islamic Republic the strong presence of the American navy in the area is a constant reminder of the imminent military threat posed by the United States. The ejection of the US from the Gulf and the promotion of a regional security architecture is one of the major declared goals of Iranian regional policy.

Whilst Iranian leaders, officials and strategists alike appear to believe that the ejection of the US navy from the Persian Gulf is a realistic goal, an objective appraisal of the pertinent facts and variables would suggest otherwise. For a start, the US appears to be more committed than ever to protecting its vital national interests in the Persian Gulf arena. So far, at least, the advent of Donald Trump and his esoteric brand of isolationism appear to have had no material bearing on this iron-clad American commitment.

Second, the US, and the broader Western, naval presence in the area continues to be warmly welcomed by both Saudi Arabia and the other Gulf states. Indeed, both Bahrain and Qatar play host to vitally important US military assets which are used to project power in the region and beyond. Bahrain is home to the US navy's fifth fleet, which was formed in 1995 to manage large-scale military operations in the area. Qatar, meanwhile, hosts the US Central Command (CENTCOM) at the Al-Udeid Air Base. This formidable military infrastructure assures complete US military dominance in the Persian Gulf, a cause of perennial worry and frustration for Iran.

Iran has a multi-faceted strategy to contain the adverse political, security and strategic consequences resulting from the strong American, and to a lesser extent British, naval presence in the Gulf. One aspect of the Iranian response is patient diplomatic and political work to try to build confidence with interlocutors on the Arab side, with a view to promoting a regional framework for security and stability. In recent years this initiative has stalled, as evidenced by the rise of political tensions between the Islamic Republic and key states on the southern side of the Gulf, notably Saudi Arabia and the UAE.

Another part of the Iranian response is to engage the foreign forces directly with a view to both immediate containment and a long-term 'waiting out' game. This aspect of the strategy calls for a degree of kinetic action, even to the point of direct engagement with American and British naval forces. This kinetic strategy is spearheaded by the naval forces of the Islamic Revolutionary Guard Corps (IRGC), composed for the most part of small converted fast-attack boats. The sight of these small boats coming within collision distance with large US warships is illustrative of the huge power disparity between the US and Iranian militaries.

Power disparity notwithstanding, the IRGC navy has proven remarkably effective against the might of the US navy. This was brought into sharp relief in January 2016, when Revolutionary Guards speed boats interdicted two US navy riverine command boats which had strayed into Iranian territorial waters near Farsi island situated in the northern part of the Persian Gulf. The IRGC navy detained ten US sailors aboard the boats and made them kneel down with their hands behind their backs. The humiliation of the US navy was complete when an American sailor was shown on camera crying.[2] Another video showed the navy lieutenant commanding the boats apologising for straying into Iranian territory and praising Iran's treatment of the captured American sailors.

Stunts of this kind are not just about propaganda, even though the public relations aspect of such incidents is hugely important to the IRGC. Beyond the propaganda level, the IRGC is keen to assert that despite the power disparity, it has the ability to impose a measure of dominance in the Persian Gulf, albeit at an asymmetric level. The Revolutionary Guards are also making it clear that they are in the game for the long haul, with a view to exhausting the US navy through attritional psychological warfare.

This strategy has been relatively successful to date in part because it is subsumed into a broader, and more legitimate, Iranian containment strategy. This broader strategy, which is enforced by the regular Iranian navy in addition to the IRGC, involves robustly defending Iranian territorial waters, particularly against potential incursion by American and British warships.[3] In the past, similar humiliating treatment has been meted out to British marines and sailors, as demonstrated by the seizure of fifteen Royal Navy personnel off the Iran–Iraq coast in March 2007 and their subsequent detention for thirteen days.

Partial success notwithstanding, key questions remain about the sustainability of the IRGC's kinetic strategy, particularly if US naval commanders, directed by their political masters in Washington, change the US navy's rules of engagement vis-à-vis confrontations with Iranian speed boats. Donald Trump famously said during his presidential campaign that he would 'shoot' Iranian speed boats out of the water if they made improper 'gestures' at American navy vessels.[4] This tough rhetoric may be in part responsible for the dramatic decline in potentially dangerous stand-offs between the US navy and IRGC vessels in the first year of the Trump presidency. To be sure, the IRGC strategy does not involve militarily engaging US warships; not only is the immediate outcome of such encounters predetermined, but such an encounter might embolden the US to retaliate disproportionately by targeting a wide range of IRGC assets in the Gulf and possibly even on the mainland.

Thus, in the Persian Gulf arena the Islamic Republic faces an exceptionally tough political, diplomatic and military environment, composed of a complex and evolving interplay between regional and global interests. There is no doubting that the United States constitutes Iran's primary adversary in this arena and the Islamic Republic's aspiration to be the dominant power in the region cannot be fully realised as long as the US maintains significant military assets in the region.

In the long term, the key to any potential breakthrough by Iran in this area will depend on the extent to which it can successfully engage and influence the regional states, big and small, through a mix of soft power tactics, including trade, diplomacy and positive cultural outreach. Thus, a case-by-case analysis of Iran's relations with regional states is critical to understanding the challenges and opportunities that lie ahead for Iran in the Gulf arena.

Saudi Arabia: Is Conflict Inevitable?

The Kingdom of Saudi Arabia (KSA) is undoubtedly Iran's main rival in the Gulf arena and further afield in Syria, Yemen and to a lesser extent Iraq. The rise in bilateral tensions can be traced to the toppling of Saddam Hussein in April 2003 and the political emancipation of Iraqi Shias. The end of minority Sunni rule in Iraq was bad enough, but the fact that the emancipation of Iraqi Shias proved to be a harbinger of Shia empowerment across the region presented the Saudi leadership with a potential national security crisis.

For years tensions had been steadily increasing, but not to the point that the two sides have come close to a direct (even if limited) confrontation. Diplomacy and engagement were still a possibility and indeed occurred from time to time as both sides sought to prevent tensions from crossing a dangerous threshold.

The game changer was the ascension of Salman bin Abdulaziz Al-Saud to the head of the Saudi royal family in January 2015. Salman's predecessor as king, Abdullah bin Abdulaziz Al Saud, had firmly stuck to the old rules of Saudi diplomacy, which necessitated avoidance of escalation whenever possible. Moreover, the former King Abdullah favoured a degree of accommodation with Iran, even though at the same time he was firmly committed to containing Iran's regional ambition.

By contrast, King Salman has proved to be hawkish—if not personally, at least the real decision makers around him have opted out of the old rules of diplomacy. Aged eighty-two and ailing, Salman is widely known as merely a figurehead with real power residing in the hands of his son, Mohammad bin Salman (MBS), who was appointed crown prince in June 2017. The 32-year old MBS effectively became Saudi Arabia's strongman immediately after his father's ascension to the throne when he was appointed defence minister in late January 2015.

Upon assuming control of the Kingdom's military, and in effect foreign policy, MBS immediately embarked on an aggressive approach, thus rewriting the rule book for Saudi diplomacy. MBS's first move was in Yemen, where he spearheaded a military campaign against the Houthi movement which had seized the capital Sana'a the previous September. By launching a war against Yemen, MBS was signalling a radical departure from traditional Saudi diplomacy and strategy, which to the greatest extent possible sought to avoid direct conflict. Thus, MBS's leadership began on a high note of confidence and a promise to change Saudi Arabia, not only in terms of the Kingdom's strategic posture but also in terms of domestic politics, by making the country more modern and clamping down on bureaucratic inefficiency, corruption and unhelpful traditions.

From the outset MBS made clear that he was going to take the fight to Iran by ensuring the regional struggle for influence unfolds 'inside' Iran as opposed to Saudi Arabia.[5] This was a clear indication that the new Saudi leadership was intent on turning Iranian 'subversion' (as the Saudis understand it) on its head by re-deploying it against the point of origin. For decades the House of Saud has feared Iranian subversion within its borders, notably Iranian outreach to the Kingdom's embattled Shia minority in the oil-rich Eastern Province. From the Saudi perspective, by fomenting unrest within Saudi borders, Iran not only desires the diminution of the House of Saud but in fact ultimately aspires to its disintegration.

As part of its own subversion strategy, the new Saudi leadership has reached out to different branches of the exiled Iranian opposition. This approach was dramatically underscored when former Saudi intelligence chief, Prince Turki al-Faisal, spoke at a Mojahedin-e Khalq rally in July 2016.[6] This was a significant escalation, not only because of the MeK's association with terrorism, but also because of the direct intervention of Turki al-Faisal, who is not only hugely influential within the Kingdom but also well-connected to Western intelligence services. The Iranians consider the shrewd and wily prince as the unofficial head of Saudi diplomacy.

There are signs that the Saudis have reached out to other exiled groups, including Iranian Kurdish separatists based in Iraqi Kurdistan. Saudi funding[7] is thought to be partially responsible for a decision in early 2016 by a well-established Kurdish separatist group, the Democratic Party of Iranian Kurdistan (PDKI), to resume armed struggle.[8] The PDKI was active in the 1980s but its armed struggle largely fizzled out after Iranian intelligence assassinated its iconic leader, Abdul Rahman Ghassemlou, in Vienna in July 1989. Ghassemlou's successor, Sadegh Sharafkandi, was in turn assassinated in Berlin in September 1992.

Officially Iran pretends that it is unimpressed by MBS, whom they dismiss as young, immature and hot-headed. There are signs of confusion in Tehran as the Iranians scramble to come to terms with the KSA's newly energised and confrontational foreign policy. Iranian fears and uncertainty are compounded by two additional factors. First, in tandem with a muscular regional policy, MBS appears to be making a serious effort at reforming the Kingdom, albeit in an autocratic manner which does not threaten the power bases of the House of Saud. For example, the clampdown on corruption and the introduction of a degree of socio-cultural liberalisation—as illustrated by allowing women to drive—are important developments in a country where change has traditionally taken place at a glacial pace. At minimum, a less traditional Saudi Arabia undermines Iranian propaganda which tries to paint the Kingdom as the bastion of atavism and barbarism.

Second, MBS's courting by Donald Trump has improved Saudi–US ties, especially after a downturn during the Obama presidency. Moreover, there are signs that Trump is conducting a form of personalised parallel diplomacy with Saud Arabia through his son-in-law Jared Kushner.[9] The net result is that US and Saudi positions on Iran are now more aligned than they ever have been in the past four decades. This bodes ill for Iran as it increases the risk of the US intervening to bolster the Saudi position in regional proxy wars. This is already happening in Yemen, where the US is actively aiding the Saudi war effort.

It also raises the question of whether the US would intervene directly to help Saudi Arabia in the event of a direct military confrontation with Iran. Hitherto, the two sides have clashed by proxy in multiple arenas, including in Iraq, Syria, Lebanon and Yemen. Whilst the possibility of a direct clash is not high, it cannot be ruled out altogether. Indeed, there is a small and barely remembered precedent for direct military engagement, but it occurred more than three decades ago during the Iran–Iraq War. Iranian F-4 Phantom fighter jets occasionally engaged with Saudi F15s in 1984–1985, the early phase of the tanker war in the Persian Gulf. The only known kinetic engagement occurred in early June 1984 when Saudi F15s shot down two Iranian F-4s in the north-eastern part of the Gulf.[10]

On that occasion the US actively assisted the Saudi air force, not only by refuelling the F-15s in flight, but also by providing surveillance information which enabled the Saudi F-15s to detect and shoot down the F-4s. Whilst this limited air combat took place more than thirty years ago, it is a probable template for any future limited military engagement between the KSA and Iran. This engagement is likely to begin in the air, an arena where the Saudis have a clear advantage. The Saudi air force boasts nearly 300 operational cutting-edge fighters and interceptors, including F-15s (both interceptor and fighter varieties), Eurofighters and Tornados. By contrast, the backbone of the Iranian air force is still composed of F-4s, F-5s and F-14s supplied more than forty years ago.

A short and sharp engagement in the air is likely to quickly assert Saudi air superiority—and possibly air supremacy if the US extensively assists the Saudis—and thus force Iran to open an arena in which it has a clear advantage: firing ballistic missiles at targets on the Saudi mainland. Whilst the accuracy of Iran's missiles has yet to be fully tested, there is little doubt that the IRGC can wreak substantial devastation in the Kingdom by attacking both military and civilian targets. The latter is likely to induce panic and thus sabotage Saudi morale, all with a view to swiftly concluding hostilities on Iran's terms. The large-scale deployment of ballistic missiles has the added advantage of deterring the United States from entering the conflict whole-heartedly on the Saudi side. In that explosive situation the primary US concern would be to avoid escalation and to bring hostilities to a speedy conclusion. Iran's ballistic missile capability ensures that the US has to take the Islamic Republic's bottom lines into consideration in any immediate conflict resolution strategy.

Arguably, Iran has already deployed ballistic missiles against Saudi targets, albeit by proxy. In early November 2017 Yemen's Houthis fired a ballistic missile at Riyadh's King Khalid International Airport. Although the missile—reportedly a Burkan 2-H—just missed the target, initial Saudi claims to have destroyed the missile with the Patriot missile defence system may have been false.[11] This was followed in December by another ballistic missile fired at Riyadh, this time targeting the official residence of the Saudi king;[12] again the Saudis claimed to have successfully intercepted the missile. An additional attempted missile strike took place in January 2018, this time aimed at the southern province of Najran.[13]

The US was sufficiently alarmed by this escalation in the Yemen War to try to bring Iran's alleged involvement in the Houthis' acquisition of mid-range ballistic missiles to attention. Indeed, the US ambassador to the United Nations, the hawkish Nikki Haley, gave a dramatic presentation in December 2017 at the headquarters of the Defence Intelligence Agency in Washington whilst standing in front of debris and missile fragments of an alleged Iranian ballistic missile. But Haley's over-confident and aggressive presentation failed to impress many experts and the jury is still out as to what extent (if any) Iran has facilitated Yemeni acquisition of short- to mid-range missiles.[14]

Going forward, another way in which Iran can hit back against the new aggressive Saudi leadership is to try to foment unrest inside the Kingdom. This would necessarily involve greater outreach to dissident, and possibly militant, networks in the Shia-majority Eastern province. Despite a heavy-handed Saudi crackdown, and the marginalisation of key dissidents since 1993,[15] the Saudi authorities have not managed to stamp out dissent and protests altogether. Indeed, according to informed sources in the London-based Saudi opposition, the Eastern Province is awash with underground dissident networks, some with the potential to engage in militant activity under the right conditions. Furthermore, Iranian intelligence agencies, both in the form of the IRGC and the Ministry of Intelligence and Security (MOIS), maintain agent networks in the Eastern Province, primarily for the purpose of intelligence gathering, though there is always the option of directing some of these networks toward militant or sabotage activities, if circumstances call for it.

Options notwithstanding, the preference of Iranian leaders and strategists alike is to desist from dangerous escalation with the Saudis. The prevailing policy is to manage the multiple proxy wars in a manner that avoids direct confrontation. Iran would be hesitant to foment unrest inside the Kingdom for fear of intensifying Saudi outreach to Iranian opposition, militant and separatist groups. Indeed, Iranian vulnerabilities in this arena are greater than the Saudis', as illustrated by the sheer range of anti-Iranian groups active in the region and in the West. By contrast, Saudi Arabia's Achilles heel is mostly limited to the restive Eastern Province, as this is the only arena where Iran can realistically expect to find sympathisers. The prospect of the Islamic Republic successfully reaching out to non-Shia dissidents, for example to Saudi liberals or hardline Salafis, is remote to say the least.

If sudden escalation occurs it is likely to be instigated by the Saudi leadership. MBS has form on this, as demonstrated by the execution of Shia cleric Sheikh Nimr Baqir al-Nimr in early 2016. Nimr's execution was an example of grave provocation which led to the severing of diplomatic ties between the KSA and Iran, following attacks on Saudi diplomatic facilities in Tehran and Mashhad. Additional provocative acts, for instance a Saudi attack on Iranian shipping off the coast of Yemen or the shooting down of an Iranian plane near the area, will likely elicit a direct reaction from Tehran. Incidents like these could trigger a limited military confrontation. Iran's strategy in this scenario would be to deliver short sharp pain on Riyadh using 'swarming' tactics, by unleashing dozens, if not hundreds, of ballistic missiles on the Saudi capital.

Gazing into the distant future, any lasting form of regional security requires Iran and Saudi Arabia to place their relations on a stable footing. Whilst the prospect of 'stable' relations between Tehran and Riyadh looks remote at present, a look at the distant past reveals a form of relationship which, whilst not tension-free, was stable enough to allow for a degree of cooperation, or failing that non-confrontation, which ensured peace and security in the Gulf arena.

As stated earlier, during the Pahlavi era Iran–Saudi relations were relatively stable for two main reasons. First, the Iranian state was not ideological; second, the sectarian dimension of the relationship was minimal. Both factors were turned on their head following the Iranian revolution. Needless to say, the collapse of the Islamic Republic would impact hugely on bilateral ties, likely resulting in an improved relationship with the KSA if Iran were to revert to secular rule and give up the role of defending oppressed or disenfranchised Shias across the region. But that prospect is remote; even in the event of major political changes in Iran, foreign policy is unlikely to change beyond recognition. Broadly speaking, Iran's regional policy has been successful, and a new administration will want to keep large chunks of it intact.

Iranian–Saudi relations also depend to some extent on the stability of the Gulf Cooperation Council (GCC) as an alliance. If the GCC retains internal cohesion and manages to craft regional security and strategic policies that promote stability—without over-reliance on foreign powers like the United States—then it can act as a counter-weight to Iran. But for the moment, the future does not look bright for the GCC, at least not in terms of security and strategic positioning. The bloc is divided on a number of issues, as demonstrated by the spat with Qatar which dramatically burst into the open in the summer of 2018. This division is even more entrenched in respect of Iran, as at least two states—Qatar and Oman—dissent from the hardline KSA position on the Islamic Republic.

One small GCC state which is pivotal to Iran–Saudi tensions is Bahrain. In fact, no other state in the region can upset the balance of power between Tehran and Riyadh more than the tiny Kingdom of Bahrain. If Riyadh loses control of Bahrain, the KSA will have effectively been defeated by Iran in the Persian Gulf arena. This is why Saudi Arabia alongside the UAE, intervened decisively in March 2011 to extinguish Bahrain's Arab Spring moment. But continuing political unrest in Bahrain, alongside the potential for militant activity, suggests a prolonged period of low-level instability which may yet present opportunities for Iran.

Bahrain: An Iranian Province?

Hossein Shariatmadari is a creature of the Islamic Republic through and through. The 70-year-old newspaper editor is a former senior member of the political-ideological division of the IRGC with strong links to the intelligence sections of the Sepah. Moreover, he has friends in high places at the country's main intelligence agency, the MOIS. But his real importance lies in his proximity to the country's leader, Ayatollah Khamenei.

As the managing editor of *Kayhan*, the country's most conservative newspaper, for over two decades, Shariatmadari is expected to reflect the views of the clerical establishment. But he does more than that, as he is also regarded as Ayatollah Khamenei's personal representative at *Kayhan*, Khamenei himself appointing him to that role. For this reason, Shariatmadari's pronouncements on foreign policy are watched closely by regional and Western intelligence services in the belief that they at least partially reflect the positions of Ayatollah Khamenei.

Thus, Shariatmadari raised eyebrows in early February 2018 when he claimed that Iran 'owns' Bahrain.[16] In fact, Shariatmadari has form on Bahrain. He made exactly the same remark ten years earlier, eliciting a sharp rebuke from the Bahraini media. What are we to make of such statements? Are they a reflection of official policy, or do they at minimum reflect the dreams and aspirations of Iranian leaders, notably Ayatollah Khamenei? Certainly, the Bahrainis, and the GCC politicos in general, interpret them as reflecting the viewpoints and aspirations of Iranian power centres. They cannot be blamed for reaching this conclusion as *Kayhan* is an important, albeit not necessarily very popular, media platform.

Founded in early 1943, at the height of Iran's occupation by the Allied powers during the Second World War, the paper embodied the views of Iran's emerging modernist and progressive classes. Pro-Western from the outset, the paper gradually transformed into a pillar of the establishment, a process that accelerated in the wake of the August 1953 coup which ousted Mohammed Mossadegh. As an unequivocally royalist paper *Kayhan's* core mission was to defend and justify the Shah's domestic and foreign policies, ranging from the 'White Revolution'[17] to the Shah's alliance with the United States.

Not surprisingly, the paper's core mission changed beyond recognition following the revolution. In one respect, though, the paper remained the same: its proximity to the establishment and key power centres. In fact, the post-revolutionary *Kayhan* broke new ground by forming special ties with security and intelligence agencies. It has long been rumoured that Shariatmadari worked as an interrogator in the 1980s and strove to create *tavaban* or 'repentants'. Moreover, *Kayhan* specialises in the publication of embellished security-centred stories on both internal dissidents and foreign adversaries. The source of these stories is widely believed to be the intelligence services.

Irrespective of whether he is speaking in an official capacity or not, Shariatmadari's views on Bahrain are not uncommon in Iran. They represent a nationalist perspective that has failed to come to terms with Bahraini independence in 1971. It is an ahistorical view as it imagines the region prior to the forceful entry of the British Empire. Furthermore, at least as far as Shariatmadari is concerned, the position on Bahrain is also a swipe at the former Shah, as the latter was quick to relinquish Iranian claims on Bahrain in the early 1970s.

The context for the Shah's position was Britain's fateful decision to withdraw from the Persian Gulf in 1971. It has been widely suggested that the Shah was intent on resolving all territorial disputes with the UK prior to the formal end of British domination in the region. Both the British and the Iranian governments approached the United Nations in 1969 with a view to resolving the issue of Bahrain's legal and political status. The result was an independence survey carried out in 1970, the results of which were presented as a referendum on independence. The UN passed a resolution on the issue in May, following which Iran formally renounced its claim to the island.

Bahrain declared independence in August 1971, and formally became an independent state on 16 December 1971.

To Iranian nationalists of all stripes, the Iranian government had been too quick to renounce claims to the island. However, to the nationalist camp in the Islamic Republic, and indeed to all Iranian nationalists opposed to the monarchical regime, the Shah's decision smacked of treason and was further proof of the monarch's subservience to Western imperialism. After all, the nationalist camp argues, the Shah's decision to relinquish Bahrain without a fight was primarily informed by his desire to avoid conflict with the British and the Americans.

Whilst there is more than a grain of truth to these arguments, the bottom line is that the people of Bahrain had decided to opt for independence as part of a complex international process, involving two powerful states in addition to the United Nations Security Council. If Iran had refused to heed UN Security Council Resolution 278 (which endorsed the results of the independence survey), it would have found itself at odds with the international community. It is difficult to see how any Iranian government—let alone the pro-Western administration of the Shah—could have countenanced such a challenging scenario.

At any rate, the Islamic Republic has mostly respected the legal and treaty obligations signed by the previous royalist administration. This includes the decision to recognise Bahraini independence following the results of the independence survey. But accepting Bahraini independence does not automatically translate to a belief that this independence is necessarily permanent. This is the point at which the Islamic Republic's position on Bahrain diverges from that of the Shah's regime, which had essentially given up hope that Bahrain could one day be re-integrated into Iran.

The dominant view in the Islamic Republic is that force should never be used to alter Bahrain's legal and political status. Any change to Bahrain's status must necessarily flow from the people's will, a prospect which at least some Iranian leaders believe is realisable. This belief is founded on the fact that not only is the majority population of the Emirate Shia, but that a substantial proportion of the demographic is Iranian in origin. In that respect, Shariatmadari's outspoken views on Bahrain are a reflection of the aspirations of an important segment of the Iranian elites. In principle, Bahrain is potentially a 'part' of Iran, as long as the locals can be persuaded to accept this idea. From this perspective, the long process that can lead to such an outcome will be informed by a combination of domestic strife and foreign tyranny.

This is why Bahrain's political crisis is so important to Iranian regional calculations. It is not only about the rivalry with Saudi Arabia; the prospect of major political changes in Bahrain can potentially pave the way for reintegration with Iran, or failing that a close alliance bordering on protectorate status. But despite the high stakes involved, Iranian policy on Bahrain since the beginning of the Kingdom's political unrest in early 2011 has largely been a failure. Indeed, more than eight years after the start of Bahrain's version of the Arab Spring, the ruling Al-Khalifa royal family has managed to crush dissent by dissolving the main opposition party (Al-Wefaq) and sidelining the country's main Shia leader Sheikh Isa Qassim by stripping him of Bahraini nationality.

The upshot is that Bahrain is one arena where Saudi Arabia holds the upper hand in its regional rivalry with Iran. But this outcome has far less to do with Saudi strategic brilliance than with the confluence of powerful international interests in Bahrain. Indeed, both the US and the UK are strongly committed to the stability of the Al-Khalifa clan and by extension the ruling establishment, despite the latter's human rights abuses and discriminatory practices toward the Shia majority. Bahrain hosts the US navy's fifth fleet, an important fact which commits the US to defending 'stability' in the Kingdom, a policy that essentially amounts to the preservation of the status quo. Meanwhile, for a combination of economic, commercial and political reasons, the UK is heavily involved in Bahrain's security sector, by providing training and assisting with intelligence collection and exploitation.[18]

Yet, despite these big challenges, Iranian leaders and strategists believe they can still end up on top in Bahrain, provided they plan ahead for a long struggle. Bahrain's political and structural crisis—where the majority feels disenfranchised by the existing institutions—indicates that major political changes cannot be ruled out. Such a change could have occurred back in early 2011 had it not been for the Saudi-led military intervention. The same outcome may be obtained next time, too, unless Iran is sufficiently strong to deter a decisive Saudi intervention.

Kuwait: Uneasy Friendship

Like Bahrain, Kuwait is also home to a substantial Shia population, some of whom are of Iranian origin. Whilst Shias do not constitute a majority of the Kuwaiti population, they are sufficiently numerous (perhaps comprising as much as 40 per cent of the native population) to be considered as the most striking demographic feature of the Emirate. But unlike in Bahrain, Kuwaiti Shias are neither disenfranchised nor subject to systematic discrimination. Whilst Shia-led political parties in Kuwait are under-represented in the country's National Assembly,[19] there are no institutional barriers to their ability to campaign and mobilise.

Kuwait also ranks as the most liberal member of the GCC, with a high degree of female emancipation and a relatively free press. The Emirate's unique geographical position of close proximity to three regional giants—namely Iran, Iraq and Saudi Arabia—greatly complicates Kuwaiti diplomacy. It calls for a degree of subtle balance of power diplomacy interspersed with divide-and-rule tactics. This is not an art that comes naturally to Kuwait's rulers, the House of Sabah.

For nearly three decades, Kuwait had a pro-Soviet policy, and was the first to do so amongst the GCC states. Kuwait's pro-Soviet tilt was in part a reflection of the Emirate's ties to Iraq, despite the imminent threat which Iraq posed to Kuwaiti sovereignty. This threat was loudly expressed by Iraqi strongman Abdul Karim Qasim at the moment of Kuwaiti independence in 1961. Qasim's claim that newly independent Kuwait should be incorporated into Iraq prompted a concerted British campaign—known as Operation Vantage—to deter Iraq from invading its tiny southern neighbour.

The threat from Iraq was serious enough for Britain to maintain active contingency plans until 1971 in order to respond to any potential Iraqi aggression. Iraq–Kuwait relations improved considerably after the Iranian revolution, as Kuwait's leaders—similar to Saddam Hussein—had identified the newly formed Islamic Republic as a potential existential threat. In view of its substantial Shia population, and relatively hollow institutional base, Kuwait felt vulnerable in the face of the new Iranian leadership's revolutionary rhetoric. Active measures were taken against Shia activists—particularly those deemed to be receptive to Iranian propaganda—but in fairness the repression was nowhere near as drastic as in neighbouring Iraq.

The outbreak of the Iran–Iraq War in September 1980 drew Kuwait even closer to Iraq, and the two countries even developed an informal alliance. Kuwait was Iraq's main financier during the war, providing billions of dollars in grants and low-interest loans. Kuwait also transported Iraqi oil through the Persian Gulf—a vital strategic service in view of the fact that Iraq was virtually landlocked and was also unable to export oil via the Mediterranean Sea as Iran's ally Syria had blocked that route. This prompted Iranian retaliation against Kuwaiti tankers, beginning in the spring of 1984, following Iraq's repeated attacks on Iran's main export facility at Kharg island.

The situation escalated following Operation Earnest Will, which involved US naval protection for Kuwaiti-owned oil tankers. In late summer and autumn 1987, Iran increased attacks on Kuwaiti tankers to the point of launching silkworm missiles against Kuwait's main oil port.[20] In terms of a direct military threat, the situation for Kuwait had become critical following Iran's capture of Iraq's Al-Faw Peninsula in February 1986. The success of Iran's Operation Valfajr-8 had brought Iranian forces within only several kilometres of Bubiyan, Kuwait's largest island. Moreover, by deploying Chinese-made Silkworm missiles at the southern tip of the Al-Faw Peninsula, Iran was in a better position to threaten Kuwaiti-owned oil tankers.

Although the Iraqi invasion of Kuwait in August 1990 was not entirely surprising—as offensive Iraqi momentum had been building up for several months prior to the invasion—it produced a deep sense of betrayal in the Arab Gulf nations for the simple fact that the GCC states—led by Kuwait—had dutifully acted as Iraq's financial lifeline during the fateful years of the Iran–Iraq War. Moreover, the invasion flew in the face of CIA analysis, which in the late 1980s was pontificating that one of the main threats to Kuwait's stability could result from a potential alliance between Palestinian residents of Kuwait and pro-Iranian Shia elements.[21] As it turned out, many Palestinian residents welcomed the Iraqi invasion, whilst the Shias were at the forefront of resistance against Iraqi invaders.

Following the liberation of Kuwait in early 1991 by a US-led military alliance, Kuwaiti attitudes and policy toward Iran have been influenced by a degree of atonement. Indeed, there was widespread recognition across the Emirate—from the royal family to average people on the streets—that Kuwait had spectacularly miscalculated by wholeheartedly backing Iraq during the war. This attitudinal shift has resulted in the occasional pro-Iranian statements by Kuwaiti politicians. For example, in July 2008 the then speaker of the National Assembly, Jassem Al-Kharafi, said that the West was 'provoking' Iran on the nuclear issue.

But relations are far from cordial, not least because Kuwait remains close to Saudi Arabia and generally toes the GCC line on Iran. Kuwait regularly detains Iranian 'spies', the most famous recent case involving the so-called 'Abdali cell' which was allegedly uncovered after Kuwaiti security forces raided a farmhouse outside Kuwait City in 2015.[22] According to Kuwaiti authorities the cell was part of a broader network which sought to destabilise the Emirate at the behest of Iran and Lebanese Hezbollah. As part of the fallout from this case Kuwait closed down the Iranian cultural mission and expelled fifteen Iranian diplomats.[23]

Furthermore, Kuwait is home to a lively Salafi community[24] which often incites against Iran. Taken together, these factors, notably Kuwait's proximity to the KSA, its faithfulness to the GCC position, and the presence of a Salafi counter to the Shia community, indicate that Kuwait and Iran can never be natural friends. However, in view of lingering guilt over Kuwait's original sin of backing Saddam Hussein, and the Emirate's perennial need to balance its powerful neighbours, Iran is likely to continue to treat Kuwait as potentially one of the weakest links of the GCC.

Qatar: A Potential Ally?

If Kuwait is a potential weak link in the GCC bloc, Qatar is arguably the weakest link. This reality was brought into sharp relief following the outbreak of the Gulf crisis in June 2017. With Saudi and UAE encouragement the GCC imposed a blockade on Qatar. To date, at least two non-GCC states—Egypt and Jordan—have also joined or at minimum supported the blockade. The rationale behind the move is Qatar's alleged support for terrorism, sponsorship of political Islam and desire to forge links with Iran.

The blockade was initially supported enthusiastically by the Trump administration, which is generally strongly supportive of the new aggressive Saudi leadership led by Mohammad bin Salman. Indeed, Trump went as far as accusing Qatar of 'sponsoring' terrorism, a move that caused deep alarm inside the US diplomatic, defence and intelligence establishments. After all, Qatar is an ally of the US and host to US Central Command. Indeed, the largest concentration of American military personnel is located in Qatar, southwest of Doha at the Al-Udeid air base.[25]

It took the US foreign policy community some effort to correct Trump's parallel diplomacy. The result was the signing of a new arms deal and a strong re-affirmation of the longstanding military and security ties between the Emirate and the United States. Thus, despite Trump's peculiar brand of arson diplomacy, the US managed to assert its traditional position during the Qatar–GCC crisis: a neutral stance (when the antagonists are all friendly nations) which calls for the speedy resolution of the dispute and the return of stability.

But for Iran, the Saudi-led embargo of Qatar presented a rare opportunity to undermine the wide-ranging Saudi effort to isolate the Islamic Republic at the regional level. The formation of the GCC in May 1981 was in part designed to contain Iran's regional influence in the wake of the Islamic Revolution. It was a recognition by the regional states of Iran's radically altered strategic profile from one of policeman of the Gulf to potential spoiler. Not surprisingly, the US has supported the GCC from the outset, in the hope that it would grow into a cohesive supra-national political and security body.

By any measure, Qatar is a peculiar case. A tiny country—both in terms of geographical size and population—it wields a striking level of influence in the region and across the Arab world. A conservative Emirate—Wahhabism is the state creed—which partially enforces Sharia law, Qatar is also the hub of regional innovation in the education, training and media sectors. Through big research and media organisations, such as the Qatar Foundation and the Al-Jazeera broadcaster, Doha has made a huge impact, not just regionally, but on a global scale.

Qatar's dispute with Saudi Arabia and the UAE boils down to differences over a single aspect of foreign policy: Qatar's sponsorship of political Islam as embodied by the Muslim Brotherhood. Both Saudi Arabia and the UAE are extremely sensitive to the Muslim Brotherhood and have ruthlessly clamped down on the group at a domestic level, whilst sponsoring the Egyptian strongman Abdel Fattah el-Sisi to wage a war of eradication against the core of the Brotherhood movement in Egypt. Qatari sponsorship of the Brotherhood has wider ramifications, one of the most worrying being Qatar's proclivity to support militant Sunni Islamist groups, particularly in Syria. In that respect, Saudi and Emirati objections to Qatari foreign policy are not entirely irrational.

With respect to Iran, Saudi and Emirati accusations that Qatar is cosying up to the Islamic Republic are more about rhetoric than substance. But the accusations also reflect fears of potentiality, specifically that an over-confident Qatar might break with the GCC consensus by pursuing accommodation with Tehran. There is certainly a high degree of confidence underpinning Qatari foreign policy, as demonstrated, for example, by its informal alliance with Turkey, which involves the deployment of Turkish troops at a military camp in southern Doha. In due course, up to 3,000 Turkish soldiers may be deployed to Qatar,[26] thus deterring the Saudis and Emiratis from fomenting regime change in Doha.

Iran's relations with Qatar are dominated by a joint project to develop the largest offshore natural gas field in the world. Known as 'South Pars' in Iran and 'North Dome' in Qatar, the project has far-reaching ramifications for the energy policies of both states. Despite protestations to the contrary, South Pars/North Dome clearly has a geopolitical dimension, as it connects Iran at a profound level to a GCC member state. Whilst Iran has extensive trading relations with other GCC member states—notably with the UAE—these relations cannot be compared to the bilateral structural depth resulting from the South Pars/North Dome project.

Qatar's spat with the KSA and the UAE notwithstanding, Iran is wary of developing strong political ties with a small country boasting an over-ambitious and at times contradictory and volatile foreign policy. Indeed, whilst Qatar reaches out to Islamists of all stripes, it simultaneously extends the hand of friendship to Iran's arch-enemy Israel. Moreover, Qatari policy in regional hotspots is often inimical to Iranian strategic objectives. The best recent example is the Syrian conflict, where Qatar has been supporting an array of militant Islamist groups, including the local al-Qaeda affiliate originally known as the Nusra Front.

Qatar's inherent limitations notwithstanding, at minimum Iran sees the Saudi-led embargo as an opportunity to deepen schisms within the GCC and to prevent it from developing a strong regional posture. As a rival to Saudi Arabia, Qatar is potentially a friend of Iran. The strength of this friendship will depend to a large extent on Qatar's ability to develop a more conceptually coherent foreign policy and to show some willingness in accommodating Iranian interests and concerns across the region.

UAE: Engagement or Confrontation?

'Ansar Allah fires missile at Riyadh, next target is Dubai'—thus ran the incendiary headline of the ultra-conservative *Kayhan* on 6 November 2017. Ansar Allah refers to the Houthi movement in Yemen, which only two days earlier had fired a missile at Riyadh's King Khalid International Airport. The headline was too sensationalist—even by *Kayhan* standards—for the authorities to ignore, and elicited a two-day ban for the hardline daily paper.

Dubai had drawn the wrath of *Kayhan* due to the United Arab Emirates' deep involvement in the Yemen war. Indeed, as the war enters its fourth year, the UAE—as opposed to Saudi Arabia—is now widely considered to be the most influential foreign power in Yemen. Unlike Saudi Arabia, the UAE has deployed significant numbers of ground forces to Yemen.

Moreover, the UAE appears to be more engaged with key Yemeni stakeholders and thus in a better position to shape the war-torn country's politics. For instance, the UAE backs the Southern Resistance Forces (SRF), the armed wing of the Southern Transitional Council (STC), the primary secessionist movement in south Yemen. The SRF took full control of Aden in early February 2018 after days of bloody street fighting with forces loyal to the internationally recognised government led by President Abd-Rabbu Mansour Hadi.

The UAE's active participation in the Saudi-led war on the Houthis, as well as its apparent ability to shape Yemen's politics, places it firmly at odds with Iran's strategic objectives in the country. Whilst UAE-backed forces may have little desire (for now) to march on Sana'a to oust the Houthis, the fact that they are preparing the ground for yet another round of secession in Yemen bodes ill for Iran's plans. The Islamic Republic seeks a united Yemen—symbolically, at least—that is perennially at odds with Saudi Arabia. The idea is to create a long-term political and security headache for the Saudis. Secession undermines that vision as it threatens to embroil Yemeni parties in prolonged civil war.

The UAE's prominent role in Yemen is a clear sign of the Emirates' growing weight in the region. This development holds both peril and promise for Iran, as a more assertive UAE is bound to confront Tehran more boldly whilst at the same time maintaining a degree of distance from Riyadh. Long considered an extension of Saudi Arabia on key regional issues, the war in Yemen clearly demonstrates that the Emirates has developed a set of interests, goals and policies that are markedly distinct from those pursued by Riyadh.

However, there is unlikely to be any breakthrough in Iranian–UAE relations in the short term as the Emirates takes a dim view of Iran's regional ambitions, in particular the Islamic Republic's attempt at creating a sustainable sphere of influence in the Levant. However, unlike the KSA and Qatar, the UAE is not known to have extended financial and logistical support to militant Islamist groups in Syria. This has been in keeping with the UAE's idiosyncratic approach to the Syrian conflict, as illustrated by its dispatch of South American mercenaries to Syria to fight alongside the coalition battling the so-called Islamic State group.[27] Furthermore, the UAE's policy in Syria has diverged from that of the KSA as the former has been careful not to single out Iran as the only bad actor in the Syrian conflict (as the KSA often does). Rather, the UAE has expressed concern at the 'colonial' role of Turkey as well as Iran in Syria.[28]

Regional flashpoints aside, Iran and UAE have deep differences at the bilateral level. Indeed, the UAE is the only GCC member state embroiled in a territorial dispute with Iran. This dispute centres on three islands in the Persian Gulf: Abu Musa and the Greater and Lesser Tunbs. The genesis of this dispute goes back to the manner of British withdrawal from the region in 1971. The UAE gained independence from the UK in late 1971, at around the same time as Bahrain. It is widely believed that the Shah made a deal with Britain over Bahrain, pledging to respect Bahraini independence as long as the UK turned a blind eye to Iran's seizure of the three islands.

Whilst the newly formed UAE immediately contested the seizure, the issue lay dormant for more than twenty years before it was suddenly revived in the spring of 1992. Whilst the UAE does not appear to be overly determined to seize back the islands, at the same time it is reluctant to relinquish its claims altogether.

It is noteworthy that there is a degree of division in the Emirates as to the seriousness of the issue, with Dubai apparently not keen on pressing the sovereignty claim, whilst Sharjah and Ras al-Khaimah hold the opposite view. Nevertheless, the issue makes headlines occasionally and creates diplomatic headaches for both sides. This happened most recently in April 2012, when the then Iranian president Mahmoud Ahmadinejad visited Abu Musa, thus provoking a furious response from the Emirati side.

But Iran–UAE bilateral ties also have a positive side, as evidenced by the hundreds of thousands of Iranians who have made the Emirates their home. This substantial demographic acts as a cultural bridge, in addition to facilitating trade and commerce, which continues to increase year on year. In fact, the UAE is currently Iran's second biggest export destination (after China) and accounts for 17 per cent of all Iranian exports.[29]

Looking ahead, Iran will be keen to strengthen trade links and to use that as leverage in managing political disputes with the UAE, including the territorial dispute centred on the three Persian Gulf islands. More broadly, Iranian diplomacy will be alert to any opportunity which has the potential of creating a rift between the UAE and Saudi Arabia on key regional issues. Barring any sudden and dramatic shifts in attitudes and resultant positions, the current trajectory suggests that the two sides can gradually move away from intermittent confrontation to place bilateral ties on a stable footing. But this shift is likely to unfold over decades, as opposed to years.

Oman: Enduring Friendship

The Sultanate of Oman counts as the only GCC member state, and one of only a few Arab states, to maintain long-term cordial relations with

Iran. This enduring friendship is important to Tehran for three reasons. First, Muscat is able to present Tehran's views and concerns at the GCC level, thus introducing at least a minimal degree of balance and objectivity to GCC proceedings. Second, the strong ties with Oman break the Arab consensus against Iran and undermine the myth that Syria is Iran's only true friend in the Arab world. Third, owing to its close ties to key Western powers, Oman can mediate between Iran and the West on the most sensitive issues.

The context for Iranian–Omani friendship is Iran's military intervention in the Dhofar rebellion in the early and mid-1970s. The first deployment of Iranian forces took place in 1973 with the dispatch of 1,200 troops, alongside heavy weapons and attack helicopters. By the following year the Iranian intervention had expanded into a full-fledged taskforce (known as the Imperial Iranian Task Force) numbering just over 4,000 military personnel and support staff. This was Iran's first military expedition in the modern era and its timing coincided with the rapid expansion and modernisation of the Iranian armed forces. Indeed, the intervention gave the Iranian armed forces the opportunity to test new concepts, skills, strategies and, of course, weaponry, freshly supplied by the US and the UK.

Notwithstanding the fact that the Iranian intervention occurred toward the tail end of the Dhofar rebellion—with the rebels mostly on the back foot by the early 1970s—the Imperial Iranian Task Force is widely credited with speeding up the conclusion of the conflict. The conflict officially ended in January 1976, even though sporadic clashes continued for several more years. The Iranian intervention was entirely in keeping with Iran's orientation and commitments at the time. Indeed, as the unofficial policeman of the Persian Gulf, and an avowed ally of the United States, it was in Iran's interest to team up with Britain to defeat a leftist rebellion which enjoyed the support of left-wing and revolutionary forces across the region. In addition, the Dhofar rebels also had the qualified support of Saudi Arabia, at least in the early phase of the campaign. Therefore, blocking Saudi intentions in Oman was an additional incentive for Iran to intervene decisively in the conflict.

The Iranian intervention earned Oman's enduring respect, not only because it removed a threat to the integrity of the state, but equally because it incentivised Oman to make the radical reforms necessary in order to modernise and function as a truly independent state. At the diplomatic and military levels, the Iranian intervention set the context for a decades-long mutual understanding and cooperation. Oman is the only GCC member state which cooperates with Iran at a military level, as demonstrated by regular high-level contacts between the Iranian and Omani navies.

Bilateral ties are sufficiently strong that Oman has consistently resisted pressure by Saudi Arabia and the United States to adopt a critical stance on Iran. Beyond issues of friendship and an enduring debt of gratitude, there is a clear understanding in Muscat that the country needs to balance its relations with powerful regional and extra-regional states with a view to safeguarding its core national security interests.

But there is another dimension to this story, namely that the West, in particular the United States, actually values Oman's proximity to Iran, as it means that Muscat can act as a bridge between the two sides on a wide range of strategic, tactical and operational issues. At the strategic level, Oman is widely credited for hosting the initial secret talks which paved the way for the nuclear deal or JCPOA. This role can only be performed because of the high level of trust that all sides maintain in Oman, and speaks to Muscat's ability to play the role of honest broker as well as patient host.

Tactically and operationally too, Oman is useful to both sides. During periods of acute stress, Muscat can help defuse tensions. In this respect the close partnership between the Iranian and Omani navies is crucial, as important tactical and operational level information can be conveyed to the Iranian, American and British sides, in a timely and efficient manner. Oman has also intervened to resolve non-military but security-related issues between Iran and the US, and to a lesser extent also with the UK. For example, in September 2011 Oman helped secure the release of two American hikers who were detained along the Iran–Iraq border in July 2009 and subsequently sentenced to eight years in prison on spying charges. A third American had been released a year earlier, also as a result of Omani mediation.

At a broader level, the cordial relations between Iran and Oman rest on a degree of cultural understanding and respect. In religious terms, Oman differs from other Arab Gulf states in that it is not, strictly speaking, a Sunni state. The dominant school of Islam in Oman is *al-Ibadiyyah* (or Ibadism) which diverges in several important respects from the four schools of Sunnism. In strategic terms, Oman's profile as a non-Sunni state allows the Sultanate to completely detach itself from the region's sectarian undercurrents and thus adopt an authentically neutral position on the Iranian–Saudi spat.

By all credible accounts, the Iranian–-Omani friendship is set to continue as both sides are fully cognisant of the wide-ranging benefits which accrue from this partnership. Nevertheless, it is important to recognise Oman's limitations as a small country (in terms of population) with a relatively modest foreign policy. Iran cannot rely on Oman to break the GCC's will in countering Iranian interests and positions. But in the years ahead, the Islamic Republic may decide to test the friendship to its limits by relying on Oman to help secure Iran's position in neighbouring Yemen. To that end, there have already been unconfirmed reports that Oman has helped facilitate the transfer of arms to the Houthis in Yemen.[30]

ISRAEL
FRIEND OR FOE?

At first glance, the title of this chapter might seem far-fetched, as it is conventional wisdom in many circles that Iran and Israel are deadly foes set on each other's destruction. But it was not always that way. Before the Iranian revolution the Israelis maintained an active diplomatic presence in Tehran, headed by the capable diplomat and intelligence officer Yuri Lubrani.

To this day there are plenty of Iranians who believe that far from being natural enemies, Iran and Israel are in fact potentially natural friends. Their argument often rests on the assumption that as non-Arab powers surrounded by supposed Arab 'enemies', Iran and Israel should cooperate, as opposed to being at loggerheads.

History is also cited to support this position. For example, the rescue of the Jews from Babylon by the founder of the Persian Empire, Cyrus the Great, is used to argue for a supposedly 'special' relationship between the Jews and the Iranians.

It is difficult to know how widespread these views and feelings are in Iran, but they are certainly not the majority opinion. The broad mass of Iranian public opinion continues to sympathise with the Palestinians and their plight. Iranians may not all agree with the hardline anti-Israeli position of their government, but by the same token most have little time for pro-Israeli sentiment.

Yet residual pro-Israel sentiment—which goes hand in hand with pro-American instincts—flares up in the country, often on the sidelines of anti-government demonstrations. This was evident in June 2018 when much of the Bazaar erupted in protest in the wake of the currency crisis. Some demonstrators—apparently unconnected to the Bazaari merchants—were heard chanting 'death to Palestine'!

This extreme slogan is less a reflection of anti-Palestinian sentiment than annoyance with the government's near-daily pro-Palestinian propaganda on the state broadcaster and other outlets. Moreover, this extreme segment of the protesters—in line with more mainstream protesters—have identified foreign policy as the Achilles heel of the Islamic Republic. By taking aim at specific foreign policy choices (such as support for the Palestinian cause), the protesters believe they are engaging in a delegitimising exercise whose ultimate aim is the overthrow of the political system.

From the outset, the Islamic Republic identified Israel as an ideological foe. This was hardly surprising as the central forces of the revolution—as embodied by the Shia Islamists clustered around the leadership of Ayatollah Khomeini—had opposed the State of Israel from its foundation in 1948. Militant groups like the Fedayian-e Islam (Devotees of Islam), whose ideology lives on in the conservative grouping Hezb-e-Moatalefeyeh Eslami (Islamic Coalition Party), staked out their anti-Shah platform at least in part on the latter's perceived support for Israel.

These suspicions cannot be reduced to conspiracy theories. By all credible accounts, the Shah's regime had established links with Israel almost since the latter's foundation in 1948. In subsequent decades, the Israelis got involved in many aspects of Iranian governance, especially in the agricultural sector. Most controversially of all, the Israelis helped the Shah to develop a sophisticated security state, as embodied by the SAVAK secret police and intelligence agency. Iranian intelligence personnel connected to SAVAK and other agencies were sent to Israel for training. Israelis also came to Tehran to offer expertise and advice to SAVAK.

Indeed, an important part of Yuri Lubrani's mission in the 1970s was to build on these ties and forge ever closer intelligence cooperation between Iran and Israel. These ties infuriated the revolutionaries and help to explain, at least in part, the anger and hatred directed at Israel during the momentous events of the Iranian revolution.

In a highly symbolic move, the revolutionaries handed the Israeli diplomatic mission in Tehran to the Palestinian Liberation Organisation (PLO) whose then leader Yasser Arafat became the first foreign dignitary to visit revolutionary Iran. This was followed by Ayatollah Khomeini's designation of Quds (Jerusalem) Day on the last Friday of the fasting month of Ramadan. In the past four decades, this occasion has emerged as the most visible sign of the Islamic Republic's opposition to the state of Israel.

Huge rallies are held across Iran and the wider region to condemn Israel's continuing occupation of Palestinian lands and to call for the restitution of Palestinian rights. The Quds Day rallies are also staged in the West, with the UK's capital London as the primary venue for Iran-aligned pro-Palestinian demonstrators. The considerable time and resources invested in organising these rallies speaks to the Islamic Republic's strong desire to furnish its anti-Zionist credentials and to keep it very much in the public eye, both at home and abroad.

Beyond Quds Day, anti-Israeli sentiment is on full display at almost all official public gatherings. Friday prayer assemblies are a favourite venue to vent anti-Israeli and anti-American feelings, as encapsulated by the slogans of 'Death to America' and 'Death to Israel' which permeate these events. These slogans are important both in terms of political affirmation in the domestic sphere and as demonstrating continuing public approval of the state's foreign policy.

These slogans are so widespread—and have been expressed for so long—that it is difficult to imagine the Islamic Republic without them. It is easy to dismiss the obsession with Israel as demonstrating the Islamic Republic's need for a perennial enemy, the 'other', at which public anger and frustration can be directed. From this point of view, the state's anti-Zionist ideology is also a clever diversionary tactic as it helps to divert public attention away from domestic woes.

But these reductive descriptions at best capture only a small part of the picture. Anti Zionism and opposition to the state of Israel are so ingrained in the Islamic Republic's culture, its view of itself and how it views the outside world that Iranian leaders would be loath to give it up. Whilst there is a lively debate in academic circles regarding the extent to which this opposition is driven by ideology, as opposed to strategic necessity, there is no denying that an inimical posture vis-à-vis the Jewish state is the driving force of Iran's regional policy, at least in ideological terms. It is the raison d'etre of the so-called 'Axis of Resistance' which defines the Iranian-led alliance in the Middle East.

Ideological or Strategic?

A minority opinion promotes the view that the enmity between Iran and Israel is essentially strategic in nature as opposed to ideological. The strongest proponent of this view is Iranian-Swedish activist and scholar Trita Parsi, whose book *Treacherous Alliance*[1] was widely regarded as ground-breaking in this area.

Similar ideas were propagated—albeit with less vigour—by the Israeli journalist Ronen Bergman in his book *The Secret War with Iran.*[2] According to Bergman, at least some of the resentment of Iranian revolutionary leaders toward Israel revolved around financial disputes, as Israel refused to honour its pre-revolutionary debts. These were loans which Israel had obtained from Iran during the Shah years.

Iran and Israel are indeed strategic rivals; in that sense the Shah's regime was mistaken in its belief that the two countries' vital national security interests converge. The perceived enmity of Arabs towards them and a shared sense of isolation in the Middle East region is not sufficient to generate long-term commonality of interest.

To illustrate this point, plenty of the elites and common people in the Arab world have a dim view of Iran, but this has no negative impact on the solidarity many Iranians have with fellow Muslims, particularly with the Palestinians. A significant constituency amongst the Palestininans supported Saddam Hussein during the Iran–Iraq War, but again, this had no material impact on Iranian sentiments towards the Israeli–Palestinian conflict.

As Nathan Thrall has pointed out, a major flaw in Parsi's book is that it ignores the role of ideology, ethnicity and religion in the foreign policy of states. In this case, it is a mistake to ignore the part that the ideological nature of the Islamic Republic plays in its confrontation with the Jewish state. After all, Iran is also locked in strategic competition with Saudi Arabia, Egypt and Turkey, but does not aspire to bring about the demise of these states.

Another major problem with the strategic rivalry argument is that Iranian leaders, policy makers and strategists have never framed the confrontation with Israel in such terms. In fact, all the key stakeholders in Iran go out of their way to bring Israel's lack of strategic depth to attention. From the Iranian point of view, the effort to draw a strategic equivalence between Iran and Israel is essentially an attempt to denigrate Iran's actual and potential strategic reach.

Stripped of hubris and pride, this viewpoint nonetheless has an objective basis in facts. Israel is after all a small state with limited resources. It is surrounded by unfriendly countries and since its foundation it has fought a losing battle in trying to win over segments of public opinion in neighbouring countries, as well as in the wider region. Indeed, Israeli leaders, military commanders and strategists readily attest that their country lacks strategic depth.

The notion that Iran and Israel have deep national security interests in common stems at least in part from Israel's 'Alliance of the Periphery' doctrine. Developed soon after the foundation of the Jewish state in 1948, this doctrine called for the development of ties to non-Arab nations on the periphery of the Middle East. It was specifically targeted at Iran, Turkey and Ethiopia.

By the late 1970s this doctrine, and associated strategy, had scored significant successes, as Israel enjoyed good relations with all three targeted states. The cultivation of ties with Muslim-majority Iran and Turkey was especially significant as it helped dispel the notion that Israel is by nature unable to develop friendly relations to Muslim states.

Needless to say, the Iranian revolution dealt a body blow to this Israeli strategy, as it removed the most important target state from the equation. But the doctrine—albeit in a modified form—continues to play a role in Israeli strategic thought. It is noteworthy that Israel's ties to Turkey have proven to be lasting and appear to be sustainable for the long-term, even in the context of an insidiously Islamising Turkey under the rule of the Justice and Development Party.

To this day, Israeli leaders never tire of proclaiming their support for the Iranian people and their desire to restore the status quo ante by normalising Iranian–Israeli relations. Israeli Prime Minister

Benjamin Netanyahu has taken this politics of effusive gestures to theatrical extremes, as demonstrated by his 2018 video messages to the Iranian people.

In the first video, in late May, Netanyahu praised Iranian 'brilliance' and expressed the hope that one day Iranian and Israeli entrepreneurs can work together for the 'betterment' of all humanity.[3] In the second video, in June, Netanyahu offered water management expertise to Iran.[4] This was a clever gesture aimed at bringing Iran's water crisis into sharp relief and exploiting the vulnerabilities that flow from this sense of deep crisis.

In the third video, later in June, the Israeli prime minister expressed support for anti-government protests, whilst at the same time congratulating the Iranian national football team for its relatively good performance in the 2018 FIFA World Cup in Russia.[5]

Even by Netanyahu's flamboyant standards, this peculiar form of public diplomacy is ground breaking. The Israeli prime minister is the first Western leader to address the Iranian people in a consistently direct manner. Moreover, Netanyahu demonstrates tremendous political acumen in identifying and exploiting Iran's core vulnerabilities.

However, the underlying logic driving the latest Israeli public relations stunt could not be less original. Netanyahu's direct messages to the Iranian public—over the heads of Iran's government—are based on the (perhaps hopeful) understanding that there is a big divide between the people and the 'regime', which a foreign power can exploit to its advantage. By addressing the Iranian people directly, Netanyahu is trying to insert himself into this putative conflict.

It is unlikely that Iranian leaders and officials are overly worried by these PR stunts. Israel may appeal to a small constituency in Iran, but the idea that Israeli leaders can markedly influence Iranian public opinion, let alone shape events inside the country, is far-fetched.

But this reality will not stop Israeli leaders from trying to have an input into the social and political unrest which appears to be a fixed feature in Iranian national life for the foreseeable future. The Trump administration has the same aspiration, believing that Western intervention can exacerbate Iran's socio-economic and political woes.

This is a profound miscalculation which takes no heed of recent history. One of the primary drivers of the Iranian revolution was opposition to the pro-Western stance of the country. The late Shah only realised the depth of this opposition toward the end of his rule, and by then it was far too late. The Shah's increasingly independent role in the Organization of the Petroleum Exporting Countries (OPEC) and his occasional jabs at the West unfolded in the context of this late realisation.

Whilst a significant strand of public opinion—if not the majority of the population—wants stable relations with the West, this does not translate to accepting the role of a vassal state. One of the enduring achievements of the Iranian revolution is that it has internalised a sense of fierce independence. It is a collective psychological state that no political force can shake off.

Many in the Arab world are keen to continually draw attention to Iran's indirect—and, according to some, direct[6]—dealings with Israel in the 1980s, as part of a broader propaganda offensive against Iran. The objective is to discredit the ideological foundations of the Islamic Republic by striking at the core of that ideology, namely its uncompromising stance towards the Jewish state.

Loud propaganda by Iran's Arab foes aside, there is little doubt that the Islamic Republic had indirect contact with Israelis, through a chain of arms dealers and similarly undesirable types. The setting was the Iran–Iraq War, and Iran's need for arms, particularly spare parts for its largely American-made equipment, forced the Iranian government to look far and wide for suitable markets.

Motivated by profit, intelligence collection and a desire to gain a foothold in Iranian defence-related organisations, the Israelis tried hard to address some of Iran's war-time requirements. This was particularly the case in the early stages of the Iran–Iraq War (1980–1981), when the newly restructured defence ministry lacked the resources and expertise to identify and exploit illegal international arms markets. Indeed, in many cases the Iranians were not even aware that they might be dealing with Israelis or Israeli-connected networks.

The situation changed as the war dragged on and the Iranians built up expertise and resources suitable for engaging with international arms merchants. From the mid-1980s onwards, the Ministry of Intelligence and Security (MOIS) took the lead role in identifying and approaching suitable arms dealers. Working in partnership with specialised procurement networks in the Ministry of Defence, the MOIS was able to satisfy some of Iran's critical defence-related needs, notably spare parts for F-4s, F-5s and F-14s.

The Iran–Contra scandal of 1986–1987—and the Israeli role in it, in the form of the flamboyant journalist and counter-terrorism advisor Amiram Nir—revealed the lengths to which Iran was forced to go in order to satisfy basic war-related needs. For example, the procurement of BGM-71 TOW[7] anti-tank missiles was critical to Iran's relative successes in the Karbala-4 and Karbala-5 offensives of late 1986 and early 1987. These weapons were procured under exceptionally difficult circumstances and in many cases at exorbitant costs. It has been suggested that in some cases the Iranians paid six times the market value of weapons.

In view of the lucrative nature of this business, it is of little surprise that a wide range of countries, organisations and individuals sought to exploit this market. Israel was no exception to this rule as Israeli agencies and individuals scrambled to make a profit at the expense of Iran's sanctioned arms procurement industry. The only remarkable note about the Israeli involvement in the arms shipments was the hope by Israeli leaders and officials that they could potentially engage in outreach to certain elements of the Iranian establishment. This was at best a forlorn hope and as the course of subsequent events showed, it came to nothing.

It is difficult to make a coherent argument against Iran's commitment to the anti-Israeli cause by drawing attention to indirect dealings with Israelis during a period of acute national stress. As the Iran–Contra affair demonstrated, Iran's position in the war was becoming increasingly desperate. Sanctioned by the world's major powers, Iran's plight was only made worse by the fact that its enemy Iraq had ready access to practically all the weapons and equipment it desired.

Indeed, Iraq was able to source arms and equipment from both Western and Eastern sources at will. The Iraqi air force was well supplied by both the Soviet Union and France, with the latter even suspected of 'loaning' Iraq fighter pilots to fly the much-vaunted Super Étendards. These planes were given to Iraq on a temporary lease and were used by the Iraqis to attack Iranian tankers and merchant ships in the Persian Gulf.

The Iranians could only look on with envy and resentment at Iraq's easy ability to replenish and reinforce its war-related stocks. A half-hearted joke in the Iranian air force at the time was that for every fighter jet Iraq lost, it got two in return from the Soviet Union. This was not far from the truth, as evidenced by the ever-expanding Iraqi air force. Indeed, the Iraqi air force nearly doubled during the course of the war, transformed into one of the world's largest air forces by the summer of 1988.

But what about Israel's deepest motivations and calculations during the war? For example, some in the Arab world believed that deep down, Israel wanted Iran to have the upper hand in the war, if not to win it outright. This argument is based on the belief that Israel regarded Baathist Iraq as a 'real' and 'permanent' enemy, whereas Iran was considered only a 'temporary' one. Once the revolutionary fervour had subsided in Tehran—the proponents of this theory argue—the Israelis could once again look forward to cultivating Iran as a potential ally.

Proponents of this theory can point to the fact that Israel took direct military action against Iraq, whereas none was taken against Iran, even though pro-Iranian elements in Lebanon regularly clashed with Israeli soldiers from 1982 onwards. The Israeli attack on the Iraqi nuclear reactor Osirak in June 1981 was so controversial that it even elicited condemnation from powerful quarters in the United States.

This theory gains more traction in the light of the fact that Iran had bombed the same reactor eight months earlier, in the opening days of the Iran–Iraq War, but the Iranian F-4 phantoms had managed to inflict only minor damage on the reactor. This daring Iranian mission—which deliberately avoided bombing the heart of the facility for fear of producing radioactive fallout—was the first ever strike on a nuclear reactor.

Over the years allegations have been made that the two strikes (Iran's Operation Scorch Sword in September 1980 and Israel's Operation Opera in June 1981) had been co-ordinated through joint meetings between Iranian and Israeli experts and planners. These allegations have weak sources and are probably motivated by a political desire to contrive Iranian–Israeli collaboration.

For example, Trita Parsi in *Treacherous Alliance* cites a former Israeli intelligence officer turned arms dealer, Ari Ben-Menashe, to claim that the Iranians had met the Israelis one month prior to Operation Opera and had even offered to allow Israeli jets to land at Tabriz airbase in the event of an emergency. These are bold claims and are, on the face of it, highly improbable. Absent much stronger sources, it is difficult to treat them seriously.

By all credible accounts, Israel was interested in prolonging the Iran–Iraq War to the greatest extent possible with a view to exhausting the protagonists. The Israeli rationale for this policy was simple: it considered both countries to be enemies of the Jewish state and wished to see their military capabilities severely diminished. The facilitation of arms deliveries to Iran must be seen as part of a broader strategy to prolong the Iran–Iraq War. After all, Iran needed arms and spare parts to sustain its war effort.

This Israeli strategy was in keeping with broader Western policy to prolong the Iran–Iraq War. The United Kingdom, for example, was also interested in prolonging the war, a view candidly set out by the late Alan Clark, a maverick Tory minister under Margaret Thatcher. The UK sold arms to both protagonists, even though Iraqi procurement networks were far more active on UK soil than their Iranian rivals were.

Israel may have considered Iraq a more proximate threat—for both geographical and ethno-cultural reasons—but there is little evidence that the Israeli leadership was to any extent soft on Iran. Indeed, as events in Lebanon had demonstrated, Iran was shaping up to become a major adversary to the Jewish state and a formidable long-term threat. It is doubtful that the Israelis were not cognisant of this long-term threat in the 1980s.

For its part, Iran did not allow the Iran–Iraq War to distract it from pursuing its anti-Zionist strategy. If Iranian leaders and strategists viewed Israel as a potential friend during the war, they did a tremendously good job at hiding their feelings. Indeed, throughout the war the Iranians continued to produce strong anti-Israeli rhetoric and propaganda. They even depicted their Iraqi enemies as part of the Zionist project, as expressed by the bombastic description of Saddam Hussein's Iraq as the 'Baathist–Zionist regime'.

At the practical level too, Iran advanced its anti-Zionist agenda through concrete actions on the ground. Lebanon was the primary venue, following the Israeli invasion in June 1982. Iran had sparred with Israeli proxy forces in Lebanon even prior to the invasion, as evidenced by growing hostility between pro-Iranian elements and the Lebanese Phalange forces led by Samir Geagea. The latter struck a big blow to Iranian influence and prestige in Lebanon by abducting three Iranian diplomats and a reporter barely a month after the Israeli invasion.

The legacy of that abduction continues to haunt Iranian diplomacy, not least because officially Iran maintains the men are still alive and being held in an Israeli prison. According to most accounts, the Iranian diplomats and reporter were probably murdered by the Phalangists soon after their abduction.

Iran's behaviour during the Iran–Iraq War demonstrated that whilst the Islamic Republic was more than willing to exploit Israeli strategic doctrines (and wishful thinking), for instance by procuring arms from Israeli-connected circles, Iranian leaders never lost sight of the bigger picture. As demonstrated by Iranian war-time propaganda, the Iranian leadership consistently depicted Israel as a far graver threat than Iraq's Baathists.

Israel is the one case where the ideology of the Islamic Republic completely supersedes any actual or potential strategic benefits or trade-offs. To that end, it is noteworthy that much of Iran's anti-Israeli infrastructure and resources was developed during the Iran–Iraq War. The Hezbollah movement which emerged from Israel's invasion of Lebanon in 1982 was essentially developed in the mid- to late 1980s. And there is every indication that Iranian strategists and planners had the distant future in mind when they invested considerable resources in their ideological compatriots in the Levant.

The scale and complexity of Iran's anti-Israeli infrastructure—and the nature of Iran's outreach to anti-Israeli groups—are at the heart of Iran's challenge to the Jewish state. This infrastructure has been designed to withstand attritional warfare. It is not designed to deliver short, sharp shocks or even a killer blow to the Israeli state.

Moreover, a careful study of this infrastructure reveals that it has been designed and developed in a way that is consistent with Iran's stated policy of ultimately abolishing Israel through peaceful means, that is to say through a referendum—or some other consensual means—which votes the Jewish state out of existence. To that end, at least at the policy level, the Islamic Republic is not committed to the physical destruction of Israel. Setting out these nuances in detail is key to understanding Iran's anti-Israeli strategy.

Outreach to Palestinians

From the very outset revolutionary Iran has extended support to the Palestinians. The former leader of the PLO, Yasser Arafat, was the first foreign dignitary to visit Tehran in February 1979 following the overthrow of the Shah. In a highly symbolic move the building housing the Israeli mission in Tehran was handed over to Arafat and the PLO.

For his part, Yasser Arafat could hardly hide his glee at such an unexpected outcome. Only a few weeks before, Iran was Israel's tacit ally, cooperating with the Jewish state in several spheres, including the supply of oil. There was plenty of clandestine cooperation as well, as evidenced by Mossad's advisory role to the SAVAK. The overthrow of the Shah had turned all that upside down, and Arafat was clearly intent on fully exploiting the new reality.

Declaring Iran his 'second home', Arafat proclaimed that Iranians and Palestinians represented 'two revolutions in one revolution and two peoples in one people'.[8] The former Palestinian leader clearly believed that he could count on the new Iranian leadership to provide significant resources to his organisation. But his ambitions went further; even during that early visit he alluded to his influence amongst Iranian revolutionary factions, notably the fiercely militant Mojahedin-e Khalq.

George Habash's Marxist Popular Front for the Liberation of Palestine, a rival wing in the PLO, exercised influence over the overtly Marxist-Leninist Iranian Fedayian-e Khalq. Arafat appeared to believe he could mediate in the disputes between the rival peripheral factions of the revolution, with a view to maximising their influence with the inner core of the revolution centred around Ayatollah Khomeini and his inner circle. This was blatant interference in internal Iranian affairs and one whose potential fruits would be denied to Arafat.

Whilst marginal groups like the Mojahedin-e Khalq and the Fedayian-e Khalq appeared to be prepared to allow the PLO to interfere in Iranian domestic affairs, the Iranian revolutionary authorities were not so positively disposed toward the political and strategic ambitions of the Palestinian leader.

For a start, Ayatollah Khomeini and the leading clerics in the Council of the Islamic Revolution (Shurayeh Enghelab-e Eslami), such as Seyed Ali Khamenei, Hashemi-Rafsanjani and Ayatollah Beheshti, were suspicious of the secular and nationalist ethos of the PLO. Whilst the council recognised the leadership role of the PLO, this was a grudging acceptance, for lack of a viable (that is, Islamic) alternative.

The Iranian revolutionary authorities were also well aware of Arafat's regional ambitions and his desire to play off the new revolutionary authority in Iran against the conservative regimes of the Persian Gulf and the wider Arab dominion. It suited Arafat that conflict should prevail between these powers, a messy state of affairs which the Palestinian leader could exploit in favour of the PLO and for his own personal ambitions.

The upshot was that the Iranian revolutionary leaders did not consider the PLO a suitable partner in their quest to confront Israel. Arafat and the PLO were default allies, whose temporary utility was predetermined by a range of ideological and political considerations.

The outbreak of the Iran–Iraq War in September 1980, and Arafat's effusive support for Saddam Hussein, confirmed the worst fears of Iranian leaders. Consequently, relations with the PLO were downgraded, but never completely severed. Arafat and the main Fatah factions of the PLO were subjected to regular criticisms—and at times blistering attacks—by the Iranian media, not only for siding with Iraq but for not being fully committed to an uncompromising confrontation with Israel.

The PLO presence in revolutionary Iran had always been highly exaggerated. For example, the Shah's last prime minister, Shapour Bakhtiar, had once claimed that there were up to 20,000 PLO advisors seconded to various revolutionary organisations, notably the Islamic Revolutionary Guards Corps (IRGC). But a CIA report, which was declassified in 2010, claimed that as few as half a dozen PLO military officials were attached to the Revolutionary Guards in August 1980.[9]

By early 1981 the PLO presence in Iran was negligible and did not exceed the personnel based at the Palestinian 'embassy' in Tehran. As the decade progressed, a role reversal gradually took shape. The Islamic Republic, which had been fearful of PLO influence over domestic Iranian affairs, began to take concerted steps aimed at developing strong and lasting influence over the various Palestinian factions. Iranian intelligence organisations sponsored various influential figures within all the PLO organisations, including Fatah.

Whilst Iran could not alter Fatah's pro-Iraq position, it could at least keep open channels of communication with the Palestinians with a view to gaining influence over the anti-Zionist struggle. A careful review of the Iranians' behaviour and choices beginning in the early 1980s strongly suggests that Iran had its eyes on Israel all along. What happened inside Palestinian factions, and their impact on the Palestinian people, was of secondary importance.

The emergence of Hamas in 1987 greatly expanded Iran's range of options. On the face of it, Hamas was unabashedly Islamic and thus a viable alternative to the secular and nationalist Fatah. Hamas also heralded the potential of a far more effective Palestinian leadership in the struggle for Palestinian rights and ultimately Palestinian statehood. It had been evident for a long time—in fact even before the victory of the Iranian revolution—that the PLO was an atrophying organisation whose commitment to a full-fledged struggle against Israel was in dispute.

Certainly, the Iranian revolutionary leadership was always fearful that Arafat would eventually 'sell out' to the Israelis by entering into comprehensive peace negotiations. The long shadow of Anwar Sadat and the Camp David Accords of September 1978 continued to haunt Iran's revolutionary leadership.

The Iranians' fears were two-fold. Foremost, a comprehensive peace agreement with Israel legitimised the Jewish state and severely curtailed—if not removed—the ability to abolish it in the long term. Second, a lasting peace agreement undermined the Iranians' ability to export the Islamic Revolution across the region. The Iranian leadership had identified the ripple effects flowing from the Arab–Israeli conflict as a potential primary driver of revolutionary and radical action across the region.

The PLO's decisive move toward peace with Israel did not unduly unnerve the Tehran leadership as they had anticipated such an outcome all along. The Oslo Accords were preceded by the 1991 Madrid Conference, which was sponsored by both superpowers, even though by that stage the Soviet Union was at death's door.

Iran countered the Madrid Conference with its own event, which was staged shortly before the international gathering in Spain. Officially dubbed the International Conference on Supporting Palestinian Intifada (ICSPI), this rival gathering brought together die-hard Palestinian factions opposed to Fatah's move toward serious negotiations with the Israelis.

It was also attended by other Arab radicals aligned to Tehran, including the then leader of Lebanese Hezbollah Abbas al-Musawi. The Hezbollah secretary-general was assassinated by Israel in an Apache helicopter attack in southern Lebanon only four months after the Tehran conference.

The ICSPI has been held periodically since the inaugural conference in autumn 1991. There was a ten-year hiatus before the conference was reconvened in April 2001. Subsequent to that it has been held in 2006, 2009 and 2011. Whilst later conferences have been characterised by a formulaic and even perfunctory attitude to the issues at hand, the inaugural conference in October 1991 was important insofar as it demonstrated Iranian initiative and resolve on the Palestinian issue.

The Iranian leadership was confident of the eventual failure of Oslo. Aside from an underlying and deep-rooted lack of faith in the utility of 'talks' with the Israelis, events on the ground in the occupied territories bolstered the confidence of Iranian leaders. The outbreak of the First Intifida in December 1987 was exactly the type of protest movement which Iranian leaders favoured, not only in terms of confronting Israel, but also challenging so-called 'corrupt' regimes in the Arab world.

The Iranians perceived the Intifada as being closely modelled on Iran's own revolution, as it demonstrated people power in the face of seemingly impossible odds. The Palestinian Intifada had the added advantage of pitting an occupied people against a foreign power. In that context, it was logical to believe that a brutal Israeli crackdown would only serve to harden Palestinian attitudes and resolve and thus prompt an unbreakable momentum toward Palestinian political emancipation.

At deeper levels the Islamic Republic hoped that the Intifada would weaken the PLO, and specifically Fatah, even though Arafat and his immediate circle had assumed leadership over the protest movement. The Iranian rationale was based on the assumption that there was a fundamental tension between a street-based protest movement and a tired leadership set on compromise with the Israelis.

The fact that the outbreak of the First Intifada coincided with the emergence of the Islamic Resistance Movement (Hamas) was treated as an additional advantage by the Iranians, who had long sought to institute a rival leadership to Arafat's towering presence in Palestinian politics.

Hamas, of course, is not organically tied to Iran and its emergence in late 1987 had nothing to do with Iranian design or planning. But another Palestinian Islamic faction, the Islamic Jihad Movement in Palestine (PIJ), was unapologetically pro-Iranian. Founded in 1981, the PIJ was committed to armed struggle as the sole viable means of breaking the Israeli occupation. The PIJ leaders' commitment to armed struggle, in addition to their strong support for Iran's Islamic revolution and the leadership of Ayatollah Khomeini, invited Iranian financial and logistical support.

The group was at the forefront of militant anti-Israeli activity from the mid-1980s onwards. It staged its first 'suicide attack' in July 1989 by targeting a bus and killing sixteen civilians. This was not a suicide bombing, as the attacker took control of the bus and drove it into a ravine. Nevertheless, it was an iconic moment that is widely regarded as the first Palestinian 'suicide attack' against an Israeli target, even though the attacker survived his mission.

The PIJ leadership edged closer to Iran following their exile to Lebanon in 1988. The Iranians paid special attention to Dr Fathi Shaqaqi, who alongside Sheikh Abd al-Aziz Awda is regarded as one of the main founders of the PIJ. Shaqaqi's leadership qualities was considered to be impeccable by the Iranians, who held out high hopes that he would one day play a major role in Palestinian national life. Shaqaqi's assassination in Malta in October 1995 by Mossad was a major blow to Iran's Palestine strategy.

Following the outbreak of the Second Intifada in September 2000 Iran edged closer to Hamas. Whilst the Islamic Republic had always admired Hamas' militant approach—and invariably applauded its attacks, including suicide bombings, throughout the 1990s—the latter's roots in the Muslim Brotherhood complicated Iran's political outreach to the group. Although by and large the Iranians have a favourable view of the Brotherhood, they are wary of atavistic strands within the movement, particularly those which are perceived to be partial toward Salafism.

The bond with Hamas strengthened following the latter's seizure of power in the Gaza Strip in June 2007. The takeover of Gaza by Hamas meant that Iran could focus on supporting a distinct Palestinian entity, an opportunity which had hitherto eluded the Islamic Republic. Although Hamas had not managed to displace Fatah—as the Iranians initially hoped that it would— by mid-2007 the Islamic Resistance Movement had emerged as a political and strategic equal to the Palestinian secular and nationalist leadership embodied by Fatah.

The relationship with Hamas has been sufficiently strong to withstand the crisis engendered by the Syrian War. Hamas broke with Damascus in early 2012 to openly side with the Syrian rebels. Inevitably this placed enormous strain on its relationship with Iran and Lebanese Hezbollah. But by the beginning of 2016, a cash-strapped Hamas was seeking to mend ties with Iran.

Whilst continuing to support Hamas, the Islamic Republic also remains fully invested in the PIJ, which it regards as an ideological ally, if not a full-fledged ideological compatriot. The current PIJ leader, Ramadan Shallah, is close to the Iranian leadership and helps to mediate in disputes with Hamas. In view of this strong nexus, the Islamic Republic appears to have a sustainable foothold in the Gaza Strip.

The Ahmadinejad Phenomenon

The rise to power of Mahmoud Ahmadinejad in 2005 led to the accentuation and development of several important trends in Iranian politics, ranging from the growth of a new form of conservatism (at the time dubbed as the Iranian neo-conservatives) to Ahmadinejad's peculiar leadership style. Underpinning it all was a populist approach to politics, which defined the Ahamadinejad presidency (2005–2013).

The Ahmadinejad administration was advised by several unconventional thinkers, notably Esfandiar Rahim Mashaei, who served as chief of staff of the administration for five years (2009–2013). For a brief period following the June 2009 disputed presidential elections, Mashaei was appointed as vice president but he was forced to stand down following a strong backlash from the conservative establishment. In fact, the issue was so heated that the leader Ayatollah Khamenei had to write to Ahmadinejad to force Mashaei's demotion. Ahmadinejad resisted at first but eventually had no choice but to heed the supreme leadership's wishes.[10]

The conservative establishment accused Mashaei of heading a 'deviant' current within the administration. This was largely on account of Mashaei's eccentric religious views, notably an intense belief in the imminent return of the Twelfth 'hidden' Imam, the Mahdi, as predicted in Shia eschatology. But many believed the main reason for the establishment's dislike of Mashaei was his lack of sufficiently strong faith in the Shia clergy and in its supreme political role.

Mashaei also came under fire in 2008 after he claimed that 'no nation' in the world is Iran's enemy and that Iran is a friend to the 'nations' of Israel and America.[11] Not surprisingly, this caused a firestorm in the Iranian media, with the conservative and principlist press attacking Mashaei for trying to subvert the Islamic Republic's biggest taboo: engagement with the 'Zionist entity'. Mashaei subsequently corrected his statement by suggesting that he only meant the 'people' of Israel, as opposed to the Zionist establishment.

But the damage was done, and the conservative establishment never forgave Mashaei his grave error of judgement. The former vice president was arrested a decade later in March 2018 by the intelligence organisation of the IRGC. This was preceded by Mashaei's increasingly bold attacks on the establishment, in particular the judiciary, on social media. On the face of it, Mashaei's detention appears to be, at least in part, an act of retribution by the establishment against a once loyal servant of the state.

Mashaei's unusual position on Israel was all the more remarkable as his boss Ahmadinejad had come to be recognised as a virulent anti-Zionist and even an anti-Semite by some international circles. Ahmadinejad launched a blistering attack on Israel in October 2005 by proclaiming that it should be 'wiped off the face of the earth'.[12] This caused outrage in the West and raised fears of a renewed burst of radicalism in Tehran.

In the context of the Islamic Republic's world view—if not stated policies—there was nothing unusual in Ahmadinejad's proclamation. He may have stated his views more candidly and forcefully than other Iranian leaders, but the substance of his views was fully in keeping with established tradition.

Indeed, the late revolutionary leader Ayatollah Khomeini had repeatedly set out this position, by for instance stating that Israel should be removed from the 'page of time'. Moreover, slogans consistent with this view were emblazoned on walls and billboards in the Iranian capital and other major cities. 'Israel must be destroyed', read one of these billboards.

The Iranian foreign policy establishment had to work hard to soften this position and to justify it in a manner that placated international public opinion. Thus, Iranian diplomats were at pains to explain that Iran did not seek the physical destruction of the Jewish state, but only its abolition through democratic means. This usually centred on the 'right of return' principle. Put simply, this principle demands the return of all Palestinian refugees and their descendants who were displaced by the creation of Israel and its aftermath. Following their return, a referendum would be held to determine the political status of the holy land. In view of the Palestinians' demographic advantage the results of this hypothetical referendum are predetermined.

What made Ahmadinejad both unusual and radical on the Israeli issue was his apparent embrace of Holocaust denial. The foreign ministry under Ahmadinejad organised a two-day conference in December 2006 to ostensibly explore the West's sensitivity on the issue. Officially dubbed the International Conference to Review the Global Vision of the Holocaust, the event attracted a number of prominent Western Holocaust deniers including Frederick Toben, David Duke and Michele Renouf.

Not surprisingly the event drew widespread international condemnation, including from the highest levels of the US and UK governments. Established Holocaust scholars accused conference organisers of attempting to cloak anti-Semitism in scholarly discourse. Arguably, the conference succeeded in its goal of attracting maximum publicity and causing outrage in the West.

The mastermind behind the conference was a little-known Iranian ideologue by the name of Mohammad Ali Ramin. A long-time resident of Germany, Ramin had been pressured to leave the country by German security agencies who suspected him of ties to Iranian intelligence. Although not part of Ahmadinejad's immediate circle, Ramin was a key presidential advisor and was rewarded with an official job as deputy minister of culture, despite the fact that many considered him to be unsuitable for the role.

Although Ramin was clearly invested in Holocaust denial, the same cannot be said of Ahmadinejad and his immediate circle. Ahmadinejad's main priority was rather to go on the cultural and ideological offensive against the West and to expose what he believed was the West's hypocrisy and double standards over free speech. The president and his supporters quipped that while Western politicians and ideologues promote the view that no idea or value is sacred (and hence off-limits to scrutiny and criticism) as part of their strategy to attack the foundations of the Islamic faith, the same politicians and ideologues cried foul when the events of the Holocaust were called into question. Ahmadinejad's aim was allegedly to show that all cultures have taboos.

There was also a larger strategy in play, namely to go on the discursive offensive against the West generally. The West often placed the Islamic Republic on the defensive by criticising its human rights record and related issues. Instead of remaining on the defensive (as previous Iranian administrations had done) Ahmadinejad and his team believed that Iran should go on the offensive by highlighting Western vulnerabilities and sensitivities.

Viewed in this framework, the Ahmadinejad administration was certainly radical, but not aberrant in the Islamic Republic, in terms of its views and position on Israel.

Intelligence Wars

In June 2018 it was dramatically announced that a former Israeli energy and infrastructure minister and one-time parliamentarian had been detained on charges of spying for Iran. By any standards, Gonen Segev has lived a remarkable life. With an impressive government record and a stint in the legislature, he is also a practising physician. His license to practise medicine in Israel was revoked following his conviction in 2005 on drug smuggling charges. According to the charge sheet the former minister had conspired to smuggle 30,000 ecstasy tablets into Israel from the Netherlands.

Besides drug smuggling, the 62-year-old Segev is alleged to have committed additional crimes including passport forgery and credit card fraud. According to Israeli investigators Segev had reached out to the Iranian intelligence service in Nigeria whilst he was living and working there. Although no longer in government, Segev still maintained extensive ties to government and defence officials. It appears that the Iranian intelligence service—most likely the MOIS in this case—was mostly focused on tapping into this network.

Segev's exposure as a possible Iranian spy (his trial opened in early July 2018 and concluded in January 2019 with Segev sentenced to eleven years imprisonment) sheds light into the intense intelligence war between the two foes. It is often assumed that Israel has the upper hand in the intelligence dimension of the conflict, as demonstrated by the Mossad's penetration of the heart of Tehran in pursuit of key elements of the Iranian nuclear programme.

The revelations surrounding Segev somewhat undermine this assumption as they hint at a much broader Iranian effort to target serving and former Israeli officials. Before Segev's arrest, most of the alleged Iranian spies caught in Israel had been fairly low-level operatives, usually of Iranian origin. In April 2015 a middle-aged Belgian national of Iranian origin was sentenced to five years' imprisonment on charges of spying for Iran. According to Israeli investigators the 55-year-old Ali Mansouri had been recruited and managed by a branch of the IRGC intelligence establishment.

Iranian intelligence services, and their allies in the intelligence organisation of Lebanese Hezbollah, scored a moderate success back in October 2000 when the latter abducted a reserve colonel in the Israel Defence Forces (IDF) in Dubai and subsequently flew him to Lebanon on a private plane. The then 44-year-old Elhanan Tannenbaum reportedly held an important position in the IDF's Northern Command (responsible for the defence of the borders with Lebanon and Syria) and was allegedly privy to important military secrets.

Hezbollah Secretary-General Hassan Nasrallah announced Tannenbaum's 'capture' on the al-Manar TV station, thus commencing a long process of bargaining and negotiations which eventually led to the IDF officer's release in January 2004. In return for Tannenbaum's release (and the repatriation of three corpses of slain IDF soldiers), Hezbollah secured the release of 435 prisoners. By any measure, the Hezbollah-led intelligence operation, which began in Israel (after a Hezbollah intelligence agent made contact with Tannenbaum) and involved Brussels and Frankfurt, before concluding in Dubai, was a resounding success.

Like Segev, Tannenbaum had been lured into an intelligence operation because of his criminal activities. He had reportedly agreed to travel to Dubai to participate in a drug-dealing operation. All sophisticated intelligence organisations are adept at identifying and exploiting a target's vulnerabilities. In this case, it appears that Iranian and allied intelligence organisations have developed specialised skills in identifying and exploiting important Israelis with criminal talents or intentions.

If Israel has the upper hand in the intelligence war then it is likely a marginal advantage. Certainly, in terms of human sources (as opposed to technology-based espionage), the Iranian intelligence services are on a par—if not superior—with their Israeli adversaries. Besides aggressively targeting serving and former Israeli officials, the Iranian services are known to target members of Iran's Jewish community who have established livelihoods in Israel.

More broadly, Iranian intelligence services systematically target Israeli organisations and Israeli-linked individuals around the world, particularly in Western Europe. The scale of this spying partially came to light in January 2018 when German police raided the homes and offices of ten alleged Iranian 'spies' in Berlin. According to German investigators the Iranian spies had been mostly focused on 'Jewish' institutions in Berlin, notably the American Jewish Committee.[13]

This dramatic raid came on the heels of the conviction of a Pakistani national by a German court in March 2017 on charges of spying for Iran. It was reported that Haidar Syed Mustafa had collected intelligence on the former head of the German-Israeli Association and a French-Israeli professor working in Paris. Syed Mustafa was sentenced to more than four years' imprisonment.

It was widely alleged in the German and Israeli media that both the targets of the January 2018 raids and the convicted Syed Mustafa had been recruited and managed by an intelligence agency affiliated to the IRGC. The Qods Force was often touted as their probable handler, but in view of the theatre of operations (Western Europe) it is likely that an even more specialised branch of IRGC intelligence had recruited and managed these agents.

If the IRGC is indeed running extensive intelligence operations in the heart of Europe, that is important for a number of reasons. First, it speaks to competition between Iranian intelligence agencies for recruitment, result and successes on European soil. This type of operation used to be the exclusive domain of the MOIS, but it appears that in recent years the intelligence ministry has steadily lost its monopoly.

Second, it raises questions about the real intentions behind the intelligence activity. The MOIS operates in Western Europe mostly to gather intelligence which can be used to gain political and diplomatic advantage over Iran's adversaries and rivals. As far as we know, the MOIS has never targeted foreign organisations and foreign individuals in kinetic operations. The intelligence ministry used to assassinate Iranian militants and dissidents in the West but these operations came to a crashing halt in 1997 following the so-called Mykonos trial. As a governmental department the MOIS is acutely sensitive to any diplomatic fallout following military activity on European soil.

Certainly, the intelligence wars between Iran and Israel have a deadly twist. There is indirect conflict when Iran confronts Israel via proxies, notably Lebanese Hezbollah, which has had deadly ramifications across the globe. For instance, the Israeli assassination of former Hezbollah leader Abbas al-Musawi in February 1992 set off a chain reaction whose ramifications were felt as far away as South America.

A month after Musawi's assassination, the Israeli embassy in Buenos Aires, Argentina was attacked by a pick-up truck driven by a suicide bomber. The resulting explosion killed twenty-nine people, including four Israelis, but most of the dead were Argentine civilians. The bombing was widely blamed on Lebanese Hezbollah, with allegations of Iranian complicity and even foreknowledge of the attack thrown in for good measure.

Even though no one was prosecuted for that attack, Argentine authorities implicated several Lebanese and Iranians, amongst them Iranian diplomats. The embassy bombing was Argentina's deadliest terror attack to date, before it was superseded by the AMIA (Argentine Israelite Mutual Association) bombing in July 1994. A suicide bomber drove a van carrying nearly 300kg of explosives into the Jewish Community Centre building, killing eighty-five people, most of them Argentine Jews.

The suicide bomber was later identified as one Ibrahim Hussein Berro, a 21-year-old Lebanese allegedly recruited by Hezbollah's external security organisation. The bombing touched off a quarter-century of internal divisions and wrangling in Argentina as to the identity of the culprits behind the attack. A section of the Argentine establishment has been determined to implicate Iran in the attack, even though there is no evidence to suggest a link.

At the centre of the anti-Iran camp was Argentine federal prosecutor Alberto Nisman, whose death in January 2015 merely created more doubt and wrangling. Initially ruled a suicide, Nisman's demise is now widely believed to have been a murder. But Nisman's central accusation that Iran had ordered the AMIA bombing to retaliate against Argentina's decision to suspend nuclear-related cooperation between the two countries has been widely discredited. For a start, a nuclear technology contract was never terminated (as Nisman alleged) and at the time of the bombing Iran and Argentina were on the threshold of reinvigorating all existing agreements.

Nevertheless, the AMIA bombing has cast a long shadow over Iran's relations with Argentina, with powerful forces in Israel and the US attempting to implicate the Islamic Republic in the bombing. It is the most powerful example of how the conflict with Israel has severely complicated Iran's global diplomacy.

Iran and Israel also spar directly in the kinetic sphere. The assassination of Iranian nuclear scientists in Tehran, allegedly by the Mossad, brought the kinetic side of the intelligence wars into sharp relief. Between January 2010 and January 2012 at least five Iranian nuclear scientists were targeted for assassination, with one surviving the bombing of his car.

The first known victim of this assassination campaign was the highly distinguished elementary particle physics professor Massoud

Alimohammadi, who was assassinated in January 2010 by a remote-controlled bomb attached to a motorcycle. Although it was initially denied that Alimohammadi had any links to the nuclear programme, his wife contradicted official accounts in a 2014 interview by disclosing that her slain husband had been involved in 'clandestine' work.[14]

In November 2010 nuclear scientist and engineer Majid Shahriari was assassinated by means of a C-4 plastic explosive bomb attached to his car door. On the same day a similar assassination method was attempted on Fereydoon Abbasi-Davani, a professor of nuclear physics at Shahid Beheshti University. Abbasi-Davani survived the assassination attempt and was later appointed as head of the Atomic Energy Organisation.

In July 2011 Daryoush Rezaeinejad, an electrical engineering postgraduate believed to be involved in nuclear research, was shot dead in front of his wife. The final hit occurred in January 2012 when Mostafa Ahmadi Roshan, the deputy director of the Natanz enrichment facility, was blown up by a magnetic bomb attached to his car door.

The assassination of so many key figures in the Iranian nuclear effort spoke of tremendous ground work by the Mossad and allied intelligence services. As every major global intelligence service knows, Iran offers an exceptionally tough operational environment as Iranian counter-intelligence is regarded as highly competent. To pull off such dramatic assassinations—targeted at figures who were to varying degrees subject to protective measures—required not only the recruitment of high-calibre agents but just as importantly many months of preparatory work in the heart of the Iranian capital. This would have entailed many days of careful surveillance and practice runs, all under the noses of Iranian counter-intelligence.

It is believed that most (if not all) of the agents that had conducted the groundwork in Tehran—and triggered the explosions or fired the shots—were Iranians. By mid-2012 Iranian officials claimed that this network had been dismantled, a claim validated by the fact that no more assassinations were carried out. The televised confessions of one of the assassins, Majid Jamali Fashi, offered a fascinating insight into the type of people that were targeted for recruitment by Mossad.

A professional kickboxer, the 24-year-old Fashi appears to have been recruited in the Republic of Azerbaijan before being flown to

Israel for extensive training at Mossad-run facilities. Part of his training allegedly involved practising using a replica of Alimohammadi's house, which had reportedly been meticulously reconstructed by the Mossad down to the finest detail. Fashi was executed in May 2012 for killing Professor Alimohammadi.

The depth and breadth of the breach necessitated an Iranian counter-attack. The attacks on Israeli diplomatic targets in India and Georgia in February 2012 were widely attributed to an Iranian desire for retaliation. Mimicking the Mossad-directed attacks in Tehran, a motorcyclist attached a sticky bomb to the car of the wife of the Israeli defence attaché to India, wounding her, the driver, in addition to two bystanders.

Meanwhile in the Georgian capital Tblisi, a car connected to the Israeli embassy was discovered to have a bomb attached underneath it. The planned attack was foiled after the bomb was defused. The failure of both attacks was mainly put down to the fact that they were hastily arranged, supposedly with a view to exacting a speedy revenge.

The covert war between Iran and Israel grinds on relentlessly and will almost certainly result in additional kinetic measures by both sides.

Open Warfare?

On Thursday, 10 May 2018 a barrage of rockets was fired into the Israeli-occupied Golan Heights. Israel immediately blamed Iran for the attack and went on the offensive, reportedly striking the entire Iranian establishment in Syria. This intense series of tit-for-tat strikes was the first time the two foes had come into direct military confrontation.

The confrontation had been brewing for months following the downing of an Israeli F-16 by Syrian air defences in February. The Israeli jet was part of a larger dispatch attacking a range of Syrian and Iranian sites following the detection and subsequent downing of what Israel claimed was an Iranian drone inside Israeli air space.

That significant confrontation was followed in April by an Israeli air strike on the T-4 airbase in Homs, home to the IRGC's aerospace division in Syria. As many as seven Iranians were killed in the strike, reportedly including the head of the IRGC drone force in Syria. The strike was a grievous blow to Iran, which, owing to the military disparity and a wide range of political and strategic considerations, could not immediately reciprocate in kind.

Although Iranian officials and military commanders deny involvement in the rocket barrage aimed at IDF forward positions just inside the occupied Golan Heights, most seasoned observers concluded that the attack was Iran's response to months of Israeli attacks and provocations.

In purely military terms, the alleged Iranian counter-attack could not even begin to compare with Israeli assaults on Iranian and Iranian-aligned positions in Syria. In 2018 alone, these air strikes had exacted a considerable toll in lives and material losses. The disparity in fire power is even starker when we consider that since 2012, Israel has carried out at least 100 air strikes on Iranian or pro-Iranian targets.[15] Most of these strikes have targeted what Israel has consistently claimed is the transfer of advanced weaponry to Lebanese Hezbollah.

Israel may exercise military superiority in the Levant but it cannot use this advantage to achieve its core strategic objectives. Israel's stated objective in the final phase of the long-running Syrian War is the ejection of Iranian forces from Syria. This appears to be an impossible task, not only in view of Iranian determination to reap the rewards of its intervention in the Syrian conflict, but equally because of the dense operational environment inside the war-torn country.

The latter phase of the Syrian War has seen the two largest military powers, Russia and the United States, deploy considerable forces inside the country. In addition, Turkey has deployed forces in Syria's north-west, ostensibly to contain the irredentist ambitions of Syria's militant Kurds, who are aligned to the United States.

The situation in north-west and north-central Syria is emblematic of the dizzyingly complex operational, strategic and diplomatic dynamics in play in the closing stages of the conflict. Nato allies Turkey and the US are fundamentally divided over the future role of the PKK-aligned Kurdish militias who have so far been considered to be amongst the winners of the Syrian conflict. Turkey wants to see the Kurds' proto-state—dubbed Rojava—destroyed, whereas the US views the entity as a bulwark against radical Syrian rebels as well as a counter to the Syrian government.

The situation between Iran, Russia and Israel is no less complicated. Whilst nominally Iran's ally in Syria, Russia has consistently accommodated Israeli military concerns, effectively turning a blind eye to repeated Israeli air strikes on Iranian and Syrian targets.

Russia plays a careful balancing role in Syria, and its ultimate intention is to secure its own long-term national security interests, notably long-term access to Tartus naval facility (which ranks as the Russian navy's sole overseas base) in addition to newly acquired bases, including the Hmeimim airbase. To that end, Russia opposes Israeli demands for the full ejection of Iranian forces from Syria.

The consolidation of Syria as Iran's strategic depth can only be bad news for Israel as the entire arena can be used to engage the Jewish state in prolonged attritional warfare. To illustrate the point, Israel's military superiority has consistently failed to remove Hezbollah's Lebanese-based military threat. It can hardly be expected to decisively defeat a direct Iranian military presence in Syria.

Full-scale warfare remains unlikely for the foreseeable future. But the low-intensity conflict is set to continue and it will create more and more dramatic outbursts in the near future.

THE USA
CONFRONTING 'THE GREAT SATAN'

In modern international relations few inter-state relationships are as complex as that between Iran and the United States. This is a relationship in which emotion, strategic rivalry and ideological disputes are mixed up in one combustible whole.

The most remarkable thing about this deeply entrenched stand-off is not that it has occasionally led to kinetic activity but that it has not degenerated into full-scale war. Despite the decades of heated rhetoric and countless threats, it would appear that both sides are keen to avoid a military confrontation.

By the same token, both powers appear to be equally keen to avoid a resolution to this four-decades-old animosity. There have been at least two occasions where a partial resolution—if not a full settlement— seemed within reach. Iran's assistance to the US during the Afghan campaign of October–December 2001 was an important factor in America's ability to topple the Taliban with relative ease. In view of Iran's long-established outreach to the so-called Northern Alliance, the Islamic Republic's cooperation was even more important to the subsequent political stability phase of the campaign.

Yet George W. Bush rewarded this tentative Iranian outreach by branding the country as part of an 'axis of evil' in his State of the Union Address in January 2002.[1] This remarkable public humiliation, made only worse as it came on the heels of unprecedented—albeit limited—Iranian–American cooperation in a battlefield setting, only confirmed Iranian leaders' belief that the United States simply cannot be trusted.

More than a decade later the centrist administration of Hassan Rouhani entered into direct negotiations with the US, as a spinoff of the multilateral JCPOA nuclear deal negotiations. This budding relationship was epitomised by the warm rapport between Iranian Foreign Minister Javad Zarif and US Secretary of State John Kerry. In those heady days back in 2015 there was even some expectation that Iran and the US could build on the momentum generated by the JCPOA to achieve breakthroughs in other areas of their fraught relationship, perhaps even coming to an arrangement on regional influence building.

But those hopes came crashing down following the electoral victory of American nationalist Donald Trump in the November 2016 US presidential elections. During his campaign Trump had vowed to tear up the JCPOA, which he had famously called the 'worst deal in history'. Throughout 2017 Trump ratcheted up the pressure and the threats, finally withdrawing from the deal in May 2018.

From an Iranian point of view, the collapse of the JCPOA is less to do with the mercurial leadership style of Donald Trump than with the inherently untrustworthy nature of the US. There is little wonder then that hard questions are being asked of the Rouhani government, specifically as to why it had trusted the Obama administration when it was fully cognisant of the real risk of American treachery. This is especially ironic in view of the fact that Rouhani's foreign policy and national security teams are composed of battle-hardened diplomats and securocrats with decades of experience behind them.

The rise of Trump and the collapse of the JCPOA have reduced Iranian–American relations to their lowest point yet. With Iranian–US tensions rising, especially in a region where multiple tension points are inflamed, there is a real sense that the two powers are heading toward a shooting war. These fears are reinforced by Trump's unequivocally tough rhetoric on Iran and the domination of his national security team by notorious Iran hawks, such as national security advisor John Bolton, Secretary of State Mike Pompeo and Secretary of Defense James Mattis.

The sense of foreboding is made worse by the Trump administration's stated policy of imposing the 'strongest' sanctions in history on the Islamic Republic. This determined effort, coupled with a barely concealed policy of regime change, hints strongly at the confrontational intentions of the current US administration. Secretary of State Pompeo's presentation of twelve demands to Iran in May 2018 was a stunning display of twenty-first-century gunboat diplomacy.

The issuing of the demands was effectively a call for surrender and a barely concealed desire to reduce Iran to the role of vassal state. Some of the more outlandish demands include allowing the International Atomic Energy Agency 'unqualified' access to all sites in the country and a demand on Tehran to end support to 'Lebanese Hezbollah, Hamas and Palestinian Islamic Jihad'.

Back in the real world, the Trump administration is preparing the ground for the economic strangulation of Iran, by applying maximum pressure on friend and foe alike to cease or massively downgrade trade and commerce with Tehran. With full sanctions taking effect in early November 2018, the greatest point of concern for the Iranian leadership is Trump's stated goal of divesting Iran of its ability to sell oil. This has led Iranian political and military leaders to threaten the closure of the Strait of Hormuz. In view of the fact that 30 per cent of the world's oil supply passes through the Strait of Hormuz, the realisation of this threat would almost certainly trigger an Iranian–US military confrontation.

As President Rouhani pointed out in July 2018, it makes no sense for other countries to export oil through the Strait of Hormuz if Iran is shorn of this opportunity. What Rouhani stated diplomatically, Iranian military commanders have set out in stark terms. Addressing Trump directly, Qasem Soleimani, the legendary Qods Force commander, proclaimed that if need be, he and Qods Force 'alone' would confront the US military. The setting—a gathering in the Western city of Hamedan to commemorate a famous operation of the Iran–Iraq War— amplified the significance of Soleimani's challenge to the US president.

The war of words between Trump and Iranian political and military leaders is unprecedented even in the context of forty years of rancour and acrimony. They are the surest sign yet that something is about to happen which my prove to be a radical departure from the

'Cold War' that has characterised the Iranian–US relationship since the Iranian revolution.

However, there were military clashes between the two powers in the Persian Gulf, notably during the latter phase of the Iran–Iraq War. During US Operation Praying Mantis in April 1988, the US navy reportedly destroyed a quarter of the Iranian navy in a day's worth of ferocious military activity in the Gulf. The confrontation was the culmination of months of tension, specifically activity by the Islamic Revolutionary Guards Corps (IRGC) navy against merchant shipping in the Persian Gulf. This involved both the laying of mines and attacking tankers with converted speedboats.

Earlier in April the guided missile frigate USS *Samuel B. Roberts* was struck by an Iranian mine and sustained heavy damage. Praying Mantis was ostensibly a retaliatory measure. In October 1987, during Operation Nimble Archer the US navy had destroyed two Iranian oil platforms in the Persian Gulf as a retaliatory measure against IRGC speedboat attacks on reflagged Kuwaiti oil tankers. The reflagging was part of US Operation Earnest Will, which was ostensibly designed to protect Kuwaiti shipping in the final phase of the Iran–Iraq War.

These military encounters were essentially limited in nature and incidental to the broader narrative of the Iran–Iraq War. There is evidence that neither side wanted a confrontation and when a serious confrontation did take place (Praying Mantis), both sides quickly adopted a de-escalatory posture in order to ease pressure and to disengage.

The encounters were a rude awakening for the Iranian navy, which lost two vessels in the fighting: the *Joshan* fast attack craft and the frigate *Sahand*. Another frigate, the *Sabalan*, sustained major damage, but it was repaired and eventually returned to service. The IRGC navy also lost at least three speedboats and was forced to evacuate two oil platforms, Sassan and Sirri. In just under twenty-four hours the US navy had destroyed a quarter of Iran's naval forces and would have inflicted further damage had de-escalation not occurred.

The Iranians drew important lessons from that encounter, principally the overriding requirement to avoid a direct military clash with the much larger and capable US naval forces in the Persian Gulf. The clashes led the IRGC navy in particular to develop asymmetric naval warfare capabilities, most of which focus on closing the Strait of Hormuz for as long as possible, and by extension thwarting the US navy's attempt at reopening it.

Qods Force commander Qasem Soleimani was hinting at this strategy in late July 2018 when he told Trump that he would not be facing Iran's regular armed forces, but his forces alone. Part of this message can be interpreted as a frank admission of the impossible odds stacked against Iran's conventional military forces in an armed confrontation with the US. Therefore, in any future military confrontation Iran will need to rely primarily—if not solely—on unconventional methods to contain and subvert America's military superiority.

But the relationship can also swing the other way. More than once Trump has hinted of his desire to secure a new deal with Iran, albeit on America's terms. Moreover, Trump's peculiar leadership style—as demonstrated by his penchant for dealing with autocrats—has given rise to hopes that he might seek a comprehensive agreement with Iran, or even a summit with the Iranian leadership, on a par with the June 2018 summit with North Korean leader Kim Jong-un.

According to this perspective, the war of words between Trump and the Iranian leaders may be a prelude to a breakthrough in the logjam that has defined Iranian–American relations for four decades. Heated rhetoric, steadily rising tensions, bold brinkmanship, even a limited skirmish in the Persian Gulf, may be just what is required to break out of the 'no war, no peace' paradigm which characterises the Islamic Republic's standoff with the world's superpower.

But this is wishful thinking. For a start, Iran is not North Korea. The latter is a hermitic kingdom devoid of complex international relations. By contrast, the Islamic Republic pursues global diplomacy and harbours ambitions far beyond the region. North Korea is exclusively preoccupied with regime survival and it has developed nuclear weapons solely for that purpose. Iran, on the other hand, does not fear regime change anywhere near as much as the Iran hawks in Washington appear to believe. The Islamic Republic is intent on establishing dominance in the region with a view to potentially projecting power beyond it.

Second, Iranian anti-Americanism is deeper and more potent than the North Korean variety. To be sure, the Korean Peninsula suffered terribly during the American-led Korean War of the early 1950s, and the leadership in Pyongyang is rightfully wary of US intentions. But North Korea's relationship with the US is nowhere near as complex, tangled and emotional as the Iranian–American relationship. In that sense, the Iranian leadership is far more heavily invested in its anti-American ideology than North Korea.

Third, Iran is a democracy of sorts, or at least it has a complex polity whereby multiple factions and power centres are involved in policy making. By stark contrast, policy making in North Korea is straightforward and meets no resistance. Any serious move by the Iranian leadership toward partial rapprochement with the US will require patient consensus-building. In view of the current domestic political configuration, the economic crisis, and regional geopolitics, this consensus will be extremely hard to achieve for the foreseeable future.

Finally, there are powerful factions and lobbies in the United States who are deeply opposed to accommodation with Iran. These factions are as ideological in their motives as their adversaries in the Iranian establishment. In fact, one could make the argument that their anti-Iranianism is more potent and deep-rooted than the anti-Americanism of the Iranian right. Many influential ideologues from these factions currently serve in the Trump administration.

There is no such comparable anti-North Korea lobby in the United States. The prevailing view of North Korea in Washington is one of bemusement as opposed to irreconcilable ideological friction—that it requires long-term containment, rather than eradication. By contrast, there are plenty of influential types in the US who wish to bring about the demise of the Islamic Republic in order to satisfy ideological and national security goals.

'Death to America'

No official Iranian political gathering is complete without the perfunctory chant of 'death to America'. The slogan has been chanted for so long and so often that it is as much a demonstration of internal political cohesion as it is a statement on foreign policy. Revolutionary Iran has produced a wide range of colourful slogans, most of which direct insult, injury or death to the country's real or perceived enemies.

The veteran BBC reporter John Simpson once wryly observed that it is a measure of the radicalism of Iranian politics that there is no way to express disapproval of someone or their actions without wishing death on them.

But where does this slogan come from and why has it assumed the significance and longevity that it has? The simple answer is that is rooted in revolutionary anger at the US, the immediate cause being the US decision in October 1979 to admit the Shah to the United States, ostensibly to seek urgent medical treatment for his rapidly deteriorating cancer. Not surprisingly, the Iranian revolutionaries interpreted this American move as a clear sign of intent that the US was interested in returning the Shah to power.

Memories of the August 1953 coup—which had ousted the nationalist Prime Minister Mohammad Mossadegh and restored the Shah to power—were still fresh in Iran. To revolutionaries of all stripes the 1953 coup was a radical turning point in contemporary Iranian history, not only because it restored the Shah to power, but also because of the shift in foreign influence on domestic affairs. For decades before the coup—going all the way back to the late nineteenth century—the United Kingdom had been considered to be the most influential foreign power in Iran. In fact, the UK's intervention in domestic politics was perceived to be so decisive that many Iranians attributed all major political events, at least in part, to British volition.

However, the most important consequence of the 1953 coup and the subversion of the democratic will is widely perceived to have been a shift in influence from the UK to the US. Indeed, by the mid- to late 1950s the US was widely regarded as the most influential foreign power in Iranian domestic politics, in keeping with the US's expanding regional and global role. In historical terms, the outbreak of the Suez Crisis in 1956 and the US's strong rebuke of the UK's role in the invasion of Egypt signified a shift in the balance of power in the Middle East in favour of the Americans.

To the Iranian revolutionaries that shift was merely a continuation of colonial policies in the Middle East. The Iranians made no distinction between an avowedly colonial power such as the UK and a putatively anti-imperialist power like the US. At both policy and ideological levels, the Americans were opposed to European colonialism and

217

correctly believed that the momentum generated by the end of the Second World War would bring about the demise of the colonialist project.

But the Americans' view of themselves and their role in the world was lost to the Iranian revolutionaries who fervently believed that the US had backed the Shah to the hilt for a quarter of a century in order to obtain and consolidate a neo-colonial presence in Iran. The act of the coup itself was deeply offensive to revolutionaries of all persuasions (Islamic and secular); apart from signifying a grave breach of Iranian sovereignty, it had fully exposed the country's profound vulnerability to foreign manipulation. That memory lingers to this day and continues to cloud Iranian judgements of the US. The real messy story of the coup—and specifically of the chaotic domestic situation which facilitated it—is often brushed under the carpet in favour of a coherent narrative centred on foreign interference.

Similarly, the complexity of the US position on the Iranian revolution was mostly overlooked by the revolutionaries who had identified Washington as opposed to the interests of the revolution. Even before the embassy takeover in November 1979, the American diplomatic mission in Tehran had been attacked by gunmen on 15 February,[2] barely four days after the victory of the revolution. That attack was quickly repulsed, thus confirming the view of elements in the Carter administration that the provisional government headed by Mehdi Bazargan could be relied upon to place Iranian–American ties on a stable footing in the post-Shah era.

The desire to maintain stable relations with the provisional government partly influenced the American decision to initially block the Shah's entry to the US. Following his departure from Iran in January 1979, the ailing Shah went from pillar to post in his forlorn quest to find a secure sanctuary. This journey took him as far afield as Egypt and Morocco to Mexico and the Bahamas, before he was finally granted permission to enter the United States in October 1979.

That fateful US decision touched off real concern in Tehran, where it was inevitably perceived as a political move laden with strategic intent. The fear that the US would sponsor the Shah's return by fomenting unrest or even contemplating a military invasion of Iran was not far-fetched at the time. As it turned out, the real story of the US decision to grant the Shah sanctuary was complicated and had unfolded in the face of opposition by then US president Jimmy Carter. In fact, Carter only appears to have changed his mind once he had been fed misinformation by pro-Shah elements from within and without the administration who claimed that the Shah was gravely ill and 'at the point of death'.[3]

Carter's decision to admit the Shah to the US was the trigger behind the decision by radical revolutionaries to attack and occupy the American embassy in Tehran. There is a lively debate as to the precise causes behind that decision and the extent to which the students' decision enjoyed the support of Ayatollah Khomeini and his inner circle.

There was certainly an element of spontaneity born out of revolutionary enthusiasm. The student group which attacked the US embassy on 4 November—officially called the Muslim Students Following the Imam's Line—was primarily motivated by revolutionary goals and ideals, chief amongst them a strong desire to terminate US influence on domestic Iranian affairs. To that end, there was much to worry about, for although the US had lost a reliable ally in the Shah, Washington had not given up hope of maintaining influence in Iran with a view to determining the major features of Iran's external relations. Washington's greatest concern was that the new revolutionary government would tilt toward Moscow in order to both consolidate the revolution at home and guarantee safety and security in the country's immediate neighbourhood.

What made the students and their political backers especially nervous was the activity of the US embassy in Tehran in the nine months since the victory of the revolution in February. In some respects—for example, covert intelligence collection—the embassy had stepped up its activities in order to develop the best picture possible of political developments in Tehran. Much of this activity was later exposed by the Muslim Students Following the Imam's Line, who painstakingly pieced together secret or confidential documents that had been shredded by US embassy staff moments before the seizure of the compound.

The students' revelations implicated many Iranian politicians—some of them revolutionary figures—in surreptitious contact with the Americans. Some of these politicians were branded as spies even though the official records showed them to be merely in touch with the embassy, as opposed to passing secret or confidential information to the Americans. The students' critics accused them of releasing information selectively so as to target political figures disliked by them and their backers. It was odd, the critics argued, that the students held back from releasing files on key revolutionary figures, such as Chief Justice Ayatollah Mohammad Hosseini Beheshti, whom many also suspected of talking to the Americans before the revolution.

Many careers were ruined as a result of the students' selective disclosures. Arguably their greatest victim was Abbas Amir-Entezam, a deputy prime minister in the provisional government. Entezam was arrested in late 1979 and charged with spying for the Americans, even though the evidence against him fell short of proving espionage. Entezam was widely regarded as the longest-held political prisoner in Iran. He was fully incarcerated for at least fifteen years before being transferred to a safe house run by the Ministry of Intelligence, probably in late 1995. Shortly thereafter he was released under house arrest whose restrictions were gradually eased. But Entezam was never a fully free man, as he was recalled back to prison on several occasions—for instance in 1998, when he gave an interview to the reformist paper *Tous*—and was subject to restrictions right up to his death in July 2018.

Entezam's forlorn fate in many ways symbolised the emotionally charged turbulence of Iranian–American relations. There is a widespread belief that the authorities kept him prisoner for so long as a deterrent against politicians and diplomats advocating normal relations with the US. The tactic worked, since no serious Iranian politician has dared to seize the initiative and advocate direct talks with the Americans. What little contact has taken place during these decades has been sanctioned at the top and conducted under forensic scrutiny.

At a broader level, the Muslim Students Following the Imam's Line succeeded in bringing about the downfall of the provisional government headed by the hapless Mehdi Bazargan, the leader of the Freedom Movement of Iran. It is important to clarify that the overthrow of the provisional government was never a stated aim of the students. Moreover, as further information and new revelations come to light, it seems plausible that the government could have survived had it stood its ground. There does not appear to have been a conspiracy to overthrow Bazargan's government, even though few in the revolutionary council or amongst Ayatollah Khomeini's closest confidants mourned its fall.

A thoughtful and well-intentioned man, Bazargan lacked sufficient political acumen and toughness to navigate the treacherous waters of revolutionary politics. By resigning, he saved himself and his government from greater embarrassment and potential harm. Although Bazargan served as a member of parliament in the first Majlis (1980–1984) he remained a marginal figure in post-revolutionary Iran. However, he was relatively free from harassment and maintained the respect of key revolutionary leaders, including Ayatollah Khomeini and his successor Ayatollah Khamenei, right up to his death in 1995.

By the time the embassy crisis had been resolved in January 1981, it had taken a terrible toll on bilateral relations. It had destroyed any trust and confidence that remained and even taken the two countries close to war, as demonstrated by Operation Eagle Claw, a failed plan by the Americans to rescue the hostages in April 1980. The crash of a US helicopter in the heart of the Iranian desert in Tabas, resulting in the death of eight US servicemen,[4] was a source of deep humiliation for the Americans, a feeling made worse by the fact that the charred corpses of the fallen airmen were shown on Iranian television.

The resolution of the crisis left an enduring legacy in bilateral ties, especially on the possibility, and even desirability, of making 'secret' deals to overcome troublesome issues. The Iranian revolutionaries had preferred to strike a secret deal with incoming US Republican President Ronald Reagan, partly from a desire to further humiliate the Democrat Jimmy Carter. Indeed, only four years after the resolution of the embassy crisis, the Iranians and Americans were once again secretly talking and making deals as part of what became known as the Iran–Contra scandal.

If the embassy crisis had set down the foundation for decades of mistrust and animosity, the outbreak of the Iran–Iraq War in September 1980, and specifically US support for Saddam Hussein, provided the visible structure that kept both powers estranged for decades. In the words of Iranian leaders, the US had erected a 'high wall' of 'mistrust' (*deevareh bolandeh bi-e'etemadi*) which would prove next to impossible to scale.

There is sufficient evidence that Saddam Hussein's decision to invade Iran in September 1980 enjoyed at least the tacit support of the United States. To be sure, Washington did not share Iraq's war aim of toppling the Islamic Republic (for fear of over-strengthening the Baathist regime in Baghdad), but at minimum the US hoped that the Iraqi invasion would contain, or more correctly divert, the energy of the Iranian revolution.

At the time this was not a controversial policy objective as all other Western powers were keen to keep revolutionary Iran in check. Across the ideological divide, even the Soviet Union shared Washington's objective of containing Islamic Iran, albeit for different reasons, including to preserve the balance of power in favour of Baathist Iraq, which was a tentative Soviet ally.

There is evidence that as early as spring 1982 the US was supplying battlefield-related intelligence to Iraq.[5] This contradicts official accounts of a US tilt toward Iraq only manifesting from November 1984 onwards, when the US restored formal relations with Baghdad. The Iranians were likely aware of the US intelligence support to Iraq and sought to alleviate its effect by not severing ties to the Soviet Union. Although officially the revolution was committed to a 'neither East nor West' foreign policy, in practice the Iranians staked out a much tougher attitude towards the West, as opposed to the Soviet Union and its satellite states in eastern Europe.

Notwithstanding early jitters, notably a spying case in 1980 involving a senior Mojahedin-e Khalq leader,[6] relations with the Soviet Union remained stable and even began to improve from 1982 onwards, especially as Moscow turned a blind eye to Tehran's attempts at sourcing arms and equipment from Soviet satellite states in eastern Europe. Even the decisive crackdown on the pro-Soviet Tudeh Party in 1983–1984 did not cause a major rupture in relations. This is despite the fact that Iranian security services claimed to have broken a Soviet spy ring inside the armed forces connected to the Tudeh Party's clandestine branch. A former commander of the Iranian navy and a leader in the Tudeh's clandestine branch in the armed forces, Rear Admiral Bahram Afzali, was executed in February 1984 upon conviction of espionage.

Resentment of the US role in the Iran–Iraq War had less to do with America's pro-Iraq tilt than with the US turning a blind eye to repeated Iraqi war crimes, specifically the deployment of chemical weapons. Even the brazen use of chemical weapons against Iraqi Kurdish civilians and Iranian soldiers in Halabja in March 1988 did not draw Washington's wrath. To the Iranians this was a clear case of US and wider Western hypocrisy and double standards with respect to international law and ethics. It was a brutal lesson that Iran would never forget. Indeed, the consequences of Iraq's liberal use of chemical weapons are still present, as evidenced by the thousands of former Iranian combatants who continue to live with scars and ailments caused by chemical weapons attacks.

The Forlorn Quest for Normalisation

Despite the heated rhetoric and animosity, it is worth remembering that every US administration since the Iranian revolution has sought to engage Iran to varying degrees, some even holding out the possibility of a partial rapprochement, if not a full-fledged normalisation. Jimmy Carter—who was the object of hatred for many revolutionaries—tried his best to come to terms with a revolution that had seemingly come from nowhere and at a stroke removed one of the US's most reliable allies. Certainly, Carter was not a natural friend of the Shah, and to this day there are plenty of die-hard Iranian monarchists who attribute the downfall of the Shah, at least in part, to Carter's decision to apply pressure on him to improve his dismal human rights record.

Ronald Reagan based his election campaign on staking out a tough position on Khomeini's Iran, and tilted US policy further in favour of Iraq during the war. But Reagan was loath to decisively move against the revolutionary regime in Tehran for a number of reasons, foremost among them being the delicate balance of power with the Soviet Union. Next to that in order of importance was Reagan's belief that a decisive Iraqi victory was not consistent with American national security interests. That view was shared across the Atlantic in London, where the continuation of the Iran–Iraq War (with a view to exhausting the protagonists) was deemed to be in line with Western interests.

Reagan had even tentatively reached out to his Iranian enemies, notably in the Iran–Contra scandal, which ultimately dealt a severe blow to US prestige on the global stage. The resolution of the embassy crisis in late 1980 (which saw the detained diplomats released in January 1981) led Reagan to believe that secret deals with Iran's new rulers could resolve sensitive issues and open doors that could be exploited for wider political and diplomatic goals. At the heart of the Iran–Contra affair was the belief in some American circles that the freedom of American hostages in Lebanon could be secured through the clandestine sale of arms to Iran.

Reagan's successor, George H. W. Bush, similarly sought to engage Iran, albeit at a less clandestine level. Bush Senior's decision to destroy the Iraqi war machine during Operation Desert Storm (January–February 1991) could not have been made without considering its consequences for the regional balance of power. Bush Senior and his team would have been all too aware that destroying Iraq's offensive capability would primarily benefit Iran, which continued to regard Iraq as its most proximate national security threat. This was one reason that Bush Senior and his advisers did not go all the way to Baghdad in March 1991 and in fact gave a green light to Saddam Hussein to crush the Kurdish and Shia-led rebellions in the north and south of his country.

Besides the dramatic shift in the US attitude on Baathist Iraq, the freeing of all American hostages in Lebanon by 1991 had raised hopes of a thaw in bilateral relations. Yet, in hindsight it was far too early to start serious engagement. For a start, memories of the Iran–Iraq War were still fresh in the collective psyche of the nation. The closing stages of the war had seen the US navy engage Iranian forces in the Persian Gulf during Operation Praying Mantis, which proved to be the US navy's largest battle since the Second World War. Moreover, just a few weeks before Ayatollah Khomeini's acceptance of United Nations Security Council Resolution 598 (which called for a ceasefire in the Iran–Iraq War), the US navy–guided missile cruiser *Vincennes* had shot down an Iranian airliner over the Persian Gulf, killing all 290 people on board. The US claimed the shooting was an accident but the Iranians were convinced it was an intentional act designed to coerce Iran into accepting ceasefire terms with Iraq.

In January 1993, the advent of the first Democrat US administration since Jimmy Carter's doomed presidency was met with a degree of uncertainty and even anxiety in Tehran. Hitherto, the Islamic Republic had dealt with Republican administrations, save for the first few years after the revolution when it had faced off against Jimmy Carter. There was a sense in Tehran that the Democrats were out for revenge as they blamed Iran for Carter's dramatic loss in the November 1980 presidential election. At any rate, Iranian leaders and key institutions such as the foreign ministry and the IRGC had not had to deal with a Democrat administration since the consolidation of the revolution. Their lack of experience merely added to the sense of anxiety.

Iranian fears were not eased by the Clinton administration's first major foreign policy initiative, the so-called 'dual containment' policy, formally announced in February 1994, which was ostensibly designed to contain Iran and Iraq simultaneously. The Iranians were less fearful of the actual practicalities of this policy than they were deeply insulted at being equated with Iraq. To the Iranians, it seemed that the US was intent on humiliating the country by not only negating its heritage, but also attempting to prevent it from playing a regional role consistent with its size, resources and potential. This perceived lack of respect goes to the heart of the Iranian–American estrangement and until it is adequately addressed by the Americans there is unlikely to be any significant shift in the nature of the relationship.

In keeping with established US policy, the Clinton administration sought to deny Iran a role in regional security arrangements. The context was especially worrying for Tehran, as the degradation of Iraq's offensive capability—coupled with the major military, diplomatic and political restrictions that were placed on Baghdad as part of the Gulf War settlement—had created a vacuum, which the Iranians felt they should fill. The George H. W. Bush administration had ignored Tehran's concerns and the Clinton administration followed suit.

Moreover, Clinton went further than other administrations by imposing new sanctions on the Islamic Republic in the spring of 1995 that sought to sever all US trade and investment with Iran.' This was followed by the Iran and Libya Sanctions Act of 1996 (modified to the Iran Sanctions Act in 2006), whose provisions targeted foreign firms that invested more than $20 million in the Iranian energy sector. By any measure, this was a major shift in US policy as it aggressively targeted Iran's most important industry. It was clearly designed to impede the modernisation of the Iranian hydrocarbon sector by blocking the transfer of knowledge and technology. In the diplomatic sphere, the sanctions of 1995–1996 effectively put paid to any expectation in Tehran that Washington might consider accommodating some of the country's legitimate concerns and interests.

Tensions rose further following a terrorist attack in Khobar, Saudi Arabia in June 1996 which killed nineteen US air force personnel. This terror attack had come on the heels of another attack on a US-run military training centre in Riyadh in November 1995 which resulted in the deaths of four US servicemen. Sections of the Clinton administration—in tandem with sympathetic elements in the US national security establishment—initially pointed the finger at Iran by implicating the local Hezbollah chapter in the Khobar Towers bombing.

In 2006 a US court found Iran and Hezbollah guilty by default, even though an exhaustive investigation by several US law enforcement and intelligence agencies had failed to throw up any incriminating evidence against the Islamic Republic. At any rate, the prevailing view in the US national security establishment is that this attack was planned and executed by Sunni jihadists affiliated to the then embryonic al-Qaeda network.

The electoral victory of reformists in the Iranian presidential election of May 1997 raised hopes that tensions might abate, and even of a determined move toward a partial rapprochement. By the time Mohammad Khatami had been sworn into office in August 1997, he and his team had already set out a foreign policy based on 'tension reduction' (*tanesh zodai*). Khatami had developed a metanarrative centred on the so-called 'dialogue of civilisations', which in practical terms meant an abundance of talks on religious and cultural understanding. Beyond vague promises and fancy theories, the reformists had few original ideas in the foreign policy sphere.

Whilst the Clinton administration was not necessarily displeased by the political supremacy of reformists in Tehran, the US was deeply reluctant to offer Iran anything that remotely resembled a concession. Indeed, sanctions remained in place and the US continued to 'contain'

Iranian influence in the region. Moreover, the US alliance with Israel remained as solid as ever and both countries continued to identify Iran as the primary spoiler in the Israeli–Palestinian peace process. Furthermore, it did not help that many of the reformists—particularly those active in the foreign policy sphere—were originally from the hard-left factions of the Islamic Republic. These were the same people who had planned and organised the seizure of the US embassy back in November 1979 and who had contributed the lion's share to the development of the revolution's anti-American creed.

These ideologues included Abbas Abdi and Ebrahim Asgharzadeh, both of whom were considered to have played leadership roles in the organisation known as the Muslim Students Following the Imam's Line. Whilst both men appeared to regret their actions as part of this movement—with Abdi at times seeming extremely repentant[8]—they were still deeply suspicious of US motives. Furthermore, their mere presence in the Khatami camp was regarded by hardliners in the US as a sign of residual anti-Americanism in the Iranian reformist movement.

Whilst Khatami waxed lyrical on the 'dialogue of civilisations', the reformist position on normalisation of ties to the US was gradually taking shape. The hard-left ideologues of the 1980s, who rebranded themselves as 'reformists' post-1989, wanted the US to make a substantial gesture, weighty enough that it could puncture a hole in the glacier that had frozen relations for two decades. In keeping with their left-wing heritage, the reformists were still exercised by the US role in the August 1953 coup that had toppled Mossadegh's nationalist government.

Although officially the Islamic Republic shunned Mossadegh and the political heritage associated with him, the left wing of the regime had distant ideological links to various strands of Iranian nationalism, including even Mossadeghism. To the establishment Mossadegh was anathema as he was identified as insufficiently Islamic, if not a full-fledged secularist. Moreover, as a descendant of the Qajar dynasty, Mossadegh was not deemed to be a truly anti-monarchical political figure. According to this point of view, Mossadegh's opposition to Mohammad Reza Shah—and the Pahlavi dynasty more broadly—was rooted in tribalism rather than political convictions. Furthermore, the clerical establishment had some historical axes to grind as Mossadegh was a political opponent of Ayatollah Abol-Ghasem Kashani, whose nationalist credentials was just as strong as Mossadegh's.

Nevertheless, not even the most die-hard ideologues of the Islamic Republic could afford to overlook the events of August 1953. For all his faults, Mohammad Mossadegh is undoubtedly a national figure in the strict historical sense. He led the drive for oil nationalisation and as a result became an inspiration to nationalists across the region. Whilst in Iran opinion is sharply polarised between those who adore him and those who loathe him, no credible Iranian political movement can afford to ignore Mossadegh's historical role.

It is in this context that Bill Clinton's secretary of state, Madeleine Albright, acknowledged the US role in unseating Mossadegh without offering an apology.[9] This was never going to be enough—not for the reformists, and certainly not for the establishment, which had always called for a full official US apology. Of course, that is unlikely to happen in the foreseeable future and thus one of the structural obstacles to a breakthrough in relations remains firmly in place.

The return of the Republicans to the presidency after George W. Bush's narrow victory in the November 2000 US presidential race signalled a decisive return to the status quo ante. A hawk in foreign policy terms, George W. Bush was always going to prove to be tough on the Iranian leadership, if only to satisfy the neo-conservative elements of his electoral base. The 11 September 2001 terrorist attacks on the Twin Towers in New York and on the Pentagon dramatically strengthened the hands of neo-conservatives in US national security circles. It was in part due to neo-conservative influence that Bush included Iran in the 'axis of evil' club during his State of the Union Address in January 2002. The speech was a body blow to Khatami and the reformists, who had gone out of their way to persuade the Iranian military to offer a degree of cooperation to the Americans in the operation to topple the Taliban.

Relations continued to deteriorate following the US-led invasion and occupation of Iraq in 2003, even though on the face of it Tehran should have been pleased with the overthrow of the Iraqi Baathists. Indeed, on one level the Iranians were elated by the ouster of Saddam Hussein, which threw up enormous opportunities for Iran's Shia allies in Iraq. But at a deeper level, the deployment of tens of thousands of American and British troops was a source of acute concern, as these troops posed an immediate threat to Iranian national security. It is important to remember the spirit of the times, with the US government and public alike fixated on 'preventative' wars so as to remove potential threats to US national security. Indeed, there was plenty of talk of preparing the ground for a military strike on Iran. In hindsight this can be understood as just talk and it can be seen that there was never a serious determination in Washington to engage the Islamic Republic at a military level.

Bush's tough rhetoric on Iran, coupled with the neo-conservative ascendance in Washington, was a major contributory factor to the loss of reformist influence in Tehran. In fact, it is arguable that it played an important role in the rise to power of the populist Mahmoud Ahmadinejad. The latter was supported by Iran's own brand of neo-conservatives who mixed radicalism with a vociferous form of populism. These Iranian neo-conservatives, most of whom had developed their networks during the formative years of the Iran–Iraq War, constituted a radical departure from mainstream conservatism as they called for social justice in the context of a return to the revolution's ideals. By contrast, the conservative establishment had long before abandoned the quest for social justice, rhetoric notwithstanding.

In the foreign policy sphere, Ahmadinejad and his inner circle believed in adopting an offensive posture and in that respect they were a suitable match for Bush and the neo-conservatives in Washington. By 2005 the reformists' foreign policy was widely regarded as a failure. By appearing to be soft in international affairs and to be willing to eschew revolutionary values for the sake of 'tension reduction', the reformists had only emboldened the hawks in the United States. That was the definitive view of both the conservative establishment and the emergent 'neo-conservatives' led by the maverick Ahmadinejad.

Bush's rhetorical flourish and the concerted campaign by allied neo-conservatives to push for a military strike on Iran confirmed the view held by the upper reaches of the Iranian leadership that the United States is instinctively inclined toward confrontation with the Islamic Republic. From this perspective, a conciliatory posture is tantamount to weakness and would merely embolden the Americans to push more aggressively for the implementation of their regime-change agenda.

As it turned out the confrontation between Bush and Ahmadinejad did not escalate into a shooting war (as many feared it would at the time), but it did put paid to any hopes of a breakthrough in relations. Consequently, the great wall of 'mistrust' went up even higher.

The Barack Obama presidency began with great promise, as Obama pledged to break with the attitude towards the Muslim world of the past eight years, characterised by conflict and violence on several fronts as part of the so-called 'War on Terror'. Obama was ostensibly committed to ending these conflicts with a view to placing America's relations with key Muslim-majority countries on a stable footing. His speech in Cairo in June 2009[10] gave rise to real expectations that his presidency would prove to be a radical departure from the Bush years.

In reality little changed on the ground, as Obama pursued the so-called War on Terror with the same vigour as his predecessor. In fact, in some aspects, notably the use of drones to target terror suspects, Obama proved to be more aggressive than Bush. Even his promise to close down the controversial detention facility in Guantanamo Bay was not fully discharged. Nonetheless, there was no denying that Obama's values and attitudes were different from his predecessor's. Moreover, the specific circumstances of Obama's upbringing—his birth in Hawaii, his Kenyan father and his four-year stay in Indonesia as a child—and his unmistakeable cosmopolitanism were powerful tools in the US diplomatic armoury.

In relation to Iran, Obama made an early outreach by calling on the country to unclench its fist. But these initial overtures were torpedoed by the events of June 2009, following the disputed presidential election which saw Ahmadinejad return for a second term in office. Whilst the US did not intervene in the political conflict in Tehran, Obama's rhetorical support for the protestors, particularly those who appeared to have been slain by Iranian security forces,[11] inevitably inflamed feelings and led to charges of US 'interference'.

It was only with the departure of Ahmadinejad that the Iranian national security establishment began to seriously consider engagement with the Obama administration. With the benefit of hindsight, it is now clear that secret negotiations between the two sides on the nuclear issue had begun in earnest in 2012, a year before Hassan Rouhani's election to the presidency. The site for these negotiations was Muscat,

Oman,[12] where Iranian and American delegations met secretly to thrash out the basis of what would later develop into a multilateral nuclear agreement known as the JCPOA.

Oman was a natural choice for these negotiations, as the country had played a mediating role between the two sides before, most recently as a facilitator in the release of three American hikers who had been convicted on espionage charges after illegally entering Iran from Iraqi Kurdistan. If Ahmadinejad had been a good match for Bush, then Hassan Rouhani was a more suitable match for Obama. Rouhani's long history in the national security establishment meant that he was well placed to manage delicate nuclear-related negotiations with the Americans, and later with an international delegation that included the UK, France, Germany, Russia and China.

The rapport that was established between Rouhani's foreign minister, Mohammad Javad Zarif, and Obama's secretary of state, John Kerry, was unprecedented since the Islamic revolution. When Zarif and Kerry met it seemed that Iran and the US were great friends, as opposed to longstanding enemies. This was in part attributable to the great diplomatic skills of the two men, and more broadly to the spirit of qualified cooperation that characterised their respective administrations. In the heady days of mid-2015 (with the ratification of the JCPOA), there were plenty of people who hoped that Iran and the US could build on the momentum generated by the nuclear deal to finally smash down the wall of mistrust. The dramatic rise to power of Donald Trump brought a swift and ignominious end to those hopes.

The Khamenei Factor

Many scholars and analysts have attributed the stubbornness of the Iranian–US standoff at least in part to the ideological positions of the Iranian leader Ayatollah Seyed Ali Khamenei.[13] The latter's anti-American credentials are not in doubt as he has been espousing the same world view for sixty years, well before the victory of the Iranian revolution. As a devotee of the Fadaiyan-e Islam group, Khamenei became acquainted with the ideology of the Muslim Brotherhood (which was a source of inspiration for the Fadaiyan-e Islam) at a relatively early age. Khamenei went on to translate the books of the Muslim Brotherhood ideologue Sayyid Qutb into Persian.

During the US embassy crisis of 1979–1980, Khamenei was one of the strongest advocates of the students and continually raised their concerns and points of view in the revolutionary council, of which he was a leading member. As well as being an unflinching 'Islamist', Khamenei is also a nationalist. He saw the road to Iranian independence as inevitably involving a clean break with the US, which he sees as a hegemonic power hell-bent on subjugating weaker nations across the globe. As an amateur historian, Khamenei made no distinction between the European empires of the nineteenth century and the rise of American global dominion. From Khamenei's point of view, the American discourse on liberty, democracy and free trade was essentially rhetoric deployed to create and sustain colonial spaces.

Closer to home, Khamenei saw the US as posing an immediate threat to the Islamic revolution. He was hardly alone in that feeling, as most Iranian revolutionary leaders (save for a few technocrats in Bazargan's doomed provisional government) viewed the US with deep suspicion. What made Khamenei stand out was his long-term perspective, and his consistently expressed belief from the very early days of the revolution that the US would prove to be Iran's nemesis, potentially in perpetuity. From this point of view, as long as Iran held fast to revolutionary values and sought to propagate these values beyond the country's borders, the US would remain committed to the overthrow of the Iranian revolution.

Ayatollah Khamenei's ascension to the leadership in June 1989 led to the institutionalisation of the state's anti-American ideology. In the 1980s anti-Americanism was largely a symptom of broader radicalism, as opposed to a clear-cut ideological position. It was continually sustained by the US's actual or perceived indiscretions, not least its support for Saddam Hussein. But despite the US's obvious opposition to the revolution, the Islamic Republic did not reflexively rule out a rapprochement, provided, of course, the Americans revised their attitude.

During Ayatollah Khamenei's leadership the question of re-establishing ties with the US became an issue of dogma. It was in the early 1990s that observers and analysts were increasingly talking of a 'taboo' in relation to advocating for the restoration of ties. This was a radical departure from the 1980s when no one talked about restoration of ties in those terms. To be sure, few serious Iranian politicians advocated for normalisation during that period, but simply talking to 'the Great Satan' was not regarded as taboo.

Some reformists have quipped that the reason Khamenei and the right-wing factions close to him have staked out such a dogmatic attitude on the issue is that they want to 'manage' the eventual restoration of ties on their own terms. In other words, they don't want the reformists to take credit for the breakthrough. This is at best a reductive analysis, and one that fails to take sufficient stock of the enormous complexities surrounding the issue.

For a start, aggressive US policies towards Iran actually intensified in the 1990s, as demonstrated by the harsh sanctions regime instituted by the Clinton administration. Whilst sanctions have been a prominent feature of US diplomacy towards the Islamic Republic from the very beginning, there was expectation in some Iranian quarters that following the end of the Iran–Iraq War, and as memories of the US embassy crisis faded, these sanctions would be steadily eased, and possibly lifted altogether. By the mid-1990s it was apparent that the United States viewed sanctions as the most important element of its Iran toolkit and that it would not consider significantly easing them unless and until there was a radical shift in Iranian behaviour in the region.

Second, in tandem with the extension and deepening of the sanctions regime, the US stepped up its drive to isolate Iran in the region and beyond. In the Persian Gulf arena, the US was determined to deny Iran a suitable role in emerging security arrangements following the Kuwait War of 1991. The US also appeared determined to thwart legitimate Iranian economic and commercial interests. The drive to deny Iran the opportunity to transport oil and natural gas from the Caspian Sea to the Persian Gulf dealt an important blow to Iranian prestige.[14] Besides the economic damage, it also represented a loss for Iran in strategic terms as the pipelines would have enhanced Iran's regional role by joining the Caspian Sea to the Persian Gulf.

Third, the US did not relent in its drive to bring about political changes in Iran that were consistent with US national security interests. In the 1990s the 'regime change' discourse took shape as the Clinton administration officially allocated funds to so-called 'pro-democracy' projects. The lion's share, amounting to $18 million, went to a supposedly secret CIA operation to subvert Iranian politics.[15] This was a serious escalation insofar as it committed the United States to political transformation in Iran. Again, it represented a departure from the 1980s when the US appeared to be merely coming to terms with the ramifications of the Iranian revolution. There was no consistent and coherent policy at the time to effect political changes inside Iran.

In the final analysis, whilst it is undeniably true that Ayatollah Khamenei's leadership is the key driver of the Islamic Republic's anti-American ethos, it is important to take account of the fact that this is not merely an ideological position. Nor has it crystallised in a vacuum. US actions and rhetoric have played a big part in creating the conditions that allow for a tough attitude on the US to prevail. Moreover, it is worth remembering that Ayatollah Khamenei's allies across the Iranian national security establishment point out that in reality there is no 'taboo' on the restoration of ties. They suggest that once the US relinquishes its 'bullying' attitude towards Iran and demonstrates a desire to engage on equal terms, possibilities for reconciliation will open up.

The Trump Factor

By all credible accounts, Donald Trump's presidency seems to bode ill for Iranian–US relations. Trump's disruptive style of leadership, coupled with his American nationalist ideology, can potentially unsettle the complex stalemate which defines America's relationship with Iran. That may indeed be Trump's intention, as he takes pride in being a 'disruptor' and in not shying away from confrontation with states whose positions threaten key US economic and national security interests.

Trump's tearing up of the JCPOA throws down the gauntlet to Iranian leaders who have vowed not to renegotiate the nuclear deal. Moreover, the increasing alignment of US regional policies with those of Saudi Arabia and Israel is a cause of real concern for Tehran as it speaks to a developing plan to contain Iran's strategic depth with a view to reversing it. Perhaps without even realising it, Trump appears to be correcting the policies of George W. Bush that had unwittingly given fresh impetus to Iran's strategic momentum. For example, the decision to invade Iraq was a fundamental misalignment of US policy with the national security interests of key ally Saudi Arabia. Saddam Hussein's downfall empowered the Shias, which in turn complicated Riyadh's national security environment.

And of course, by his own admission Trump is consciously reversing Obama's foreign policy legacy. The nuclear deal was misaligned with Israel's national security interests and Trump's withdrawal from it adequately addresses one of Israel's key concerns about the Islamic Republic. Whilst Trump justifies this shift in US policy in terms of his American nationalist doctrine, there are plenty of influential voices in Washington who are not convinced that near-perfect alignment with Riyadh and Tel Aviv is necessarily consistent with US national security interests.

In keeping with his disruptive leadership style, Trump aspires to a radical shakeup of the way the US has managed the four-decades-old stand-off with the Islamic Republic. But how realistic is this aspiration in view of the multiple dimensions and complexities which define this most vexed of relationships? At an institutional level, both powers have grown accustomed to the 'no war no peace' stalemate of their relationship. This peculiar state of affairs is exemplified by the existing balance of power in the Persian Gulf. Despite the massive disparity in conventional military power, the IRGC navy has imposed a semblance of balance—or at least the appearance of it—through the skilful adoption of asymmetric tactics.

Any change to the US navy's rules of engagement vis-à-vis the IRGC navy could potentially spark a days-long naval confrontation. This is a real risk as the IRGC navy prides itself on closely tracking the movement of the US and British navies through the Strait of Hormuz. At times this monitoring has taken the form of harassment as the Iranian speedboats come dangerously close to US warships. Usually a warning shot is enough to encourage disengagement. However, should US warships fire on IRGC speedboats in anger, it may well set off a vicious circle of engagement and retaliation. This is one reason that unlike Trump, US naval commanders are not keen on a change to existing rules of engagement.

The US decision to impose the 'strongest' sanctions in history on Iran by November 2018, a plan which apparently includes a determination to prevent Iran from exporting oil, has prompted Iranian political and military leaders to threaten the closure of the Strait of Hormuz. The rationale is clear-cut according to Iranian leaders: if Iran cannot export oil, other countries should not be able to either. The commander of the Qods Force, Major-General Qasem Soleimani, raised the temperature further in July by addressing Trump after the US president's attack on his Iranian counterpart. Appearing to suggest that the regular Iranian military would not necessarily get involved in a conflict with the US, Soleimani told Trump that the US would exclusively be facing him and the Qods Force. 'There is not a night that goes by when we don't think about you,' Soleimani told Trump.

At a practical level, whilst the IRGC navy has the capability to close the Strait of Hormuz—possibly for several days—equally the US navy has the ability to re-open it. Any escalation from that point could see a return to the final months of the Iran–Iraq War and Operation Praying Mantis, during the course of which US naval assets in the Persian Gulf destroyed a quarter of the Iranian navy.[16] Retaliatory strikes by the IRGC Qods Force beyond the immediate operational theatre— for example terror-style attacks on US forces in the wider region— might well spark US attacks on the Iranian mainland. This form of rapid escalation, whilst unlikely, cannot be ruled out as long as Donald Trump is president.

Yet even with Trump at the helm in Washington, there is reason to be hopeful that Iran and the US will choose to avoid any form of military confrontation. For a start, key US foreign policy and national security institutions, including the Pentagon, the State Department and the CIA, are at odds with Trump on foreign policy generally, and specifically in relation to the Middle East. In view of the complexity of Iranian–US relations, it is doubtful that any of these institutions would advocate for military action, except under truly extraordinary circumstances.

This complexity encompasses mutual entanglement across the region's flashpoints, from Syria to Yemen. In Syria, for example, Iranian and US forces are based in very close proximity in some areas, notably in the east of the country. Meanwhile in neighbouring Iraq, Iran and the

US are ostensibly on the same side in terms of their mutual support for the Iraqi government. But there is no denying the deep tension, with some pro-Iranian Shia-led militia groups at times openly threatening the Americans.[17]

In other spheres too, the entanglement is deep and tortuous, as for example in the case of the American prisoners held in Iran and vice versa.[18] A military confrontation would only further complicate these fraught issues, probably setting back prospects for reconciliation by decades. But even in the absence of military conflict, there is reason to believe that this four-decades-old confrontation has yet to peak. The US is still not prepared to accept Iran as a major regional power. Absent a significant shift in Iranian attitudes and behaviour, specifically in relation to Israel, it is difficult to envisage a shift in this deeply entrenched American attitude. For its part, Iran is likely to press ahead with plans to strengthen both conventional and asymmetric military capabilities, to the point of securing immunity from US 'bullying'.

CONCLUSION

At the time of writing the Trump administration has just re-imposed punishing sanctions on Iran. These follow on the heels of Trump's decision in May 2018 to abandon the landmark nuclear accord, known as the JCPOA. The withdrawal from the JCPOA dealt a big blow to the government of Hassan Rouhani, which had staked so many hopes and expectations on the deal.

In his election campaign of May 2013, Rouhani had promised full sanctions relief in the event of a comprehensive deal. But once the deal was struck sanctions were never fully lifted as the Obama administration dragged its feet. Even so, the populace held out hope that total sanctions relief would come, and that Iran would be allowed to fully integrate into the international system.

Now that the deal has collapsed Rouhani has much to answer for. Above all, he will have to explain the naivety of his foreign policy team in trusting the United States. Over the past four decades a cardinal tenet of the Islamic Republic's foreign policy has been its lack of trust in the United States. This is a tried and tested doctrine, which originated during the revolution and is fully reflective of four decades of tension, misunderstanding and mistrust. The same feeling prevails in Washington where animosity toward Iran straddles the political divide.

In view of this history it is remarkable that a seasoned national security apparatchik like Rouhani, alongside his team of highly experienced diplomats led by Mohammad Javad Zarif, took the bold step of reaching out to the Obama administration. The Rouhani team was consistently warned not to trust the United States, yet it chose to ignore this advice in the belief that the dividends flowing from a successful deal outweighed the fall-out from a failed process.

The collapse of the deal is a personal tragedy for Rouhani and the leading members of his government, and effectively reduces his role for the remainder of his second term to that of a lame duck president. More broadly, the entire process of negotiating the JCPOA culminating in its eventual rejection by the US has been a traumatic experience for Iranian diplomacy. It is one of the harshest lessons of the past forty years, and its legacy and repercussions will likely continue to unfold for years to come.

Trump's decision to withdraw from the nuclear deal has set back the prospect of bilateral rapprochement for many years, possibly decades. Any future Iranian government is likely to exercise far more caution before engaging in serious diplomacy with the US.

At this point there are two pressing issues confronting Iran. The first one is the impact of the sanctions and the extent to which they will damage the economy. When the Obama administration imposed tough unilateral sanctions in January 2012, the effects were sufficiently far-reaching that many analysts and commentators saw them as at least partly responsible for Iran's decision to enter talks in earnest. Another point to be made about the last round of tough sanctions was their relatively short duration—just over 18 months—before they were incrementally eased from autumn 2013 onwards.

Of course, the Iranians denied that sanctions had any role in their decision to enter talks, initially held secretly in Oman and only with the US and then becoming part of a multilateral negotiating process, which eventually produced the JCPOA. However, strenuous denials notwithstanding, there can be little doubt that fear of the future impact of sustained sanctions, if not their actual effects, was a major factor nudging Iran toward a compromise posture.

This time around, the situation is even more serious. The widescale protests and rioting that took place in late December 2017 and January 2018 were provoked by specific economic and financial factors, including widespread unemployment at the provincial level, environmental factors,[1] unfair distribution of resources, collapsing credit institutions and the fear of collapse of pension funds.

Those protests took place before the US pull-out from the JCPOA and the re-introduction of sanctions. Since May 2018 the Iranian currency has been in freefall and the price of gold has soared. The combined effect of this economic instability led to protests in June, with intermittent and random protests continuing throughout the summer.

One of the key goals of the Trump administration is to foment social and political unrest in Iran through the application of sanctions. The Trump team believes that unrest on the streets will force Iran's leaders to reconsider their position and to return to talks on American terms.

As sanctions begin to bite, with a concomitant fall in purchasing power and living standards, there may well be an uptick in social unrest. How expansive and sustained this will be remains to be seen but on their current trajectory random protests, lacking in identifiable and credible leadership, no matter how big are unlikely to have a major political impact. Moreover, the security forces will likely nip them in the bud before they have the opportunity to expand.

The second issue relates to the political and strategic calculus of Iranian leaders, and specifically the issue of whether they will reconsider their position in the light of the tough sanctions regime. On the face of it, this seems unlikely, at least for the duration of Trump's presidency. Trump is seeking not only a revision to the terms and conditions of the nuclear deal, but a much more expansive agreement that covers both Iran's ballistic missiles programme and the country's regional posture.

Both issues are close to the heart of Iranian leaders, who are loath to submit to any restrictions on these fronts, let alone controls dictated by Washington. Both issues are central to Iran's national security and any Iranian government would consider concessions, let alone major restrictions, at its own peril. Moreover, any concessions on these issues would require consensus across Iran's complex state machinery, meaning a degree of alignment between the avowed state and the parallel state—agreement that would take a long time to thrash out.

At any rate, sanctions alone, no matter how punitive or crippling, are unlikely to change Iran's regional posture. The Islamic Republic is deeply entrenched in Iraq and the Levant region and it has both the resources and motivation to maintain a presence in these areas virtually indefinitely.

Moreover, Iran is also deeply involved in the Israeli–Palestinian conflict, albeit indirectly. More than three decades of sustained investment on this issue have ensured an influential role for Iran, not only in terms of the Palestinians' confrontation with Israel, but also in relation to intra-Palestinian disputes.

Iran has a firm and unwavering ally in the form of Palestinian Islamic Jihad organisation and a more reluctant partner in Hamas. The latter's control of the Gaza Strip makes it a key stakeholder in the entire conflict and one whose role could potentially become dominant if the West Bank-based and Fatah-dominated Palestinian Authority continues to decline.

Whilst Iran is not a decisive outside actor in this conflict (Egypt and the United States wield far more immediate influence) and while the broader landscape pertaining to the Israeli–Palestinian dispute is extremely dense (with even small states like Qatar able to exercise influence in the Gaza Strip by supplying money[2]), the Islamic Republic can still maintain a credible role.

Hitherto, Iran has played the role of spoiler by consistently opposing a political solution based on the Oslo accords of 1993 and 1995. Iran argued from the outset that the 'peace process' and its goal of a two-state solution were non-starters, thus defying the mood of optimism and expectation of that era.

But a quarter of a century later, the two-state solution is now widely regarded as moribund. The associated deep malaise and loss of hope permeating every layer of Palestinian society speak to the profound crisis gripping the Occupied Territories.[3]

The despair and sense of crisis which grip the Palestinian landscape indicate that any outside power which seeks to remedy the situation must begin to present new solutions. Therefore, if Iran wants to maintain and even expand its influence in that arena, it must rethink its role of perpetual spoiler and offer imaginative solutions outside the two-state paradigm. Simply insisting on the destruction of Israel—if only by political means—may no longer prove enough.

In Yemen, Iran has hitherto formulated a smart policy of intervening in Saudi Arabia's backyard without committing troops or indeed much in the way of resources. The extent of Iran's support to the Houthis remains deeply contested, and beyond supplying knowhow—and possibly some materiel and spare parts—for the upgrade of Yemeni ballistic missiles, it is not clear if Iran has made or indeed needs to make a deeper intervention.

The success of the intervention comes primarily in the form of the ideological orientation of the Ansarullah movement, popularly referred to as the Houthis. What started as a parochial fight for northern Yemeni rights within the framework of greater local autonomy has developed into a national struggle with pan-regional ambitions, as demonstrated by Houthi slogans and iconography, which now bear a striking resemblance to Lebanon's Hezbollah. Indeed, the Ansarullah movement is now firmly ensconced in Iran's ideological orbit as a committed member of the so-called axis of resistance.

The Houthis and their allies in the Yemeni military continue to fend off Saudi- and Emirati-backed forces ranged against them in Aden and the south, as well as fighting the Kingdom of Saudi Arabia and the United Arab Emirates directly. Repeated ballistic missiles attacks on the KSA have achieved the desired psychological effect of painting the Saudi-led war as unwinnable. Moreover, by threatening to attack the UAE[4]—in particular Dubai—the Houthis hold out the prospect of rapid escalation in the event of intolerable pressure, for instance a UAE-sponsored assault on Sana'a.

Aside from the massive humanitarian crisis that it has engendered, the other distinctive feature of the Yemen conflict is the impotence of aspiring regional powers Saudi Arabia and the UAE. Despite committing considerable military resources to prosecuting parallel (and sometimes conflicting) military campaigns, and even going to the extent of recruiting mercenaries,[5] in addition to enjoying active support from both the US and Britain, Saudi Arabia and the UAE have hit a dead-end in Yemen. The conflict has demonstrated that these aspiring regional powers have neither the military prowess nor the strategic acumen to accomplish even minimal military and strategic objectives.

In view of the depth and breadth of Iran's regional involvement, it is difficult to see how the US can even begin the process of rolling it back without threatening a direct confrontation. But will the US—even under the leadership of the aggressive Donald Trump—really consider going to war with Iran? The answer, for now at least, would appear to be 'no', not least as the established US foreign policy community (the State Department, the CIA and the Pentagon) is opposed to it for fear of touching off unintended consequences.

Even a limited military confrontation, such as an engagement between the US navy and Islamic Revolutionary Guards Corps (IRGC) naval forces in the Persian Gulf, would lead the Iranian leadership and its strategists to militarise their thinking immediately. Kinetic action would almost certainly push the Iranian leadership to abandon the nuclear deal altogether and resume uranium enrichment and related activities in earnest. In view of the sophistication of Iran's nuclear establishment, there can be little doubt that Iran could produce a nuclear weapon, if the political decision were made to undertake such a game-changing move.

There are other scenarios in which the nuclear deal could collapse altogether. If the Europeans fail to offer Iran adequate sanctions relief—via a proposed alternative payment system referred to as the 'Special Purpose Vehicle'[6]—then Iran is likely to conclude that there is little incentive to continue complying with the terms and conditions of the JCPOA.

Additionally, if the US applies too much pressure—for instance by demonstrating resolve to reduce Iranian oil exports to zero—then the rational calculus of the Iranian leadership may be adversely affected, potentially leading to irrational choices. Of course, there are plenty of people in Iran (and elsewhere) who would argue that abandoning the JCPOA and fully resuming the nuclear programme does not constitute an irrational choice under current conditions.

Moreover, there is a significant constituency in Iran that favours the militarisation of the nuclear programme to meet extreme US threats. This group often cites North Korea as a putatively successful example of an embattled state deterring threats through nuclear parity. They also refer to Gaddafi's Libya as an example of how deeply vulnerable a state becomes once it gives up its nuclear weapons ambitions.

It is important to stress that at present there is no suggestion inside Iranian policymaking circles of opting for the nuclear option. In view of the complexity of the policymaking process in Iran and the abiding need to achieve inter-institutional consensus, both within the avowed state and between the avowed state and the parallel state, moving to such a decision would likely be slow and laborious.

The Iranian leadership and the foreign policymaking community are highly aware that any decision to escalate their nuclear programme would have huge repercussions across the region and would materially affect Iran's relations with all key regional players and the Western powers.

The biggest danger emanates from Israel, which has in the past repeatedly threated to bomb Iranian nuclear installations. Whilst Israel will in any case be anxious to attack the installations in the event of an Iranian 'breakout', it is unclear whether it actually has the capability to inflict serious damage on the Iranian nuclear establishment, let alone to destroy it.[7] Amongst defence experts there is a consensus that only the United States has the ability to deliver a 'knockout' blow to the Iranian nuclear programme, and then only temporarily.

There have been reports that Saudi Arabia may react to Iranian nuclear escalation by building its own bomb.[8] But Saudi Arabia's track record of developing sophisticated indigenous industries is not strong, particularly in the defence sector. Despite purchasing tens of billions of dollars' worth of military equipment and weapons (and spending similar amounts on training and maintenance) in the past three decades, the Kingdom ultimately remains deeply dependent on its Western allies for its security.

Saudi Arabia is much more likely to try to buy a nuclear weapon (possibly from Pakistan) than to build one. But the net result would be the same, namely the spectre of nuclear proliferation in the Middle East. At an official level, Iran is committed to counter-proliferation, as embodied by Iran's membership of the Non-Proliferation Treaty (NPT).

But Iran's deeper argument is that the greatest subversion of the NPT in the Middle East is represented by Israel's possession of nuclear weapons. Therefore, theoretically at least, an argument can be made that as nuclear proliferation has already occurred in the Middle East, additional acquisition—and particularly one that is primarily designed to achieve parity with Israel—can be construed as deterrence.

But at a legal and official level, Iran cannot realistically produce a nuclear weapon and attempt to justify it to the world as long as it remains a signatory to the NPT. Hitherto, the Islamic Republic has been compliant with its international treaty obligations, as demonstrated by its abiding by the terms of the JCPOA, and hence it would be highly aberrant behaviour if it were to brazenly violate both the letter and the spirit of the NPT.

Beyond the strategic and legal challenges, an additional obstacle is the internal battle over incorporating nuclear weapons into Iran's national security doctrine. Hitherto, the Islamic Republic has not produced a coherent national security doctrine in the manner, for example, of the UK's Strategic Defence and Security Review. We can study Iran's unwritten national security doctrine through the pronouncements of army and IRGC commanders, as well as the speeches of Ayatollah Khamenei. But internally—in terms of the ways the Iranian forces go about organising national defence—a coherent doctrine and internal debates are vital to justify the acquisition of a powerful new capability.

There is also an additional problem of managing public opinion. Hitherto, Iranian leaders have been telling their public that they are not interested in nuclear weapons. In the mid-1990s, Ayatollah Khamenei reportedly issued a *fatwa* against the acquisition and use of nuclear weapons. This alone would make the public acquisition of nuclear weapons highly problematic. Of course, Iran can try to circumvent the public relations problem by keeping its acquisition a secret, but that would fatally undermine their deterrent effect, which, as consistently argued in this book, constitutes Iran's primary motivation for developing nuclear weapons in the first place.

Given these difficulties it is fair to assume that the Iranian leadership will resist the temptation of going down the nuclear route, partly as a result of massive US pressure. But there is a degree of unpredictability—for instance, a US attack on Iran or Iranian forces in Syria could galvanise the leadership to seriously consider the acquisition of nuclear weapons, if only to deter the United States from waging full-scale war against the Islamic Republic.

The behaviour of Washington's regional allies in the next two years will also be important. If either Israel or Saudi Arabia attacks Iran directly, and the US takes active measures to support its allies, that could also touch off a radical rethink of defensive doctrine in Tehran. The outcome of such a conflict would be crucial to Iran's appraisal of its situation. In any direct conflict with Israel or Saudi Arabia, Iran is likely to rely on its arsenal of mid- to long-range ballistic missiles to inflict damage and, more importantly, to conclude hostilities in the quickest time frame possible.

If the deployment of ballistic missiles proves successful, particularly in a swarming-style attack in which hundreds if not thousands of missiles are unleashed against specific targets, then Iran is likely to maintain its current defensive posture. In other words, ballistic missiles will continue to be the country's primary means of deterrence.

Beyond the threat posed by the Trump administration and its commitment to crippling sanctions, the Islamic Republic must address a range of key domestic and foreign policy issues if it wants to defy Washington's and its allies' attempts to arrest its strategic momentum.

First and foremost, the Iranian government must adequately address the country's deep structural economic malaise. Whilst it is true that sanctions over the years have taken their toll, the real economic story of the past three decades (since the end of the war with Iraq) revolves around structural issues related to corruption, lack of transparency and above all the phenomenon of parallelism.

Parallelism refers to economic structures outside the control of the government. The phenomenon of the *Bonyads* (foundations) is rooted in the 1980s, but only began to grow out of control in the 1990s. Initially these foundations—notably the Bonyad-e Mostazafan (Foundation of the Dispossessed)—were established to manage the confiscated wealth of the ousted royal family and senior functionaries of the Pahlavi regime. In time they became large and established economic players in their own right whose activities are generally beyond the control and oversight of the government. Additionally, many of these foundations pay little or no tax.

In addition to the post-revolutionary *Bonyads*, there is also the issue of more established autonomous economic entities which continue to operate without effective oversight. The best example is the Astaneh Qods Razavi, ostensibly a charitable organisation whose mission is to administer the Imam Reza shrine in Mashhad.

In reality this Mashhad-based organisation presides over a vast business empire, employing tens of thousands of workers and reportedly turning out annual profits to the tune of $15 billion.[9] The untaxed nature of this wealth—and the associated lack of transparency as to how it is distributed and spent—is inimical to public confidence in the Iranian government's ability to formulate and implement a cohesive national economy.

Beyond the *Bonyads* and their cartel-like business structure, there is the highly vexed issue of the IRGC and its economic interests. Whilst it is true that the Revolutionary Guards' involvement in the economy has been exaggerated, there is no denying their economic role. IRGC commanders themselves often showcase their economic capabilities, as embodied by the Gharargah-e Sazandegi Khatam al-Anbiya (Khatam al-Anbiya Construction Headquarters).[10] Founded during the Iran–Iraq War, this vast engineering firm now easily qualifies as Iran's largest major infrastructure and project management contractor.

Revolutionary Guards commanders argue that the Pasdaran's involvement at the strategic heights of the economy, whether through Khatam al-Anbiya or related entities, not only does not distort the economy but is in fact filling a crucial vacuum. They argue that the IRGC is the sole organisation in the country with the resources and expertise to manage large-scale infrastructure projects. In addition, they argue that the political reliability of the Pasdaran makes them less vulnerable to corruption and inefficiency.

Whilst there is obviously some truth to these positions, the fact remains that the IRGC—in tandem with the *Bonyads* to which it is ideologically aligned—introduces a degree of parallelism to the economy, which at the very least complicates the government's aspiration to oversee the entire national economy. Absent a strong economic base, Iran cannot sustain a dominant regional position in the long-term.

Another issue of central importance to Iran's regional position and prestige is reputational management. The new revolutionary state was initially popular across the region as Middle Eastern communities admired the Iranian people's courage and resolve to overthrow a deeply established monarchy and create a new political society from scratch. Whilst Persian Gulf monarchies such as Saudi Arabia, the Emirates, Bahrain and Kuwait worked hard to depict the Iranian revolution through a sectarian lens, there was a period in the 1980s when the rhetoric and world view of the Iranian revolution held pan-sectarian appeal across the Middle East and North Africa.

In subsequent decades this appeal diminished, not only because of the propaganda of established regimes but perhaps more importantly because Iran itself began to prioritise the national interest above revolutionary values. In recent years Iran's reputation in the Arab Sunni world has taken a battering, largely because of the Islamic Republic's intervention in the Syrian conflict. Apart from the sectarian dimension of the conflict, the heavy civilian death toll and reported atrocities by the Syrian government—including the use of chemical weapons—have hardened attitudes towards Iran and its allies amongst Sunni communities in the region.

Deep and long-term engagement with the region requires proper reputational management and extensive outreach to all the region's communities and their elites. At present, sustained community outreach is not a well-established feature of Iran's regional strategy. While it is true that the Islamic Republic properly looks after its core regional constituency—primarily by allocating funds to the welfare programmes of its non-state allies such as Hezbollah—it is far less concerned with the welfare of other communities. Without a comprehensive regional outlook—and one that takes sufficient stock of humanitarian issues—Iran's intervention across the region risks being perceived in imperial terms.

Finally, Iran's own domestic stability is crucial to its regional posture. There has been at least one episode of serious instability in the last decade, in the aftermath of the June 2009 disputed presidential elections. In addition, sporadic protests and riots have taken place, most recently in late December 2017 and early January 2018.

None of these protests have threatened the legitimacy or integrity of the Islamic Republic, nor do they threaten to do so in the absence of a credible alternative to the current ruling system. Without credible opposition platforms inside the country (as opposed to dislocated and unpopular exiled groups), intermittent protests will not be able to expand into something more serious or meaningful.

But periodic outbreaks of instability incur reputational costs, which in turn undermine Iran's regional standing. If the ultimate goal of the Islamic Republic is to drive out the United States from the region in order to create a new regional security architecture, it needs to first ensure that its own house is in proper order.

NOTES

IRAN'S BACKGROUND

1. 'President Ahmadinejad turns against regime's guard in Iran', *The Times*, 5 July 2011, https://www.thetimes.co.uk/article/president-ahmadinejad-turns-against-regimes-guard-in-iran-3wkf6w9c3bp

2. *The Washington Post*, 'The Omani "back channel" to Iran and the secrecy surrounding the nuclear deal', David Ignatius, 7 June 2016, https://www.washingtonpost.com/opinions/the-omani-back-channel-to-iran-and-the-secrecy-surrounding-the-nuclear-deal/2016/06/07/0b9e27d4-2ce1-11e6-b5db-e9bc84a2c8e4_story.html?utm_term=.1557b8225d92

POLITICAL SOCIETY

1. The EDC's full name is Expediency Discernment Council of the System.

2. Iran Student Correspondents Association, 'Dr. Velayati Appointed Head of IAU Board of Trustees', 4 February 2017, http://en.iscanews.ir/news/574448

3. BBC Persian, 21 July 2017, http://www.bbc.com/persian/blog-viewpoints-40685451

4. Nasser Karimi, 'Iranian supreme leader Ayatollah Khamenei in hospital after "routine" prostate surgery', *The Independent*, 8 September 2014, http://www.independent.co.uk/news/world/middle-east/iranian-ayatollah-khamenei-in-hospital-after-routine-surgery-9717464.html

5. Yasser Okbi and Maariv Hashavua, 'Speculation over successor after Iran's Khamenei reportedly hospitalized in serious condition', *The*

Jerusalem Post, 5 March 2015, http://www.jpost.com/Middle-East/ Speculation-over-successor-after-doctors-reportedly-say-Irans-Khamenei-has-two-years-left-to-live-393007

6. The full speech can be accessed here: https://www.youtube.com/ watch?v=ToD56sFDpqM
7. The best example is the Fars news agency: http://www.farsnews.com/
8. The bulk of the MeK organisation is currently based in Tirana, Albania.
9. Human Rights Watch, 'Iran: Allow Peaceful Protests Over Lake's Destruction', 10 September 2011, https://www.hrw.org/ news/2011/09/10/iran-allow-peaceful-protests-over-lakes-destruction

ASYMMETRIC CAPABILITY

1. It has been widely reported that Yazdi wanted to return F-14 Tomcats. Had he succeeded, Iran would have been at an immediate disadvantage in the air war vis-à-vis the Iraqi air force following the outbreak of major hostilities in September 1980.
2. SAVAK stands for Sazeman-e-Eteelaat va Amneeyat-e-Keshvar, or the National Security Intelligence Organisation.
3. Some have even opined that Jahanbani's blonde hair (he was of partial Russian heritage) and his flawless good looks were a factor in his execution as the revolutionaries perceived him as the embodiment of alien influences.
4. Jon Lee Anderson, 'Tariq Aziz and the Last of the Baathists', *The New Yorker*, 8 June 2015, https://www.newyorker.com/news/news-desk/ tariq-aziz-and-the-last-of-the-baathists
5. Mohammad Sadeq al-Sadr was most famous for his work on 'tribal' jurisprudence. Indeed, he produced a body of work under that same name. As a result of his scholarly work focused on the tribes—and his attendant popularity with the urban working class (who still clung on to tribal mores)—he was perceived to be a populist cleric.
6. 'Iraq's Muqtada al-Sadr makes rare Saudi visit', Al Jazeera, 31 July 2017, http://www.aljazeera.com/news/2017/07/iraq-muqtada-al-sadr-rare-saudi-visit-170731073908238.html
7. Allegedly the fighter pilots were assassinated by highly trained teams directed by the Qods Force of the IRGC and other Iranian security/ intelligence organisations, including the Ministry of Intelligence. These teams were likely embedded in or were an outgrowth of the so-called 'Special Groups' which comprised the elite of the militant wing of the Sadrists and the elements closest to Iran.

8.   To this date the culprits behind the murder of Mohammad Sadeq al-Sadr and his two sons have not been identified. The Sadrists, alongside most politically conscious Iraqi Shias, blame the Saddam regime, despite the latter calling for the identification and arrest of the perpetrators shortly after the assassination. In view of the sensitivity of the case—not least the fact that Sadeq al-Sadr had links to parts of the Iraqi establishment—it is unlikely that a formal Iraqi intelligence service carried out the killing. Speculatively speaking, the order for the killing most likely hailed from the top of the Baathist hierarchy but was outsourced to local criminal groups.

9.   It is named after Fatima Zahra, or Fatima bint Muhammad, the youngest daughter of Prophet Muhammad and the wife of Ali ibn Abi Talib, who was the fourth caliph according to orthodox Sunni Muslims and first Imam of the Twelver Shia Muslims. Fatima was the mother of Imams Hassan and Hussein, the latter being the iconic martyr of Shia Islam.

10.   The liberation of Khorramshahr, following the Beit al-Moghadass operation, which started in April 1982, is widely considered by military experts and strategists as the defining turning point in the Iran–Iraq War. Before the spring of 1982 Iraq occupied large swathes of the south-western Khuzestan province and effectively held the advantage in the war. But beginning in March 1982 with the Fath al-Mobeen (Clear Victory) operation, followed by Beit al-Moghadass (Sacred House, i.e. Jerusalem), the Iraqis were pushed out of Khuzestan province, thus denying them their essential war aims. From June 1982 onward Iran held the upper hand in the war, a position which lasted until April 1988 when Iraq regained the initiative.

11.   The Iranian Karbala-4 offensive of late December 1986 was planned to occupy Iraq's second city Basra and thus to cut Iraq in half and force the capitulation of the Baathist regime in Baghdad. The operation was Iran's biggest military disaster of the war and resulted in at least 10,000 deaths. The subsequent Karbala-5 operation was more successful and some forward Iranian units reached the outskirts of Basra (barely 10 km away from the city centre) but they were eventually pushed back by a determined Iraqi counter-offensive. Karbala-5 is widely regarded as the toughest and costliest battle of the Iran–Iraq War.

12.   In Iran it is common practice to promote 'martyred' officers by one rank.

13.   The first intensive campaign occurred in the summer of 1985 when Iraq deployed the Mig-25 Foxbat to drop inaccurate bombs on Tehran. The Mig-25's terrific speed meant that it could evade Iran's F-14 Tomcats.

14.   CIA Directorate of Intelligence, 'Iran-Iraq: Ballistic Missile Warfare and Its Regional Implications (An Intelligence Assessment)',

https://www.cia.gov/library/readingroom/docs/CIA-RDP88T00096R000100120003-6.pdf

15. Shahab-3 is widely believed to be a modified version of the North Korean Hwasong-7 (or Nodong-1).

16. The Qiam-1 ballistic missile, test fired in August 2010, can also be considered a spin-off of the Shahab-3.

17. Paulina Izewicz, 'Iran's Ballistic Missile Programme: Its Status and the Way Forward', The EU Non-Proliferation Consortium, *Non-Proliferation Papers*, No. 57, April 2017, https://www.sipri.org/sites/default/files/Irans-ballistic-missile-programme.pdf

18. There are unconfirmed reports of Sejjil-3 in the pipeline. It reportedly has a range of up to 4,000 km. If true, this would mean that Iran is only a step away from developing ICBMs, which usually have a minimum range of 5,500 km.

19. Tamir Eshel, 'Iran Unveils Underground Bases Supporting IRGC's Ballistic Missiles', *Defense Update*, http://defense-update.com/20151014_underground_missile_base.html

IRAQ: PROXIMATE THREAT OR STRATEGIC ALLY?

1. The Lakhmids or *Banu Lakhm* were a pro-Iranian Arab kingdom.

2. This is the subject of a continuing debate and disagreements between historians. During certain periods Twelver Shias may have formed the majority in certain parts of southern Iraq prior to the advent of the Safavid Empire. At any rate, Twelver Shias constituted a more or less consistent majority for centuries before the rise of the Safavids in and around the shrine cities of Najaf and Karbala.

3. The Ottoman–Safavid wars over control of Iraq began in 1514 and concluded in 1639 with the Treaty of Zuhab, which effectively ceded Mesopotamia to the Ottomans.

4. Martin Chulov, 'From Tehran to Beirut: Shia militias aim to firm up Iran's arc of influence', *The Guardian*, https://www.theguardian.com/world/2017/jun/16/from-tehran-to-beirut-shia-militias-aim-to-firm-up-irans-arc-of-influence

5. Former US president Bill Clinton has allegedly said that his first reaction upon learning of the attacks was to think there could only be two culprits with the ability and motivation of executing an attack on that scale and magnitude: Iran or al-Qaeda.

6. In an interview with Al Jazeera on 31 August 2002, Iraqi Vice President Taha Yassin Ramadan accused 'Persians' throughout history of siding with Jews or Zionists against Arabs.

7. After the revolution, promotions above the rank of full colonel were abolished. Therefore, Iran's most senior officers were confined to colonel level. This restriction was eased following the conclusion of the Iran–Iraq War.

8. A similar air raid took place in May 1993 in response to MeK cross-border attacks targeting oil pipelines in Khuzestan province.

9. Mohammad Edalatian came from a family with strong ties to the MeK and related left-wing groups. One of his brothers had been executed in the early 1980s on account of his involvement with the MeK. Edalatian himself had been imprisoned in the early 1980s, and at some point during his incarceration had been 'turned' by the Iranian intelligence services. On his release from custody in the mid-1980s he re-established contact with the group and on the instructions of the Iranian intelligence services crossed the border into Iraq in the late 1980s in order to fully re-join the MeK. He stayed there until mid-1993, reportedly supplying his handlers in Iran with useful information on every aspect of the MeK presence in Iraq. In June 1993, Edalatian was assigned a cross-border mission, and this proved to be his opportunity to kill three MeK members before fleeing across the border. Following his return to Iran he allegedly became an instructor for the Ministry of Intelligence and Security (MOIS) and wrote a manual on the successful infiltration of the MeK. Predictably, the manual is entitled *Penetration*.

10. The MeK also carried out high-profile assassinations, notably the gunning down of Asadollah Lajevardi (a leading prosecutor and prison governor in the 1980s) in August 1998 and the killing of the legendary army commander Ali Sayyad Shirazi in April the following year.

11. The remaining camp Ashraf residents were transferred to camp 'Liberty' (west of Baghdad), which had formerly served as a US military base. MeK members based at Liberty continued to be subject to rocket and missile attacks by Shia-led militias most likely directed by the Qods Force. In 2013 alone, four separate rocket attacks struck the camp, killing over a dozen residents. A particularly deadly attack occurred in late October 2015, during which up to twenty MeK members were killed. These attacks—coupled with mounting pressure by the Iraqi government—speeded up a UN-led process to relocate the camp residents to third countries. The bulk of MeK members were transferred to Albania, which had struck a deal with the US to accommodate the MeK on its territory. By September 2016 the relocation process had been completed as the last MeK members left Iraq.

SYRIA: MISSION ACCOMPLISHED?

1. Michael Brendan Dougherty, 'Commander Of U.S. Forces In the Middle East Tells Senate That Knocking Over Syria Would Hurt Iran', *Business Insider*, 6 March 2012, http://www.businessinsider.com/commander-of-us-forces-in-the-middle-east-tells-senate-that-knocking-over-syria-would-hurt-iran-2012-3?IR=T

2. Another exception is the Palestinian Islamic Jihad (PIJ), which is openly pro-Iranian. The PIJ is an anomaly, in that it is influenced by neither the Muslim Brotherhood nor the Salafi movement.

3. Greer Fay Cashman, 'Grapevine: Uri Lubrani retires after a glorious career', *The Jerusalem Post*, 3 December 2015, http://www.jpost.com/Opinion/Grapevine-Uri-Lubrani-retires-after-a-glorious-career-436276

4. Gareth Smyth, 'Periphery: Israel's search for allies in the Middle East by Yossi Alpher', *The Guardian*, 30 April 2015, https://www.theguardian.com/world/iran-blog/2015/apr/30/periphery-israel-iran-relations-yossi-alpher-book-review

5. Islamic Revolution Documents Center, 'How CIA, Mossad helped form Savak', 11 November 2016, http://irdc.ir/en/news/26/how-cia-mossad-helped-form-savak

6. See, for example, 'Leader's View of Islamic Awakening', Khamenei.ir, 19 May 2011, http://english.khamenei.ir/news/1458/Leader-s-View-of-Islamic-Awakening

7. Author's discussion with Iranian security official.

8. Assaf Moghadam, 'Marriage of Convenience: The Evolution of Iran and al-Qaʿida's Tactical Cooperation', *CTC Sentinel*, Vol. 10, Issue 4, April 2017, https://ctc.usma.edu/posts/marriage-of-convenience-the-evolution-of-iran-and-al-qaidas-tactical-cooperation

9. The exact date of Soleimani's appointment as commander of the Qods Force is unclear, but it is believed to have taken place at some time between the summer of 1997 to the spring of 1998.

10. Jennifer Parmerlee, 'Sudan denies "Khartoum-Tehran axis' to promote Islamic regimes in Africa', *The Washington Post*, 12 March 1992, https://www.washingtonpost.com/archive/politics/1992/03/12/sudan-denies-khartoum-tehran-axis-to-promote-islamic-regimes-in-africa/bebdea34-373b-4a9c-bd89-d3b7bea7d6b3/?utm_term=.b57c58747ebe

11. Robert Block, 'US turns blind eye to Iran arms for Bosnia', *The Independent*, 3 June 1994, http://www.independent.co.uk/news/world/europe/us-turns-blind-eye-to-iran-arms-for-bosnia-1420068.html

12. 'Raids across Germany target suspected Iranian spies', Deutsche Welle, 16 January 2018, http://www.dw.com/en/raids-across-germany-target-suspected-iranian-spies/a-42165145

13. Mujib Mashal and Fatima Faizi, 'Iran Sent Them to Syria. Now Afghan Fighters Are a Worry at Home.', The New York Times, 11 November 2017, https://www.nytimes.com/2017/11/11/world/asia/afghanistan-iran-syria-revolutionary-guards.html?mtrref=www.google.com.ua&gwh=B55A388B31F81FF5B6FE9BD3A914D601&gwt=pay

14. Babak Dehghanpisheh, 'Iran recruits Pakistani Shi'ites for combat in Syria', Reuters, 10 December 2015, https://www.reuters.com/article/us-mideast-crisis-syria-pakistan-iran/iran-recruits-pakistani-shiites-for-combat-in-syria-idUSKBN0TT22S20151210

15. Ali Alfoneh, 'Iraqi Shia Fighters in Syria', The Atlantic Council, 4 May 2017, http://www.atlanticcouncil.org/blogs/syriasource/iraqi-shia-fighters-in-syria

16. 'Iran bids farewell to iconic martyr Hojaji', Press TV, 27 September 2017, http://www.presstv.com/Detail/2017/09/27/536621/Iran-Mohsen-Hojaji-Tehran-Leader-of-the-Islamic-Revolution-Ayatollah-Seyyed-Ali-Khamenei-Syria-Daesh

17. Anshel Pfeffer, 'Iran Spends Billions on Proxy Wars Throughout the Mideast. Here's Where Its Money Is Going', Haaretz, 2 January 2018, https://www.haaretz.com/middle-east-news/iran-spends-billions-on-proxy-wars-here-s-where-its-money-is-going-1.5630081

18. Bozorgmehr Sharafedin and Ellen Francis, 'Iran strikes deal with Syria to repair power grid', Reuters, 12 September 2017, https://www.reuters.com/article/us-mideast-crisis-syria-iran/iran-strikes-deal-with-syria-to-repair-power-grid-idUSKCN1BN25Y

19. 'Rojava: A Syrian Kurdish Democracy', The Kurdish Project, https://thekurdishproject.org/history-and-culture/kurdish-democracy/rojava-democracy/

20. Saeed Kamali Dehghan, 'Rouhani acknowledges Iranian discontent as protests continue', The Guardian, 31 December 2017, https://www.theguardian.com/world/2017/dec/31/protesters-who-spread-fear-and-violence-will-be-confronted-says-iran

21. Jeffrey Goldberg, '"Neither Gaza, Nor Lebanon, I Give My Life to Iran!"', The Atlantic, 18 September 2009, https://www.theatlantic.com/international/archive/2009/09/-neither-gaza-nor-lebanon-i-give-my-life-to-iran/26842/

NOTES

IRAN AND THE GULF: AN UNEASY EQUILIBRIUM

1. Persian Gulf Online, http://www.persiangulfonline.org/en/what-is-the-persian-gulf-organization/
2. Wills Robinson, 'New footage shows captured American sailor in floods of TEARS moments after his unit surrendered to Iranian soldiers', *The Daily Mail*, 10 February 2016, http://www.dailymail.co.uk/news/article-3441156/New-footage-shows-captured-American-sailor-floods-TEARS-moments-unit-surrendered-Iranian-soldiers.html
3. 'Iranian Boats Block U.S., British Navy Ships In Strait of Hormuz', Radio Free Europe/Radio Liberty, 6 March 2017, https://www.rferl.org/a/iran-block-u-s-british-ships-hormuz/28353919.html
4. Jenna Johnson, 'Trump: Iranian boats that make improper "gestures" will be "shot out of the water"', *TheWashington Post*, 9 September 2016, https://www.washingtonpost.com/news/post-politics/wp/2016/09/09/trump-iranian-boats-that-make-improper-gestures-will-be-shot-out-of-the-water/?utm_term=.62be3f2235a6
5. Sami Aboudi and Omar Fahmy, 'Powerful Saudi prince sees no chance for dialogue with Iran', Reuters, 2 May 2017, https://www.reuters.com/article/us-saudi-prince-iran/powerful-saudi-prince-sees-no-chance-for-dialogue-with-iran-idUSKBN17Y1FK
6. 'Iran says Saudis back terrorism after senior prince attends rebel rally', Reuters, 10 July 2016, https://www.reuters.com/article/us-iran-saudi-rebels/iran-says-saudis-back-terrorism-after-senior-prince-attends-rebel-rally-idUSKCN0ZQ0E5
7. Babak Dehghanpisheh, 'To Iranian eyes, Kurdish unrest spells Saudi incitement', Reuters, 4 September 2016, https://www.reuters.com/article/us-iran-politics-kurds/to-iranian-eyes-kurdish-unrest-spells-saudi-incitement-idUSKCN11A0BD
8. 'Kurdistan PDKI resumes armed resistance in Iran', Kurdistan 24, 29 February 2016, http://www.kurdistan24.net/en/news/e977cea5-a78e-458e-8dd6-759841d6c895/PDKI-resumes-armed-resistance-in-Iran-
9. Annie Karni, 'Kushner took unannounced trip to Saudi Arabia', Politico, 29 October 2017, https://www.politico.com/story/2017/10/29/jared-kushner-saudi-arabia-244291
10. Richard Halloran and Special to *The New York Times*, '2 Iranian Fighters Reported Downed by Saudi Air Force', *The New York Times*, 6 June 1984, http://www.nytimes.com/1984/06/06/world/2-iranian-fighters-reported-downed-by-saudi-air-force.html
11. Max Fisher, Eric Schmitt, Audrey Carlsen and Malachy Browne, 'Did American Missile Defense Fail in Saudi Arabia?', *The New York Times*, 4

258

December 2017, https://www.nytimes.com/interactive/2017/12/04/world/middleeast/saudi-missile-defense.html

12. Patrick Wintour and Saeed Kamali Dehghan, 'Saudi Arabia shoots down Houthi missile aimed at Riyadh palace', *The Guardian*, 19 December 2017, https://www.theguardian.com/world/2017/dec/19/saudis-shoot-down-houthi-missile-close-to-capital-riyadh

13. 'Yemen's Houthis fire ballistic missile toward Saudi Arabia', Reuters, 20 January 2018, https://www.reuters.com/article/us-yemen-security-saudi/yemens-houthis-fire-ballistic-missile-toward-saudi-arabia-idUSKBN1F90GO

14. Colum Lynch and Robbie Gramer, 'Haley's "Smoking Gun" on Iran Met With Skepticism at U.N.', *Foreign Policy*, 14 December 2017, http://foreignpolicy.com/2017/12/14/nikki-haley-yemen-houthi-rebels-iran-missiles-press-conference-pentagon-skepticism-united-nations-trump-nuclear-deal-diplomacy/

15. In October 1993 the Saudi government announced a deal with the largest Shia-led opposition group, the Reform Movement, in which the said group would desist from anti-Saudi activities in return for a general amnesty. The deal was supposed to usher in a new era of greater Saudi acceptance of Shia identity and religious practices, but according to most informed observers that part of the deal has never been realised. The deal did succeed in marginalising the most effective Shia opposition leader of the time, Sheikh Hassan al-Safar. For more information, see Youssef M. Ibrahim, 'Saudi Officials Reporting Accord With Shiite Foes', *The New York Times*, 29 October 1993, http://www.nytimes.com/1993/10/29/world/saudi-officials-reporting-accord-with-shiite-foes.html

16. 'Khamenei Representative Renews Claims On Bahrain', Radio Farda, 11 February 2018, https://en.radiofarda.com/a/iran-khamenei-shariatmadari-renews-claims-on-bahrain/29033219.html

17. *Enqelab-e Sefid* or 'White Revolution' was in essence a land redistribution programme launched by the Shah in the early 1960s to break the hold of feudal and traditional land-owning classes in the country.

18. 'UK covered up intelligence training for Bahrain police, human rights group says', RT, 7 February 2017, https://www.rt.com/uk/376588-bahrain-police-training-reprieve/

19. There are two identifiably Shia parties active on the Kuwaiti political scene. The Justice and Peace Alliance—which follows the Shirazi school of thought—has one elected member in the National Assembly. Meanwhile, the National Islamic Alliance—which has two deputies in the National Assembly—is mildly supportive of Iran.

20. John H. Cushman Jr. and Special to *The New York Times*, 'Iranian Attacks on Kuwaiti Port Called Cause for U.S. to Retaliate', *The New York Times*, 18 October 1987, http://www.nytimes.com/1987/10/18/world/iranian-attacks-on-kuwaiti-port-called-cause-for-us-to-retaliate.html
21. CIA Directorate of Intelligence, 'Kuwait's National Security Policy: The Iran-Iraq War and Beyond', https://www.cia.gov/library/readingroom/docs/CIA-RDP89S01450R000200190001-5.pdf
22. 'Kuwaiti court overturns death sentence in Iran spy cell case', Reuters, 18 June 2017, https://www.reuters.com/article/us-kuwait-security/kuwaiti-court-overturns-death-sentence-in-iran-spy-cell-case-idUSKBN1990DR
23. 'Kuwait closes Iran cultural mission, expels diplomats', Al Jazeera, 20 July 2017, http://www.aljazeera.com/news/2017/07/kuwait-shuts-iran-cultural-mission-expels-diplomats-170720112334252.html
24. Zoltan Pall, 'Kuwaiti Salafism and Its Growing Influence in the Levant', Carnegie Endowment for International Peace, 7 May 2014, http://carnegieendowment.org/2014/05/07/kuwaiti-salafism-and-its-growing-influence-in-levant-pub-55514
25. Brad Lendon, 'Qatar hosts largest US military base in Mideast', CNN, 6 June 2017, https://edition.cnn.com/2017/06/05/middleeast/qatar-us-largest-base-in-mideast/index.html
26. 'Turkey sends more troops to Qatar', Al Jazeera, 27 December 2017, http://www.aljazeera.com/news/2017/12/171227051912500.html
27. Emily B. Hager and Mark Mazzetti, 'Emirates Secretly Sends Colombian Mercenaries to Yemen Fight', *The New York Times*, 25 November 2015, https://www.nytimes.com/2015/11/26/world/middleeast/emirates-secretly-sends-colombian-mercenaries-to-fight-in-yemen.html
28. Noah Browning, 'UAE criticizes 'colonial' role of Iran, Turkey in Syria', Reuters, 29 August 2017, https://www.reuters.com/article/us-mideast-crisis-syria-emirates/uae-criticizes-colonial-role-of-iran-turkey-in-syria-idUSKCN1B91NM
29. 'Upward Trend in Iran-UAE Trade Transactions', *Financial Tribune*, 23 May 2017, https://financialtribune.com/articles/economy-business-and-markets/65083/upward-trend-in-iran-uae-trade-transactions
30. 'Just how neutral is Oman in Yemen war?', Al-Monitor, 12 October 2016, https://www.al-monitor.com/pulse/ru/contents/articles/originals/2016/10/oman-neutral-saudi-war-iran-houthis.html

ISRAEL: FRIEND OR FOE?

1. Trita Parsi, *Treacherous Alliance: The Secret Dealings of Israel, Iran and the United States*, New Haven: Yale University Press, 2008.
2. Ronen Bergman, *The Secret War with Iran: The 30-Year Clandestine Struggle Against the World's Most Dangerous Terrorist Power*, New York: Simon & Schuster, 2008.
3. 'In video, Netanyahu accuses Tehran regime of "plundering" Iranians' smarts', *The Times of Israel*, 1 June 2018, https://www.timesofisrael.com/in-video-netanyahu-accuses-tehran-regime-of-plundering-iranians-smarts/
4. 'Netanyahu offers Israeli water tech to Iran', *The Times of Israel*, 10 June 2018, https://www.timesofisrael.com/netanyahu-offers-israeli-water-tech-to-solve-irans-growing-environmental-crisis/
5. 'Netanyahu hails Iranian people's "courage" in anti-regime protests', *The Times of Israel*, 27 June 2018, https://www.timesofisrael.com/netanyahu-hails-iranian-peoples-courage-in-anti-regime-protests/
6. Many sources claim that Israel directly sold arms to Iran in the early period of the Iran–Iraq War. The highest estimate comes from Trita Parsi, who claims in his book *Treacherous Alliance* that Israel sold $500 million worth of arms to Iran in the period 1981–1983.
7. TOW stands for 'tube-launched, optically tracked, wire-guided'. Iran had purchased TOW missiles before the revolution and thus the Iranian army was familiar with the weapon system. This familiarity was the key reason for the illicit purchase of the system in 1985 and 1986.
8. Jonathan C. R. et al., 'PLO Chief, in Iran, Hails Shah's Fall', *The Washington Post*, 19 February 1979, https://www.washingtonpost.com/archive/politics/1979/02/19/plo-chief-in-iran-hails-shahs-fall/04eae6e9-d5db-4aa4-ba4b-709ed90edb9a/?utm_term=.d4e9eac2ab90
9. 'CIA Report Reveals Budding Tehran-PLO Relationship In 1979', *The Jerusalem Post*, 16 January 2018, https://www.jpost.com/Middle-East/CIA-report-reveals-budding-Tehran-PLO-relationship-in-1979-536895
10. *Chicago Tribune*, 22 July 2009, http://articles.chicagotribune.com/2009-07-22/news/0907210458_1_nationalist-iranian-anniversary-esfandiar-rahim-mashaei-tir-square
11. Dudi Cohen, 'Iranian VP: We are friends of the nation in Israel', Ynetnews, 19 July 2008, https://www.ynetnews.com/articles/0,7340,L-3570266,00.html
12. Ewen MacAskill and Chris McGreal, 'Israel should be wiped off map, says Iran's president', *The Guardian*, 27 October 2005, https://www.theguardian.com/world/2005/oct/27/israel.iran

13. 'Iranian Spies Target Jewish Centers in Berlin – Focus', Radio Farda, 20 January 2018, https://en.radiofarda.com/a/iranian-agents-target-jewish-centers-in-germany/28985805.html
14. Scott Peterson, 'Covert war against Iran's nuclear scientists: a widow remembers', The Christian Science Monitor, 17 July 2014, https://www.csmonitor.com/World/Middle-East/2014/0717/Covert-war-against-Iran-s-nuclear-scientists-a-widow-remembers
15. Amos Harel, 'Israel Struck Syrian and Hezbollah Arms Convoys Nearly 100 Times in Five Years, Top General Says', Haaretz, 17 August 2017, https://www.haaretz.com/middle-east-news/israel-struck-syrian-hezbollah-convoys-nearly-100-times-in-5-years-1.5443378

THE USA: CONFRONTING 'THE GREAT SATAN'

1. The White House Office of the Press Secretary, 'The President's State of the Union Address', 29 January 2002, https://georgewbush-whitehouse.archives.gov/news/releases/2002/01/20020129-11.html
2. Nicholas Cumming-Bruce, 'US Embassy stormed by Tehran mob', The Guardian, 15 February 1979, https://www.theguardian.com/century/1970-1979/Story/0,,106889,00.html
3. 'Why Carter Admitted the Shah', The New York Times, 17 May 1981, https://www.nytimes.com/1981/05/17/magazine/why-carter-admitted-the-shah.html
4. One Iranian civilian was also killed during the operation.
5. Seymour M. Hersh, 'U.S. Secretly Gave Aid to Iraq Early in Its War Against Iran', The New York Times, https://www.nytimes.com/1992/01/26/world/us-secretly-gave-aid-to-iraq-early-in-its-war-against-iran.html
6. Mohammad Reza Saadati was arrested in 1980 during a meeting with a Soviet diplomat. He was tried for espionage and executed the following year.
7. Todd S. Purdum, 'Clinton to Order a Trade Embargo Against Teheran', The New York Times, 1 May 1995, https://www.nytimes.com/1995/05/01/world/clinton-to-order-a-trade-embargo-against-teheran.html
8. Abbas Abdi even met one of the hostages, Barry Rosen, nearly twenty years later in July 1998. See Los Angeles Times, 1 August 1998, http://articles.latimes.com/1998/aug/01/news/mn-9089
9. David E. Sanger, 'U.S. Ending a Few of the Sanctions Imposed on Iran', The New York Times, 18 March 2000, https://www.nytimes.com/2000/03/18/world/us-ending-a-few-of-the-sanctions-imposed-on-iran.html

10. 'Text: Obama's Speech in Cairo', *The New York Times*, 4 June 2009, https://www.nytimes.com/2009/06/04/us/politics/04obama.text.html

11. Tabassum Zakaria, 'Obama calls Neda video "heartbreaking"', Reuters, 23 June 2009, http://blogs.reuters.com/talesfromthetrail/2009/06/23/obama-calls-neda-video-heartbreaking-2/

12. David Ignatius, 'The Omani "back channel" to Iran and the secrecy surrounding the nuclear deal', *The Washington Post*, 7 June 2016, https://www.washingtonpost.com/opinions/the-omani-back-channel-to-iran-and-the-secrecy-surrounding-the-nuclear-deal/2016/06/07/0b9e27d4-2ce1-11e6-b5db-e9bc84a2c8e4_story.html?utm_term=.7bdb4cf4cbf9

13. See, for example, Karim Sadjadpour's *Reading Khamenei: The World View of Iran's Most Powerful Leader*, Washington, D.C.: Carnegie Endowment for International Peace, 2009. Available at: http://carnegieendowment.org/files/sadjadpour_iran_final2.pdf

14. David B. Ottaway and Dan Morgan, 'U.S. Backs Non-Iranian, "Eurasian" Corridor West for Caspian Sea Oil', *The Washington Post*, 20 November 1997, https://www.washingtonpost.com/archive/politics/1997/11/20/us-backs-non-iranian-eurasian-corridor-west-for-caspian-sea-oil/d7aaf9f8-9e32-4583-a2c0-8883b78cb44d/?utm_term=.740f153fb986

15. Tim Weiner, 'U.S. Plan to Change Iran Leaders Is an Open Secret Before It Begins', *The New York Times*, 26 January 1996, https://www.nytimes.com/1996/01/26/world/us-plan-to-change-iran-leaders-is-an-open-secret-before-it-begins.html

16. Captain J. B. Perkins III, U.S. Navy, 'Operation Praying Mantis: The Surface View', U.S. Naval Institute, *Proceedings Magazine*, Vol. 115/5/1,035, May 1989, https://www.usni.org/magazines/proceedings/1989-05/operation-praying-mantis-surface-view

17. Laurie Mylroie, 'Iraqi militias threaten US and Israel', Kurdistan 24, 21 June 2018, http://www.kurdistan24.net/en/news/5c8883f6-be16-4ebf-95f5-a17c7fdf63dd

18. Yeganeh Torbati and Joel Schectman, 'America's unending hostage crisis with Iran', Reuters, 1 August 2018, https://www.reuters.com/investigates/special-report/usa-iran-student/

CONCLUSION

1. Scott Waldman, 'Climate Change May Have Helped Spark Iran's Protests', ClimateWire, *Scientific American*, 8 January 2018, https://

www.scientificamerican.com/article/climate-change-may-have-helped-spark-iran-rsquo-s-protests/

2. 'Qatar said providing fuel funds to Gaza via Israel, overriding PA objections', *The Times of Israel*, 6 October 2018, https://www.timesofisrael.com/qatar-said-providing-fuel-funds-to-gaza-via-israel-overriding-pa-objections/

3. Zena Tahhan, 'The complicated legacy of Yasser Arafat', Middle East Eye, 13 November 2018, https://www.middleeasteye.net/news/palestine-complicated-legacy-yasser-arafat-118507911

4. 'Yemen Houthi rebels threaten to attack UAE and Saudi airports', The New Arab, 8 November 2017, https://www.alaraby.co.uk/english/news/2017/11/8/houthis-threaten-to-attack-uae-and-saudi-airports

5. Josh Wood, 'Outsourcing war: How foreigners and mercenaries power UAE's military', Middle East Eye, 10 July 2018, https://www.middleeasteye.net/news/outsourcing-war-how-foreigners-and-mercenaries-power-uaes-military-90958187

6. Patrick Wintour and Saeed Kamali Dehghan, 'European "clearing house" to bypass US sanctions against Iran', *The Guardian*, 6 November 2018, https://www.theguardian.com/world/2018/nov/06/european-clearing-house-to-bypass-us-sanctions-against-iran

7. Whitney Raas and Austin Long, 'Osirak Redux? Assessing Israeli Capabilities to Destroy Iranian Nuclear Facilities', *International Security*, Spring 2007, https://www.belfercenter.org/publication/osirak-redux-assessing-israeli-capabilities-destroy-iranian-nuclear-facilities

8. Patrick Wintour, 'Saudi crown prince warns it will build nuclear bomb if Tehran does the same', *The Guardian*, 15 March 2018, https://www.theguardian.com/world/2018/mar/15/saudi-arabia-iran-nuclear-bomb-threat-mohammed-bin-salman

9. Gavin Serkin, 'Iran's Hidden State: Here's What Every Investor Needs to Know', Frontera, 1 June 2016, https://frontera.net/news/mena/irans-hidden-state-investor-needs-to-know/

10. https://www.khatam.com/

INDEX

Mossadegh, Mohammad, 39, 53,
55, 58, 59, 63, 168, 217, 227–8
Mosul, Nineveh, 35
Mousavi, Hossein, 63, 64
Mubarak, Hosni, 135–6
Muharram, 77
Mujahideen, 103–4
Musa al-Kazim, Imam, 78
al-Musawi, Abbas, 197
Muscat, Oman, 230–31
Muslim Brotherhood
in Egypt, 129, 132, 136–7, 175,
231–2
Khamenei and, 231–2
in Palestine, 199
in Qatar, 175
in Sudan, 145
in Syria, 128–9, 140
Mustafa, Haidar Syed, 204–5
mustakbereen, 31
mustazafeen, 31
Mykonos assassinations (1992), 205

Nagorno-Karabakh, 143
Najaf, Iraq, 24, 34, 76, 82, 119,
120, 121, 124, 254
Najibullah, 103, 104
Najran, Saudi Arabia, 164
Nasrallah, Hassan, 204
Nasser, Gamal Abdel, 131, 157
nation-state model, 133
National Defence Forces, Syria, 8
national identity, 13–18
National Liberation Army of Iran,
61–2, 110–11, 112
natural gas, 10, 175, 233
navy, 74, 159
Nazi Germany (1933–45), 38
Nehzat-e Azadi, 62, 72–3
neo-conservatives, 199, 228, 229
Netanyahu, Benjamin, 188

Netherlands, 203
New Iran Party, 56
Nigeria, 203
al-Nimr, Nimr Baqir, 165
Nineveh, Iraq, 6, 35
Nir, Amiram, 190
Nisman, Alberto, 206
Nixon, Richard, 39
Non-Proliferation Treaty (NPT),
245–6
North Atlantic Treaty
Organization (NATO), 92, 96,
209
North Dome natural gas field, 175
North Korea, 94, 95, 105, 215–16,
244
Northern Alliance, 105, 106, 211
Noureddine family, 78
Nowruz, 19
nuclear programme, 5, 244–6
Argentina and, 206
assassinations of scientists
(2010–12), 90, 206–8
Israel and, 90, 203, 206–8
IRGC and, 54
JCPOA (2015), 9, 10, 39, 96–7,
180, 212, 230–31, 234–5,
239–41, 244, 246
Kuwait and, 173
al-Nusra Front, 140–42, 152, 176

Obama, Barack, 163, 212, 230,
239, 240
oil, 10, 21, 25, 58
Anglo-Iranian Oil Company,
58
Iran–Iraq War (1980–88), 25,
163, 172, 214
Israel and, 194
nationalisation movement
(1950s), 21, 58, 228

Kuwait, relations with, 173
Lebanon, relations with, 127,
  163
MeK, relations with, 162
and missile programme, 97, 164,
  166
MOIS in, 165
Muslim Brotherhood, relations
  with, 175
al-Nimr execution (2016), 165
nuclear weapons and, 245
Oman, relations with, 179, 180
Pahlavi dynasty and, 130, 131,
  133, 166
Persian Gulf and, 158
Qatar, relations with, 173–6
Riyadh attack (1995), 226
Sadr's visit (2017), 83
Shia Islam in, 37, 75, 143,
  161–2, 165
Soleimani and, 143
Syria, relations with, 127, 128,
  149, 160, 163
Taliban, relations with, 105
United Arab Emirates, relations
  with, 36, 133, 167, 173–5,
  176–7, 178
United States, relations with,
  103, 115, 158, 163, 164, 226,
  234, 235, 246
Wahhabism, 133
women's rights, 162
Yemen, relations with, 36, 160,
  161, 163, 164, 177
SAVAK, 30, 60, 73, 81, 132, 184,
  194
Sayyidah Zaynab Shrine, Damascus,
  128, 148
Sazeman-e Mojahedin-e Enghelab-e
  Islami, 62, 63
Scud missiles, 92–3

Second World War (1939–45), 38,
  218
Secret War with Iran, The (Bergman),
  186
security-intelligence community,
  66–9
Segev, Gonen, 202–3
Sejjil missiles, 95–6
September 11 attacks (2001), 103
Shahab missiles, 94–5, 96
Shaheedan, 24, 80, 84–7, 116
Shahid Beheshti University, 207
Shahid Modaress missile base, Beed
  Kaneh, 89–90
Shahnameh (Ferdowsi), 14
Shahriari, Majid, 207
Shallah, Ramadan, 199
Shaqaqi, Fathi, 198
Sharafkandi, Sadegh, 162
Sharefeddine family, 78
Sharia law, 174
Shariatmadari, Hossein, 167–8
Sharjah, United Arab Emirates, 178
Shatt Al-Arab, 72, 74, 115
Shia Islam, 1, 18–37, 166
  in Afghanistan, 103, 105, 142,
    149
  Alawites and, 37
  Arab nationalists and, 19–20
  in Bahrain, 7, 8, 135, 137, 143,
    156, 169, 170
  clerical class, 21, 23
  and Islamic Revolution (1979), 1
  and Iran–Iraq War (1980–88),
    76–8
  in Iraq, *see* Shiism in Iraq
  IRGC and, 30
  in Kuwait, 171, 172
  in Lebanon, 6, 21, 30–33,
    78–81, 142
  Mahdi, 200